SQUARE
TABLE

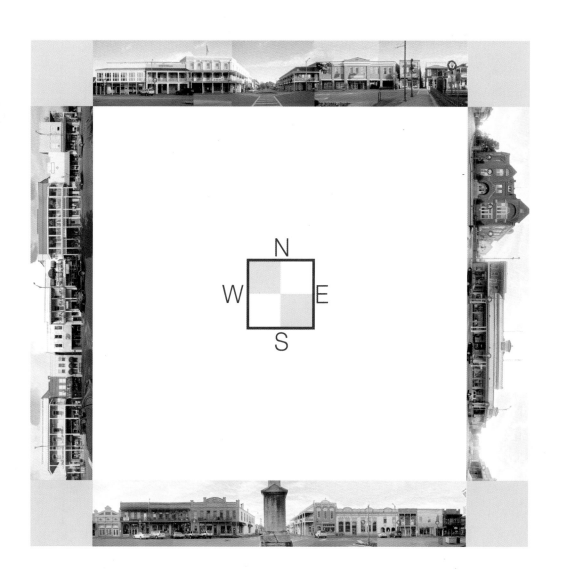

SQUARE TABLE

A COLLECTION OF RECIPES FROM OXFORD, MISSISSIPPI

yoknapatawpha

arts council

Library of Congress Control Number: 2005933004

ISBN: 0-9767314-0-1

Cover art by Jason Bouldin

Cover design by Paige Tatum

Back cover bronze by Bill Beckwith

Photography by Langdon Clay

Food Styling by Cory Lewis and Gay Graeber

Manufactured in the United States of America

First Printing: 2005 10,000 copies

WIMMER
COOKBOOKS

A CONSOLIDATED GRAPHICS COMPANY

800.548.2537 wimmerco.com

The book before you is not only a celebration of culinary, visual, and literary arts in Oxford-Lafayette County, Mississippi, but a fundraising project for the Yoknapatawpha Arts Council lovingly created by 200-plus volunteers during three years.

Founded in 1975, the non-profit Yoknapatawpha Arts Council (YAC) is the designated arts agency for the city and county with the mission of promoting the arts to all people in the region. YAC enriches the community by providing opportunities to participate in artistic and cultural activities. YAC has accomplished much in 30 years, and proceeds from this book will make possible a great deal more. Some highlights are these:

- Powerhouse Community Arts Center (160 seat theatre, gallery, classroom and meeting space, YAC office)

- Community Arts Grants given to, among many others, Theatre Oxford, *Thacker Mountain Radio Show*, Oxford Civic Chorus, Oxford Children's Choir, Oxford Shakespeare Festival, Blues Symposium, Oxford Conference for the Book, Freedmantown Cemetery Documentation Project

- Oxford Film Festival – www.oxfordfilmfest.com

- Double Decker Arts Festival – www.doubledeckerfestival.com

- YAC Web site featuring an Online Arts Calendar and Directory – www.oxfordarts.com

- Holiday Party & Ornament Auction & Membership Party

- Artists' Exhibits & Studio Tours

- Kids' Events including: Special Performances for Schoolchildren, Kids' Art Show, Drama and Puppet Workshops, Summer Arts Camp, Middle School Writing Contest and Creative Arts Fair

Square Table captures a wonderful time and place. Read, cook, and enjoy!

Elaine Abadie
Executive Director

Photo by Nathan Latil

Photo by Bruce Newman

Photo by Bruce Newman

Photo by Bruce Newman

SPONSORS

Lamar Level

*On the Square
since 1910*
www.fnboxford.com
662-234-2821

BAPTIST
Memorial Hospital
North Mississippi

Jackson Level

Becky and Ron Feder

Mary and Sam Haskell

Internal Medicine Associates

JPB Pathology, Inc.

Marchbanks Real Estate

Newk's Express Café

Oxford Insurance Agency

Carolyn Ross

Diane T. Scruggs

Smith, Turner & Reeves

Van Buren Level

Addy Photography

Bancorp South

Carole and Bill Dye

Endoscopy Center of
North Mississippi

ENT Consultants of North
Mississippi

Leighton and Campbell McCool

Dr. and Mrs. Dennis Morgan

Helen and Mike Overstreet

Oxford University Bank

Judy and Chris Riddell

Southside Art Gallery

Surgical Clinic of North
Mississippi,
Drs. King and Byars

Taylor Capital Venture

Tom Davis Insurance

TicketsXchange

Dr. and Mrs. Scott Whitaker

Franklin Williams

Wishing Tree Properties

Tyler Level

Ajax Diner

Sharon and Dwight Ball

Rebel Press and Office Supply
Co., Inc.

Cindy and Richard Sinervo

Laura and Brent Smith,
Chaney's Pharmacy

Tannehill & Carmean

Ginny and Cooper Terry

Waller Funeral Home

Fillmore Level

Crossroads Animal Hospital

Downtown Grill

G & M Pharmacy

La Mystique

Thomas C. Levidiotis

Pat and Ernie Lowe

Becky and Ed Meek

Oxford Alarm and Communications

Oxford Lung Physicians

Phil Bailey and Associates

Rosser Immigration Law

Sneed's Ace Hardware

Star Package Store

Dawn Testa Award Realty

*YAC gratefully acknowledges the ongoing support of the
Mississippi Arts Commission, National Endowment for the Arts, City of Oxford, and Cellular South.*

4

CONTENTS

WELCOME to the NEIGHBORHOOD

John T Edge

Works of the sort you hold in your hands are generally called community cookbooks, the idea being that they are products of people living in the same locality who share common interests — those interests being some sort of charity or arts endeavor or other selfless work. The aim of these books is to raise dollars and to render the raising of said dollars painless.

That last part is important. The organization — in this case the Yoknapatawpha Arts Council — gets funds, but it must also give of itself. And it must give with such gusto that parting with thirty-odd dollars is of no account.

The customary analgesic offered contributors to the cause is a cache of recipes, some good stories, a few pretty pictures. And *Square Table* delivers the drugs of choice. No doubt about that. The art alone is worth the fare. But don't judge this book by a thumb-through, even if you're swooning by page thirty-seven. Find a space for *Square Table* on your kitchen shelf. Dog-ear the pages; edit the recipes to suit your palate. Make the book your own.

A year may pass before you come to truly appreciate the effort. By then, your repertoire will include smothered doves and marmalade sweet potatoes, not to mention cream cheese jalapeño venison rolls and cornbread salad. You will have made your peace with — and eaten your fill of — angel hair flan and pepperoni spaghetti cakes.

You will claim Pat Chrestman's butter-gilded Rotel cabbage and Fairy Bell Carothers's buttermilk-dipped fried chicken as your own. You will have figured out that the Tomato Bread Pudding on page 167 complements the Country Captain Chicken on page 112. And you will have developed certain affectations, like telling friends that smoked quail stuffed with goat cheese, oyster mushrooms, and polenta is an *old family recipe*.

By then, you will have lingered over Larry Brown's chicken stew essay. And John Grisham's ode to Brunswick stew. And Ann Fisher-Wirth's confession of love by way of quesadillas. Not to mention Beth Ann Fennelly's paean to pink-velvet-cake. You will have read what William Faulkner had to say about trout and chicken, and you will have reveled in his description of the "thin plume of supper smoke windless above the chimney" from *Go Down, Moses*. Indeed, the selection of Faulkner food quotes will prove so compelling that you may wonder why the editors left out that passage from *The Hamlet* wherein he describes a sweet potato as a "moist blast of spring's liquorish corruption."

But I'm getting carried away. And hungry. So I'll bring this home. By way of this book, the people of Oxford swing wide their doors and invite you to take a seat at our collective table. These are the artworks we craft, the stories we tell, the dishes we cook. This is how we, the members of the Yoknapatawapha Arts Council, see ourselves.

Let the old guard blanch at the inclusion of angel hair flan. (The literal-minded among them might even take offense.) Let the nigglers niggle. (At least four recipes call for infernal quick instead of righteous stone-ground grits.) If you seek to understand this kinda-sorta cosmopolitan community, a year spent cooking from *Square Table* may be your best entrée.

Think about it: Where else will you find a quotation from *Light in August* — one of those gorgeous run-ons in which Faulkner employs words like lambence — cheek-to-jowl with a recipe for prosciutto-wrapped and cream cheese-slathered Asian pears?

John T Edge, director of the Southern Foodways Alliance at the University of Mississippi, writes for Gourmet, *the* Oxford American, *and other publications. He is the author of a number of books including* Fried Chicken: An American Story.

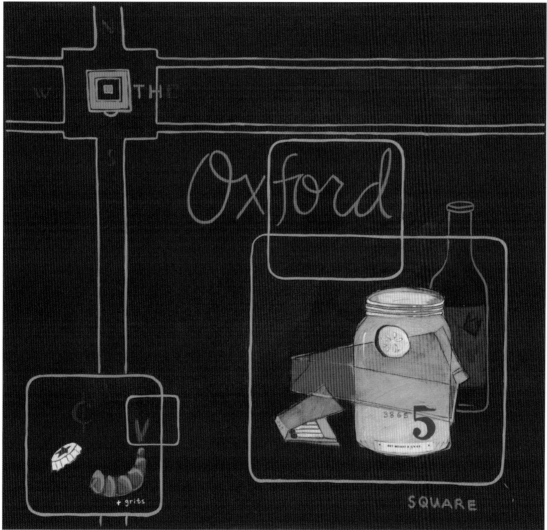

The Oxford Square   Amy Evans

Evans is a photographer, painter, and art educator in Oxford and was named one of the "most fearsome talents" in the culinary world by *Food & Wine* magazine. Her website is amycevans.com.

Garden Sandwich Cake
Goat Cheese Torta
Prosciutto Wraps

APPETIZERS

PROSCIUTTO WRAPS

6   ripe pears, cored (peeled if Asian pears) and sliced ½-inch thick

½   cup orange juice

8   ounces garden vegetable light cream cheese

60   baby spinach leaves, washed and dried

⅓   pound thinly sliced prosciutto, cut into 5 x ½-inch strips

Dip pear slices in orange juice and pat dry. Place pear on work surface, top with a small dollop of cream cheese and 1 spinach leaf. Wrap with prosciutto and place seam-side down on serving platter.

60 wraps

Photo on page 8

BLACK BEAN SALSA

1   15-ounce can black beans, rinsed and drained

1   8-ounce can white shoepeg corn, drained

1   large tomato, seeded and chopped

½   red onion, chopped

⅛   cup chopped fresh cilantro

2   tablespoons fresh lime juice

1   tablespoon olive oil

1½   teaspoons red wine vinegar

½   teaspoon salt, or to taste

¼   teaspoon pepper

   Avocado slices and cilantro sprigs for garnish

   Tortilla chips

Combine all ingredients except garnish in a large bowl. Cover and chill. Garnish, if desired, with sliced avocado and fresh cilantro. Serve with tortilla chips.

Add a few Tabasco drops and/or chopped jalapeño pepper to enhance the spicy flavor, if desired.

4 cups

Photo on page 25

Artist Jason Bouldin, Cover

Nationally regarded for his portrait work, Jason Bouldin received the Portrait Society of America's top prize for one of his portraits in 2002. His subjects include those close to home, such as former Governor William F. Winter, as well as subjects far away, such as Derek Bok, president of Harvard University. Although primarily a portraitist, he also paints landscape and still life studies, and has garnered prizes for works in that genre as well, having been selected in 2003 for the national "Sea to Shining Sea" exhibit, in 2001 for the American Artists Professional League Annual Exhibition, and twice for the National Parks Academy "Arts for the Parks" Exhibitions.

FIVE-FRUIT SALSA

2 cups chopped, fresh cantaloupe
6 green onions, chopped
3 kiwifruit, peeled and finely chopped
1 medium navel orange, peeled and finely chopped
1 medium yellow bell pepper, chopped
1 medium red bell pepper, chopped

1 8-ounce can crushed pineapple, drained
2 jalapeño peppers, seeded and chopped
2 cups finely chopped fresh strawberries
Tortilla chips

In a bowl, combine all ingredients except strawberries. Cover and refrigerate 8 hours or overnight. Just before serving, stir in strawberries. Serve with tortilla chips.

4 cups

ROASTED RED PEPPER DIP

2 large red bell peppers
2 cloves garlic, peeled
½ cup packed, fresh basil leaves
8 ounces cream cheese, room temperature

1 teaspoon lemon juice
Salt and pepper to taste
Pita chips or crackers

Preheat oven to broil. Cut peppers in half and remove seeds. Put on top oven shelf and broil until blistered, 15-20 minutes. Cover with paper towels and dish towel and let rest 10 minutes. Peel off charred skin, rinse peppers, and pat dry. In a food processor chop garlic and basil leaves. Add red peppers, cream cheese, lemon juice, salt and pepper. Pulse until well combined. Refrigerate 3-4 hours. Serve with pita chips or crackers.

1½ cups

Photo on page 25

SPICY SPINACH ARTICHOKE DIP

½ cup unsalted butter

1 medium onion, chopped, about 1 cup

2 10-ounce packages frozen, chopped spinach, thawed and squeezed dry

1 14-ounce can artichoke hearts, drained and chopped

8 ounces cream cheese, room temperature

8 ounces sour cream

1 cup shredded Monterey Jack cheese, divided use

1 cup grated Parmesan cheese, divided use

2 teaspoons Tabasco sauce, or to taste

Salt to taste

Tortilla chips or corn chips

Spinach is an excellent source of iron, vitamin C, vitamin A, folic acid, and fiber.

Preheat oven to 350°. In a large skillet over medium-high heat, melt butter and sauté onion until soft, about 5 minutes. Stir in spinach, artichoke hearts, cream cheese, sour cream and ¾ cup of each cheese. Add Tabasco and salt. Stir until blended and heated through. Pour into a greased 2-quart baking dish and top with remaining cheeses. Bake until cheese is melted, about 10 minutes. Serve with tortilla chips or corn chips.

7 cups

THAI VEGGIE DIP

This Asian-inspired dip is also good with chicken tenders.

1 tablespoon minced green onion

1 teaspoon sesame oil

¾ cup crunchy peanut butter

¼ cup lemon juice

¼ cup soy sauce

½ cup water

1 teaspoon crushed red pepper

2 cloves garlic, minced

2 tablespoons shredded coconut

2 tablespoons packed brown sugar

Fresh vegetables

In a large skillet sauté onions in sesame oil. Add peanut butter, lemon juice, soy sauce, water, crushed red pepper, garlic and coconut. Cook over low heat 4 minutes, stirring constantly. Add brown sugar, cover, and simmer 10 minutes. Add small amounts of additional water, if needed. Serve warm with fresh vegetables.

1½ cups

In the late 1930s, Oxford had an actual rainmaker. Miss Lilly Stoate of North Lamar could, with the use of prayer and sitting by a stream poking the water with a stick, make the clouds produce rain. She traveled to drought-stricken areas and got enough results to be featured in *Life* magazine.

~Will Lewis, Jr.

MUSHROOMS IN BURGUNDY

2   cups unsalted butter
1   quart hearty Burgundy wine
1   cup boiling water with 4 beef bouillon cubes
1   cup boiling water with 4 chicken bouillon cubes
1   teaspoon pepper
1   teaspoon garlic powder
1½ tablespoons Worcestershire sauce
1   teaspoon dill weed
4   pounds mushrooms, washed and dried

In a large stockpot melt butter and add wine, beef cubes with water, chicken cubes with water, pepper, garlic powder, Worcestershire and dill weed. Stir to blend well. Add mushrooms. Cook over low heat 5 minutes, then bring to a slow boil over medium heat. Reduce heat to a simmer and cover. Simmer 4-5 hours. Remove cover and continue cooking until liquid barely covers the mushrooms, another 3-5 hours. Serve in a chafing dish as an appetizer or as an accompaniment to grilled meat.

30 servings

STUFFED MUSHROOMS

1½ pounds large, fresh mushrooms
¼   cup chopped onion
3   green onions, chopped
2   cloves garlic, chopped
1   tablespoon olive oil
¼   cup dry white wine
¼   cup breadcrumbs
1   14-ounce can artichoke hearts, drained and finely chopped
½   cup grated, fresh Parmesan cheese
½   cup mayonnaise
¼   teaspoon salt
¼   teaspoon pepper

Preheat oven to 350°. Rinse and pat mushrooms dry. Remove and discard stems. In a skillet sauté onions and garlic in olive oil until tender. Add wine and cook until liquid is evaporated, about 2 minutes. Stir in breadcrumbs. Remove from heat and let cool. Combine onion mixture, artichokes, Parmesan, mayonnaise, salt and pepper. Spoon 1 teaspoon mixture into each mushroom cap. Bake 12-15 minutes.

16 servings

STUFFED CHERRY TOMATOES

Stuffing the tomatoes is time-consuming but makes a beautiful presentation.

20-30 cherry tomatoes
1 pound bacon, cooked and crumbled
½ cup mayonnaise
⅓ cup chopped green onions

3 tablespoons fresh Parmesan cheese, grated
2 tablespoons fresh, minced parsley

Cut a thin slice off each tomato top. Scoop out and discard tomato pulp. Invert onto paper towels and allow to drain. In a medium bowl, stir together bacon, mayonnaise, green onions, Parmesan and parsley until well combined. Spoon mixture into tomatoes and chill.

20-30 appetizers

Do not store tomatoes in the refrigerator, as cold air can make the flesh pulpy.

GOAT CHEESE TORTA

1 pound goat cheese, room temperature
1 cup unsalted butter, room temperature
6 ounces sun-dried tomatoes packed in oil, drained
2 cups fresh basil leaves, firmly packed
3 cloves garlic, peeled and crushed

½ teaspoon salt
½ teaspoon pepper
⅓ cup olive oil
Basil leaves and toasted pine nuts for garnish
Crackers or garlic toast

In a food processor or blender, combine goat cheese and butter until well blended and set aside. In food processor or blender, chop sun-dried tomatoes and set aside. In food processor or blender, place basil, garlic, salt and pepper. With motor running, slowly drizzle in olive oil, processing until basil is puréed. Line a 3-cup mold or loaf pan with plastic wrap. In the bottom of the mold, layer ⅓ of goat cheese mixture, all of the basil mixture, ⅓ of goat cheese, all of the sun-dried tomatoes, and the remaining ⅓ goat cheese. Refrigerate until firm, at least 3 hours. Unmold, garnish, and serve with crackers or garlic toast.

3-cup mold

Photo on page 8

13

HERBED GOAT CHEESE

Goat cheese, or *chèvre*, is lower in calories and carbohydrates than similar cow's milk products, such as cream cheese.

1 teaspoon minced garlic	¼ cup sour cream
½ tablespoon unsalted butter	1 tablespoon minced, fresh basil
8 ounces goat cheese, room temperature	1 tablespoon minced, fresh oregano
3 ounces cream cheese, room temperature	Salt and freshly ground pepper to taste
	Nasturtiums for garnish
	Crackers

In a small skillet, sauté garlic in butter until softened. Set aside. In the bowl of an electric mixer, blend goat cheese, cream cheese and sour cream until smooth. Stir in the garlic, basil and oregano. Season with salt and pepper. Garnish with nasturtiums, if desired. Serve with crackers.

1½ cups

ROSEMARY CHEESE
WITH FIG PRESERVES

8 ounces cream cheese, room temperature	4 teaspoons honey
3 ounces goat cheese, room temperature	1 teaspoon coarsely ground pepper
	Fig preserves
1 tablespoon chopped, fresh rosemary	Fresh rosemary sprigs for garnish
	Crackers

Grease 1½-cup mold or small loaf pan. Line with plastic wrap, allowing a few inches to extend over pan. In a food processor pulse cream cheese, goat cheese, rosemary, honey and pepper until smooth, about 15 seconds. Spoon into prepared mold. Cover and chill at least 2 hours. Unmold onto serving plate and remove plastic wrap. Stir preserves and spoon desired amount over cheese. Garnish with sprigs of rosemary and serve with crackers.

1½-cup mold

CHEESE AND ARTICHOKE TORTA

1   medium red bell pepper

6   ounces marinated artichoke hearts, drained and chopped

3   tablespoons minced, fresh parsley

1   tablespoon chopped, fresh basil, optional

16   ounces cream cheese, room temperature

1   1-ounce dry ranch salad dressing packet

     Crackers

Preheat broiler. Place whole pepper directly on oven rack. Broil until sides start to blister and brown. Immediately remove pepper from oven and place in a paper bag. Close bag and let stand for 20 minutes. Peel, seed, and chop pepper. In a small bowl combine chopped pepper, artichokes, parsley and basil. Set aside. In a medium bowl, blend cream cheese and salad dressing mix until smooth. Line a deep 3-cup bowl with plastic wrap. Divide cheese mixture into thirds and vegetable mixture in half. Alternate layers of cheese and vegetable mixtures, beginning and ending with cheese. Chill at least 4 hours. Invert onto plate, remove plastic wrap, and serve with assorted crackers.

3-cup mold

If Heisman trophies were awarded for tailgating, the University of Mississippi would be the favorite.

~Curtis Wilkie

CHUTNEY CHEESECAKE

12   ounces Cheddar cheese, grated

1   cup chopped pecans

½   medium onion, chopped

9   ounces cream cheese, room temperature, divided use

¼   cup prepared mango chutney

1   10-ounce package frozen, chopped spinach, cooked and squeezed dry

     Salt and pepper to taste

     Toasted pine nuts or fresh herbs for garnish

     Crackers

In a food processor pulse Cheddar cheese, pecans and onions until well blended. Press in bottom of a greased 9-inch springform pan. In food processor pulse 8 ounces cream cheese and chutney until well blended. Spread over Cheddar cheese layer. In food processor pulse remaining 1 ounce cream cheese, spinach, salt and pepper. Spread over chutney layer. Decorate with toasted pine nuts or herbs. Refrigerate 6-8 hours, unmold, and serve with crackers.

20 servings

15

Mississippi ranks number one in the nation in the production and processing of catfish.

City Grocery

CATFISH AND TASSO SAVORY CHEESECAKE

CRUST

1 cup grated Parmesan cheese	½ cup unsalted butter, melted
1 cup breadcrumbs	1½ teaspoons Creole seasoning

FILLING

1⅓ cups garlic olive oil	1 teaspoon Creole seasoning
¾ cup yellow onion, chopped	24 ounces cream cheese, room temperature
½ red bell pepper, finely diced	
1 cup tasso ham, chopped	¼ cup sour cream
¾ pound catfish fillets, baked and chopped	4 eggs, lightly beaten
1 teaspoon salt	½ cup heavy cream
½ teaspoon cracked black pepper	¾ cup grated, smoked mozzarella

Preheat oven to 350°. For crust, in a mixing bowl combine all crust ingredients until well blended. Press into a 9-inch springform pan.

For filling, in a large skillet over medium-high heat, heat olive oil and sauté onion and red bell pepper until soft. Add tasso, catfish, salt, pepper and Creole seasoning. Toss well and heat through. Set aside and let cool to room temperature. In the bowl of an electric mixer, beat cream cheese, sour cream and eggs until frothy. Add cream, mozzarella and fish mixture. Blend well and pour over crust. Bake until set, about 1½ hours.

20 servings

STILTON AND WALNUT TOASTS

8 ounces Stilton cheese, room temperature	1 baguette, thinly sliced and toasted or grilled
1 teaspoon Dijon mustard	20 walnut halves, toasted
8 ounces mascarpone	

In a small bowl mash the Stilton and blend it with the mustard and mascarpone until smooth. Spread thickly on warm baguette slices and top each with a toasted walnut.

30 pieces

TEX-MEX CRANBERRY SALSA

Serve this slightly spicy salsa with chips or cream cheese and crackers.

1   cup water

1   cup sugar

12 ounces whole fresh cranberries, rinsed and picked over

1   8-ounce can crushed pineapple in juice

3   green onions, finely chopped

2   tablespoons pickled jalapeño peppers, chopped

1   tablespoon fresh lime juice

½   teaspoon ground cumin

2   tablespoons chopped cilantro

This cranberry salsa also complements a Thanksgiving turkey.

Make a simple syrup by bringing water and sugar to a boil over medium heat in a heavy small saucepan. Stir frequently. Stir in cranberries and cook until the cranberries turn to mush, 10-12 minutes. Drain pineapple and reserve juice. To cranberries add crushed pineapple, green onions, jalapeños, lime juice, cumin and cilantro. Heat through. Add reserved pineapple juice if too spicy. Transfer to bowl and refrigerate.

5 cups

Nations' Best Catering

SUN-DRIED TOMATO-FETA CHEESE BALL

½   cup unsalted butter, room temperature

8   ounces cream cheese, room temperature

4   ounces feta cheese, crumbled, room temperature

½   cup chopped green onions

½   cup sun-dried tomato pesto

2   large cloves garlic, minced

1   tablespoon Greek seasoning blend

1   teaspoon dried basil

¼   teaspoon cayenne pepper

Toasted pine nuts or chopped fresh parsley for garnish

Crackers or crostini

In a large mixing bowl blend all ingredients except garnish until well combined. Chill 1-2 hours. Shape into a ball and roll in toasted pine nuts or chopped parsley. Serve with crackers or crostini.

12 servings

BRIE AND MANGO CHUTNEY EN CROÛTE

1	8-ounce frozen puff pastry sheet, thawed	4	tablespoons Brie
4	tablespoons prepared mango chutney	1	egg yolk, beaten

Preheat oven to 400°. Roll puff pastry sheet into a ⅛-inch thick rectangle, 15 x 10 inches. Cut sheet into 24 individual 2½-inch squares. In the center of each square, place ½ teaspoon prepared mango chutney and ½ teaspoon Brie. Fold 1 corner of pastry over filling. Repeat with opposite corner. Fold remaining corners together to form a small package, sealing edges with a bit of water. Brush with egg and bake until golden, about 5 minutes.

24 squares

LUMPIA

FILIPINO EGG ROLLS

2	pounds ground pork, cooked and drained		Salt and pepper to taste
			Soy sauce to taste
3	eggs, divided use	1	11-ounce package super-thin spring roll wrappers
1	8-ounce can water chestnuts, finely chopped	1	teaspoon water
1	medium onion, finely chopped		Vegetable oil for frying
3	cloves garlic, minced		

DIPPING SAUCE

½	cup soy sauce	½	teaspoon crushed red pepper
4	tablespoons lime juice		

For egg rolls, in a large bowl mix the pork, 2 eggs, water chestnuts, onions, garlic, salt, pepper and soy sauce together. Halve spring roll wrappers and place a tablespoonful of the pork mixture along the long edge of wrapper and roll up. In a small bowl beat 1 egg with 1 teaspoon water to form egg wash. Seal the egg roll by dipping a finger in egg wash and running it along the edge of the wrapper. Stack egg rolls in a pan with waxed paper between each layer. In a large skillet or wok, heat vegetable oil to about 375°, or until water pops when sprinkled in the pan. Fry egg rolls in oil, turning until each side is golden brown. Drain on paper towels.

For the dipping sauce, combine soy sauce, lime juice and crushed red pepper. Serve sauce with egg rolls.

60 egg rolls

CREAM CHEESE JALAPEÑO VENISON ROLLS

Serve these hot off the grill.

5	pounds venison steak, cubed
	Salt and pepper
8-12	ounces cream cheese, room temperature
	Jalapeño peppers, sliced lengthwise into strips
	Dale's Steak Seasoning
	Toothpicks

Preheat charcoal grill seasoned with mesquite or hickory. Sprinkle venison with salt and pepper. Spread cream cheese on 1 side of each venison cube. Wrap cube tightly with a jalapeño strip and secure with a toothpick. Drizzle with steak seasoning. Cook over hot charcoal fire, turning frequently, 15-20 minutes.

40 servings

CRISPY ASIAN CHICKEN WINGS

Start preparation the day before serving.

5	pounds chicken wings or drummettes
1	cup lime juice
1	teaspoon salt
1	cup tamari sauce
½	cup honey
1	teaspoon Tabasco sauce
1	teaspoon sesame oil
¼	cup peanut oil
¼	cup chopped, fresh cilantro
1	tablespoon peeled, grated, fresh gingerroot
1	teaspoon chopped garlic
1	green onion, sliced
1	very ripe, finely diced mango
	Sesame seeds and lime wedges for garnish

One day before serving, marinate chicken in salt and lime juice 10 minutes. Drain. Toss chicken with remaining ingredients except garnish and marinate overnight, covered.

Preheat oven to 400° and gas grill to medium. In a roasting pan, bake chicken, uncovered, 30 minutes. Just before serving, put chicken on hot grill and turn frequently until crispy, about 15 minutes. Sprinkle with sesame seeds and garnish with lime wedges.

30 servings

It was not unusual to see William Faulkner on the square, as unapproachable as God. He stood out in a field of blue denim, dressed as he was in herringbone jackets or sometimes in threadbare khakis. But I was surprised by the tiny size of the great man. He seemed far too short and slight to have composed such sound and fury. Faulkner had himself attended Ole Miss and later served as postmaster at the school until an inspector fired him for inattentiveness in 1924. As he stalked away from the job, Faulkner delivered a peroration we were taught in English class: "I reckon I'll be at the beck and call of folks with money all my life, but thank God I won't ever again have to be at the beck and call of every son of a bitch who's got two cents to buy a stamp."

~Curtis Wilkie

Dixie

GRILLED CHICKEN EMPANADAS

DOUGH

1	cup unsalted butter, room temperature	2¼	cups cake flour
8	ounces cream cheese, room temperature	½	teaspoon baking powder
1	egg yolk	½	teaspoon salt

FILLING

2	tablespoons olive oil	¼	teaspoon salt
½	cup chopped yellow onion	¼	teaspoon pepper
1	clove garlic, minced	¼	bunch cilantro, chopped
1	jalapeño, diced	4	ounces Cheddar cheese, shredded
3	grilled boneless chicken breast halves, diced	1	egg
		1	teaspoon water

SAUCE

2	avocados, peeled	2	tablespoons mayonnaise
¼	bunch cilantro	2	tablespoons lime juice
¼	cup chopped yellow onion	¼	teaspoon salt
1	jalapeño		

For dough, in the bowl of an electric mixer, beat butter and cream cheese until smooth. Add egg yolk, cake flour, baking powder and salt. Blend until combined. Let dough rest in a warm area 30-40 minutes. On a floured work surface, roll dough to a ⅛-inch thickness. With a 3-inch round cutter, cut out 50 circles.

For filling, in a large skillet over medium-high heat, heat olive oil and sauté onions, garlic and jalapeño until onions are translucent. Add chicken, salt and pepper. Cool mixture and toss with cilantro and Cheddar. Preheat oven to 350°. Place 1 teaspoon filling on each pastry circle. Fold dough over to make a half-moon shape. Crimp the seam with a fork. In a small bowl beat egg with 1 teaspoon water. Brush egg wash on empanadas. Bake until golden brown, 10-15 minutes.

For sauce, coarsely chop avocados, cilantro, onion and jalapeño. In a blender combine all sauce ingredients and blend until smooth. Refrigerate. Serve sauce alongside empanadas.

50 empanadas

Oxford Steak Company

SHRIMP INFUSED CREAM CHEESE

Spread on crusty bread or crackers as an appetizer, or on grilled crostini as a heavy hors d'oeuvre, topped with whole shrimp and chives. At Oxford Steak Company we serve it over filet mignon.

1 tablespoon olive oil	1 tablespoon white wine
1 pound raw shrimp, peeled and coarsely chopped	8 ounces cream cheese, room temperature
Salt and pepper to taste	Chopped fresh parsley
2 teaspoons minced garlic	

In a sauté pan over medium-high heat, heat olive oil and add shrimp. Sprinkle with salt and pepper to taste, stirring to coat. When shrimp begin to turn pink, add garlic. Cook 30 seconds. Add white wine, stir, and reduce heat to medium-low. Cut cream cheese into blocks and add all at once. Stir well until fully combined. Stir in parsley.

2 cups

The University of Mississippi Blues Archive in Oxford contains the world's largest collection of blues music.

HERBED SHRIMP POCKETS

2-3 tablespoons olive oil	1 teaspoon crushed red pepper
¾ pound medium, raw shrimp, peeled	Salt and pepper to taste
2 cloves garlic, minced	1 8-ounce sheet frozen puff pastry
3 green onions, chopped	1 egg
3 teaspoons chopped, fresh parsley	1 teaspoon water
2 teaspoons chopped, fresh rosemary	Grated Parmesan cheese

In a heavy medium skillet over medium heat, cook oil, shrimp, garlic, onions, parsley, rosemary, crushed red pepper, salt and pepper until shrimp are pink. Thaw puff pastry, flatten with a rolling pin, and cut into 25 squares. Place 1 shrimp coated with herbs on each square. Pinch ends up and around the shrimp, but do not seal. Lightly beat egg with 1 teaspoon of water and brush each pocket with egg wash. Sprinkle with Parmesan cheese, gently patting the cheese into the dough. Freeze on cookie sheet until frozen hard, about 3 hours. Store in plastic bags. To bake, preheat oven to 375°, place shrimp pockets on a lightly greased or parchment-lined cookie sheet, and bake about 20 minutes.

25 pockets

SHRIMP IN MUSTARD SAUCE

¼ cup finely chopped parsley	2 teaspoons crushed red pepper
¼ cup finely chopped shallots	1 teaspoon salt
¼ cup tarragon vinegar	Freshly ground pepper to taste
¼ cup red wine vinegar	2½ pounds boiled shrimp, 31-40 per pound, peeled
½ cup olive oil	
4 tablespoons Dijon mustard	

In a small bowl mix all ingredients except shrimp. Pour mixture over shrimp. Mix well so that every shrimp is coated. Cover and refrigerate.

8 servings

JAMAICAN SHRIMP SPREAD

1 pound medium, boiled shrimp, peeled and sliced into fourths	1 cup flaked coconut
2 cups mayonnaise	1 teaspoon cayenne pepper
1 cup finely chopped green onions	1 tablespoon lemon juice
	Crackers

Combine shrimp, mayonnaise, green onions, coconut, cayenne and lemon juice until well blended. Refrigerate to blend flavors. Serve with crackers.

4 cups

MANGO SHRIMP

2 ripe mangoes, chopped	4 tablespoons Italian vinaigrette salad dressing
2 avocados, chopped	3 tablespoons fresh lime juice
4 green onions, chopped	1 pound shrimp, cooked, peeled and chopped
2 tablespoons chopped cilantro	Tortilla chips
1½ tablespoons chopped pickled jalapeño peppers	

In a large bowl combine mangoes, avocados, green onions, cilantro, jalapeño peppers, salad dressing and lime juice. Add shrimp and toss to coat. Refrigerate to blend flavors. Serve with tortilla chips.

3 cups

PICKLED SHRIMP

5 pounds shrimp, boiled and peeled	3 cups white vinegar
2 onions, sliced	2 teaspoons salt
15 bay leaves	½ teaspoon celery seed
1¼ cups vegetable oil	1 dash Tabasco sauce
2½ tablespoons capers with juice	

In a shallow dish alternate layers of shrimp, onions and bay leaves. In a large bowl combine oil, capers, vinegar, salt, celery seed and Tabasco. Pour over shrimp and refrigerate. Drain before serving.

5 cups

Three types of shrimp are harvested along the Mississippi Gulf Coast: brown shrimp from June to October, white shrimp in the fall, and pink shrimp in winter and early spring.

■ 208 *South Lamar* ■

TEMPURA SHRIMP
WITH SOY-LIME DIPPING SAUCE

SHRIMP

Vegetable oil	1 teaspoon chopped parsley
2 cups flour, divided use	1½ cups club soda
1 cup corn starch	Flour
1 teaspoon salt	3 pounds large, raw, shelled shrimp
1 teaspoon pepper	

SAUCE

1 cup soy sauce	1½ teaspoons peeled, minced gingerroot
¼ cup fresh lime juice	1½ teaspoons crushed red pepper
1½ teaspoons minced garlic	1 tablespoon honey
1½ teaspoons minced shallots	

In a large skillet or fryer, pour enough oil to cover shrimp. Heat oil to 350° In a metal bowl stir together 1 cup flour, corn starch, salt, pepper, parsley and club soda. In a shallow bowl put remaining 1 cup flour. Dredge shrimp in flour, shake off excess, then dip into tempura batter. Drop into hot oil and fry until shrimp float.

For sauce, in a small bowl stir together all ingredients. Serve alongside shrimp.

6 servings

Crab Fingers in Citrus Vinaigrette

½ cup fresh orange juice

½ cup fresh ruby red grapefruit juice

¼ cup raspberry vinegar

½ cup olive oil

Salt and pepper to taste

1 pound crab fingers

Whisk together all ingredients except crab. Pour over crab fingers and marinate 45 minutes. Drain excess vinaigrette before serving.

3 cups

PARTY SMOKED SALMON

This salmon has a smoky, cedar flavor that comes from cooking it on a cedar plank over a charcoal fire.

SALMON

4	tablespoons unsalted butter, melted	Freshly ground pepper to taste
1	tablespoon lemon juice	Fresh dill sprigs
3	pounds salmon fillet, skin on and boned	Parsley sprigs for garnish
		Lemon slices for garnish

SAUCE

8	ounces cream cheese, room temperature	½	teaspoon Worcestershire sauce
½	cup sour cream		Lemon pepper to taste
¼	cup diced red onions		Tabasco sauce to taste
¼	cup capers		Crackers

For salmon, preheat barbecue grill. Moisten cedar plank by soaking it in water and weighting it with a heavy object to keep it submerged while grill is heating. Combine melted butter and lemon juice. Place salmon, skin side down, on the moistened plank and baste with butter mixture. Season with pepper and fresh dill. Let salmon rest 5 minutes to blend flavors. Place cedar plank and salmon in center of hot grill and close lid. The plank will start to smolder, rendering a wonderful smoke flavor. If plank starts to flame up, douse it with a splash of water. Cook about 30 minutes. To serve, roll salmon onto a platter or cutting board. Remove charred skin. Invert salmon onto a serving platter and garnish with fresh parsley and lemon slices.

For the sauce, in the bowl of an electric mixer, mix cream cheese and sour cream until well blended. Stir in red onions, capers, Worcestershire sauce, lemon pepper and Tabasco. Serve salmon with sauce and crackers.

24 servings

MENU

TAILGATING IN THE GROVE

Bloody Marys for the Grove
Bacon Tomato Cups
Black Bean Salsa
Roasted Red Pepper Dip
Broccoli Salad
Herbed Goat Cheese
Fairy Bell's Fried Chicken
Cold Pasta Salad
Chocolate Toffee Cookies
Mo's Sugar Cookies

Crawfish, also called crawdads or crayfish, are freshwater crustaceans that are at their best from March to May.

Main Street Grill, Water Valley

SHRIMP AND TOMATO CROSTINI WITH GREEN ONION OIL

GREEN ONION OIL

1	bunch green onions, chopped	1	cup olive oil
3	cloves garlic, peeled and crushed		Salt and pepper to taste

CROSTINI

10	large shrimp, peeled and boiled	1	baguette, sliced into 20 pieces and toasted
10	Roma tomatoes, seeded and diced		

For oil, in a food processor or blender, purée green onions, garlic, olive oil, salt and pepper until smooth.

For crostini, cut each shrimp into thirds. In a large bowl stir together shrimp, diced tomatoes and green onion oil. Top each baguette slice with shrimp mixture.

20 crostini

CAJUN CRAWFISH DIP

1	tablespoon unsalted butter	12	ounces cream cheese, room temperature
6	green onions, chopped	1	pound frozen, cooked crawfish tails, thawed and chopped
4	cloves garlic, minced		Crackers or toast rounds
1	teaspoon cayenne pepper		
½	teaspoon black pepper		
½	teaspoon garlic salt		

In a heavy large skillet over medium heat, melt butter. Sauté green onions in butter until soft. Add garlic, cayenne, black pepper and garlic salt. Sauté, stirring constantly, for 3 minutes. Add cream cheese and stir until melted. Add crawfish tails and heat through. Keep warm in chafing dish. Serve with crackers or toast rounds.

3 cups

Yocona River Inn

OYSTERS WITH ARTICHOKES

1	pint shucked oysters		10-12	canned artichoke hearts, drained and quartered
2	tablespoons unsalted butter		¼	cup white wine
2	tablespoons chopped shallots or yellow onions		1	cup heavy cream
1	tablespoon minced garlic		½	teaspoon black or white pepper
½	teaspoon salt			Cornbread, biscuits or puff pastry shells
1	teaspoon dried marjoram or oregano (or ½ teaspoon dried tarragon)			

Drain oysters and reserve liquid. In a large sauté pan over medium heat, melt butter and add shallots, garlic and salt. Sauté 3-4 minutes, stirring frequently. Add herb of choice, stir well, and continue cooking 2 minutes. Add artichokes, stir well, and sauté 2-3 minutes. Turn heat to high, pour white wine in pan and stir constantly, scraping the pan sides to remove browned shallots and herbs. When the wine is nearly evaporated, add cream, the reserved oyster liquid and pepper. Cook until the cream is reduced to about ⅓ of its original volume. With the heat on high and the cream bubbling, add the oysters and any liquid that is with them. Stir or swirl the pan briefly, to distribute the oysters so that they will cook evenly. The oysters are done when the ruffled side fans out, after about 2 minutes. Once oysters puff up, they are done and any more cooking will just make them shrink. Ladle over cornbread, biscuit or puff pastry shells and serve immediately.

Cream sauce may be prepared ahead and refrigerated, then brought to a boil before adding oysters.

6-8 appetizer servings

DAR LEMON SANDWICHES

3	egg yolks		1	cup pecans, ground
	Juice and grated zest of 2 lemons		20	thin slices whole wheat bread
½	cup sugar			Mayonnaise
8	ounces cream cheese, room temperature			

In a heavy medium saucepan over medium-high heat, cook egg yolks, lemon juice, lemon zest and sugar until thick, whisking constantly, about 7 minutes. Add cream cheese and pecans. Whisk until smooth. Refrigerate. Remove from refrigerator 30 minutes before making sandwiches. Trim crust from bread and spread with mayonnaise and lemon filling. Cut sandwiches diagonally.

20 sandwiches

The landscape of tents, stretching as far as one could see, now resembled the camp of a medieval army, flying red and blue pennants and lighted by lanterns and candles.

~Curtis Wilkie

on the Grove

GARDEN SANDWICH CAKE

This sandwich, filled with salads and frosted to resemble a cake, is for a special occasion. Be creative with the fillings; chicken salad, pesto or thin slices of salmon or ham work well. Use bread baked in a square, round or rectangular shape. The number of fillings will determine how high the cake is. Use a minimum of 3 layers.

Driving up Highway 7…
I sight the water-towers
of Ole Miss and the
town silhouetted on the
horizon, and then the
lights of the Square and
Mr. Bill's [Faulkner's]
courthouse, and the
loops and groves of the
campus with the Lyceum
at the top of the hill, and
the dark stadium in the
distance. All of it seems
to have sprung from
the hard red earth
for me….

~Willie Morris

"Coming on Back"

PARSLEY AND BACON FILLING

2	bunches fresh parsley or watercress, chopped
1	pound crisp cooked bacon, finely crumbled
3	tablespoons homemade mayonnaise

1	teaspoon Worcestershire sauce
½	teaspoon garlic powder
3	tablespoons unsalted butter, room temperature

EGG AND OLIVE FILLING

12	hard-boiled eggs, chopped
1	cup green olives with pimiento, chopped

2	tablespoons mayonnaise

JALAPEÑO AND PIMIENTO FILLING

3	cups Cheddar cheese, grated
1½	cups Monterey Jack cheese, grated
½	cup chopped pimientos

2	tablespoons pickled jalapeño peppers, chopped
1	cup mayonnaise
1	cup Miracle Whip

FROSTING

10	ounces goat cheese, room temperature

16	ounces cream cheese, room temperature

Large loaf white bread, unsliced

Fresh herbs, vegetables and edible flowers for garnish

- For parsley and bacon filling, combine parsley, bacon, mayonnaise and Worcestershire, stirring until well combined. In a separate bowl, mix garlic powder and butter and set aside.
- For egg and olive filling, mix all ingredients until well combined.
- For jalapeño and pimiento spread, mix all ingredients until well combined.
- For frosting, in a food processor mix goat cheese and cream cheese until creamy and of spreading consistency.
- To assemble, cut crusts from bread loaf. Slice bread horizontally into 4 layers, if using 3 fillings. Place bottom bread layer on serving plate. Spread the reserved butter mixture, from the parsley and bacon recipe, over bread layer. Spread parsley and bacon filling evenly over buttered bread. Press second bread layer over parsley and bacon filling; spread bread with egg and olive filling.

GARDEN SANDWICH CAKE *continued*

Press third bread layer over egg and olive filling. Spread jalapeño and pimiento filling over bread. Top with fourth bread layer. Frost the top and sides of sandwich cake with frosting, spreading until smooth and even. Decorate with edible flowers such as nasturtiums, pansies, Johnny jump-ups, coreopsis and violets, or with sprigs of oregano, dill, Italian parsley, rosemary and thyme. Mix herbs and flowers with vegetables such as asparagus spears to resemble a garden on the side of the cake. Refrigerate 2-3 hours and slice to serve.

12-15 servings

Photo on page 8

LOBSTER BRIE TURNOVERS

A special occasion hors d'oeuvre

4 shallots, minced	¼ pound Brie, rind on, diced, room temperature
1½ tablespoons minced garlic	
Olive oil	¼ cup chopped parsley
1 pound fresh asparagus, ends removed, cut into 1-inch pieces	Salt and pepper to taste
1 whole lobster, cooked, meat removed	1 pound phyllo dough, room temperature
⅓ cup heavy cream	Unsalted butter, melted
	Fish roe, optional

In a heavy large skillet over medium high heat, sauté shallots and garlic in olive oil until translucent. Add asparagus and sauté until not quite tender, as it will finish cooking in the turnover. Finely chop lobster, add to skillet, and cook until warm. Drain oil from pan. Add cream, heat to a simmer, and remove from heat. Add Brie and stir until melted. Add parsley, salt and pepper. Chill 3-4 hours.

Preheat oven to 350°. Brush 1 sheet of phyllo dough with butter, stack another layer on top and brush it with butter. Top with a third layer and brush with butter. With a sharp serrated knife, slice the stack of phyllo dough lengthwise into 2 rectangular strips. Place 3-4 teaspoons of lobster filling on the bottom of each strip, topping with a sprinkle of fish roe, if desired. Fold the phyllo to form a triangle, then continue folding from one corner to the opposite side to form one triangle from each strip. Continue with remaining phyllo and filling. Arrange turnovers on greased cookie sheet. Brush turnovers lightly with butter or lightly coat with cooking spray. Bake until golden brown on top, 8-12 minutes.

Shrimp may be substituted for the lobster.

16 turnovers

…Miss Sophosiba came out the door carrying a tray with another toddy on it…after a while she said how her papa always said nothing sweetened a Missippi toddy like the hand of a Missippi lady and would Uncle Buck like to see how she use to sweeten her papa's toddy for him? She lifted the toddy and took a sip of it and handed it again to Uncle Buck…

~William Faulkner

Go Down, Moses

Chutney Spread

8 ounces cream cheese,
room temperature

½ cup prepared chutney,
finely chopped

4 tablespoons
finely chopped pecans

2 tablespoons
chopped pimiento

2 teaspoons curry powder

1 teaspoon lemon juice

3 drops garlic juice

Bread or crackers

In a mixing bowl combine
cream cheese and chutney.
Blend well. Add pecans,
pimiento, curry powder,
lemon juice and garlic juice.
Serve with bread
or crackers.

1½ cups

CUCUMBER SPREAD

Begin preparing this spread the day before serving.

2   large cucumbers, unpeeled

½   cup cider vinegar

2   teaspoons salt

16   ounces cream cheese, room
     temperature

¾   cup mayonnaise

½   teaspoon garlic salt

1   teaspoon lemon juice

Grate cucumbers. In a glass or plastic bowl, place cucumbers, vinegar and salt. Stir to blend, cover, and refrigerate overnight. Wrap cucumbers in paper towels and press out all liquid, getting them as dry as possible. In a mixing bowl blend cream cheese, mayonnaise, garlic salt and lemon juice. Stir in cucumbers. Use as sandwich filling or to fill cherry tomatoes.

4 cups

■ 208 *South Lamar* ■

CRAB CAKES

1   pound jumbo lump crabmeat

1   pound claw crabmeat

1   red bell pepper, finely diced

1   yellow bell pepper, finely diced

1   green bell pepper, finely diced

1   teaspoon Tabasco sauce

1   teaspoon Worcestershire sauce

1   teaspoon dry English mustard

1   cup mayonnaise

½   cup crushed saltine crackers

2   cups Panko breadcrumbs*
     Clarified butter

Preheat oven to 450°. In a large bowl thoroughly mix all ingredients except Panko breadcrumbs and butter. In a shallow bowl put Panko breadcrumbs. Using a 3-ounce ice cream scoop, place 1 scoop of crabmeat mixture in the bowl of Panko breadcrumbs and form into a cake. In a skillet heat 1 tablespoon clarified butter until it smokes. Without crowding the pan, sauté 1 side of each crab cake until golden brown, turn over and finish heating in the oven 5 minutes. Repeat with remaining crab cakes.

*From Japan, Panko breadcrumbs are lighter and crunchier than American ones. They are available in Asian markets.

10 servings

LELLA'S PIMIENTO CHEESE

Homemade mayonnaise is the secret.

8	ounces sharp Cheddar cheese, grated	1	dash red pepper
4	ounces whole pimientos	1	dash Worcestershire sauce
	Lella's mayonnaise	1	pinch sugar
1	dash onion powder		

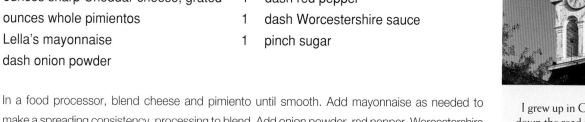

In a food processor, blend cheese and pimiento until smooth. Add mayonnaise as needed to make a spreading consistency, processing to blend. Add onion powder, red pepper, Worcestershire and sugar; process until blended. The pimiento cheese will be a solid color once the processing is complete.

1 cup

LELLA'S MAYONNAISE

1	cup oil, divided use	½	teaspoon salt
1	egg	1	tablespoon lemon juice
½	teaspoon dry mustard		Onion powder to taste
1	dash cayenne pepper		

In a food processor fitted with a metal blade, place ¾ cup oil, egg, mustard, cayenne, salt, lemon juice and onion powder. Process on high speed, very slowly pouring the remaining ¼ cup of oil in a thin stream through the food chute, or pouring the oil into the food pusher and allowing it to drip through the small hole in the pusher. Very slowly incorporating the oil will keep mayonnaise from separating. Continue processing until all oil is blended.

1 cup

I grew up in Coffeeville, just down the road from Oxford. It was and is a small, close-knit community where everyone knows almost everyone and people take care of each other. My very special aunt, Ella (referred to as "Lella" by my brother and eventually people outside our family) was famous, and I do mean famous, for her pimiento cheese. Just how closely her pimiento cheese sandwiches were associated with her is indicated by the fact that her minister mentioned them in his sweet eulogy for her. He said that he didn't know who had been making the pimiento cheese sandwiches in heaven before she got there, but they were going to have to move over now because she was going to be in charge. I called Lella and asked how she made her sandwiches. She started with "Well, first you make the mayonnaise." I interrupted her and said that I was not going to make homemade mayonnaise, just to give me the proportions on the cheese, pimientos, and spices. There was a long pause and then she said, "Well, you might as well not bother." You better believe that when I make these sandwiches—
I make the mayonnaise!

~Nan Davis

BEVERAGES

Lavender Punch

1 cup water

2 sticks cinnamon

¼ teaspoon whole cloves

3 12-ounce cans frozen
grape juice concentrate,
thawed

½ cup fresh lime juice

2 quarts ginger ale, chilled

Frozen seedless grapes
for garnish

Bring water, cinnamon
and cloves to a boil and
steep 5 minutes. Strain and
chill. Add grape juice
concentrate, lime juice
and ginger ale just
before serving.
Garnish with grapes.

14 cups

YOKNAPATAWPHA TEA

4 English Breakfast tea bags
12 large fresh mint leaves
3 cups boiling water
1 cup orange juice
⅓ cup lemon juice

1 cup sugar
6 cups water
   Sprigs of mint
   Orange slices

Place tea bags and mint leaves in a 3-quart pitcher. Add 3 cups boiling water and steep until cool. Discard tea bags and mint leaves. Add orange and lemon juices, sugar and 6 cups water to tea mixture, stirring until sugar is dissolved. Serve over ice and garnish with mint springs and orange slices.

3 quarts

Photo on page 175

OLD-FASHIONED LEMONADE

1 cup fresh lemon juice
1 cup superfine sugar
4 cups water

½ cup cranberry juice, optional
   Lemon slices and mint for garnish

Place lemon juice, sugar and water in a pitcher. Stir until sugar is dissolved. Stir in cranberry juice, if desired. Chill and serve over ice. Garnish with lemon slices and mint.

1½ quarts

GRAND HOTEL BRUNCH PUNCH

1 quart orange juice
1 quart pineapple juice
1 quart apple juice

2 cups ginger ale
   Cherry juice or grenadine
   Champagne

Combine juices and ginger ale. Add cherry juice or grenadine to color and champagne to desired amount. Chill.

20 cups

BLOODY MARYS FOR THE GROVE

¾ cup lemon juice	Pepper to taste
1 tablespoon Louisiana Hot Sauce	Celery salt to taste
1 tablespoon chili sauce	1 46-ounce can tomato juice, chilled
¼ cup Worcestershire sauce	1 24-ounce can V-8 juice, chilled
1 teaspoon Tabasco sauce	1 fifth vodka, chilled
1 tablespoon prepared horseradish	Celery sticks and small lime wedges for garnish

Combine lemon juice, hot sauce, chili sauce, Worcestershire, Tabasco, horseradish, pepper and celery salt in a pint jar. Refrigerate overnight. In a large container pour seasoning mixture, tomato juice, V-8 juice and vodka; stir until combined. Serve over ice and garnish with celery sticks and lime wedges.

25 servings

Artist Robert Malone Artwork, page 35

Educated in painting and sculpture at Memphis College of Art and the University of Mississippi, Malone has been an Assistant Visiting Professor in Ole Miss's art department since 1997. Malone's artwork shows primarily in Memphis, Oxford, and New Orleans, but his work has appeared in shows and is in private and corporate collections around the country, as well as in Australia. Originally from Trenton, Tennessee, Malone loves to cook, wok, and grill.

HAL'S BOURBON SLUSH

12 ounces lemonade concentrate	6 cups water
6 ounces orange juice concentrate	1 cup sugar
2 cups bourbon	2 cups strong hot tea

Stir all ingredients together until sugar dissolves. Freeze until slushy, 6-8 hours.

13 cups

BRANDY ALEXANDER

2 cups vanilla ice cream	3 tablespoons white Crème de Cacao
3 tablespoons brandy	Chocolate shavings for garnish

Process ice cream, brandy and Crème de Cacao in a blender until smooth. Spoon into glasses. Garnish with chocolate shavings. Serve immediately.

2 servings

Author John Grisham
Essay, page 36

John lived in Oxford while studying law at the University of Mississippi (J.D.,1981) and again from 1990 until moving to Charlottesville, Virginia, in 1999. He published his first novel, *A Time to Kill*, in 1989. His next book, *The Firm*, was his break-out hit. Since then, he has published 13 legal thrillers, three other novels and has become one of the world's best-selling authors. Several of his books have been made into films. In 1993 Grisham and his wife, Renée, funded a visiting Southern writer program that brings a new promising writer to the campus every year.

FROZEN MARGARITAS

¾ cup premium tequila
½ cup Cointreau
6 ounces frozen limeade concentrate

Zest of 1 lime
Ice
Margarita salt and lime wedges for garnish

Pour liquors, limeade concentrate and zest into blender container. Add ice to fill the container. Blend well. Serve in margarita glasses garnished with salt and lime wedges.

4 servings

PEAR MARTINI
WITH LEMON AND ROSEMARY

ROSEMARY SYRUP

1 cup sugar
1 cup water

4 4-inch rosemary sprigs

MARTINI

3 cups vodka
6 tablespoons fresh lemon juice
4 tablespoons clear pear brandy

12 ice cubes
12 small rosemary sprigs
12 thin slices of pear

Bring sugar and water to a boil in a small saucepan, stirring until sugar dissolves. Add rosemary sprigs. Reduce heat and simmer 2 minutes. Cool mixture completely and discard rosemary.

Mix rosemary syrup, vodka, lemon juice and brandy in a large pitcher. Cover pitcher with plastic wrap and place in freezer until mixture is cold, about 3 hours. Remove pitcher from freezer and add ice cubes. Stir briskly to melt the ice partially. Strain mixture into chilled martini glasses. Garnish each glass with a rosemary sprig and pear slice.

12 servings

Stormy Square by Robert Malone ▶

BRUNSWICK STEW
from INDIANA JONES

John Grisham

My wife, Renée, was born in North Carolina, as were her parents, grandparents and so on. Her great-great grandfather fought for a Carolina brigade and was killed by the Yankees during Pickett's charge at Gettysburg. No state lost as many boys as North Carolina in that great battle.

Her grandfather, Silas Jones, was born in the small town of Clayton, North Carolina, in 1900, the youngest of 11 children born to a colorful lady by the name of Indiana Jones. I attended the funeral of Silas Jones in Clayton 95 years after he was born there. Indiana Jones gets credit for the particular style of Brunswick stew that I am about to discuss.

Renée's mother is an excellent cook, which quickly became a delightful windfall once I started hanging around their house in Southaven, Mississippi. Lib, from Apex, North Carolina, prepared dishes I had never eaten. Southern dishes, but with a decidedly regional taste. The cornbread was either flat and baked, or flat and fried. (Either version was fine with me.) The squash was browned in a black skillet over several hours. The cabbage and collards were chopped. The fried chicken had a crust far thicker and crunchier than anything Colonel Sanders ever came up with. There was a coconut cake that weighed at least 20 pounds and was instantly addictive. The barbeque sauce was vinegar based with a touch of sugar.

But the signature dish was Brunswick stew, something virtually unheard of in Mississippi and Arkansas. And when I let it slip that I had never eaten Brunswick stew, Renée and her family were horrified. The romance was briefly in jeopardy.

They had little to worry about. One bowl and I was hooked.

Later, after we were married, we visited her kinfolk in North Carolina and I was offered all manner of Brunswick stew. Every serious cook has his or her own recipe. Many restaurants serve a side of the stew without even asking; it just arrives, like the ice water. And it's all delicious.

However, it is extremely difficult to locate a family recipe for the stew. A real recipe that is, not one published in a cookbook. I suspect there are two reasons for this. The first is a regional oddity. Many cooks in North Carolina consider it rude if you ask for a recipe. Downright rude. Recipes are guarded like dark family secrets, whispered down from one generation to the next. My wife has a recipe for chocolate chip cookies that will annihilate the will of even the most committed anorexic, and she will not give it to anyone. Our daughter is 18 years old and has yet to see it. When the cookies are made, no one is allowed in the kitchen.

I don't know if this is peculiar to people from North Carolina, and I'm not asking a lot of questions. It does, however, lead to some tense moments in otherwise pleasant settings when an unenlightened cook from somewhere outside of North Carolina asks my wife or her mother for a recipe. You might as well blurt out that the food tastes awful.

The second reason is that many of the recipes are simply never reduced to writing to begin with. This adds greatly to their mystery. A savory dish of this or that always tastes better if it's been cooked the same secret way for many generations.

When Silas Jones was alive he was in charge of making the Brunswick stew, and it was a ritual that engulfed the entire family. At the first hint of cold weather he would announce, "Tomorrow, I'm making Brunswick stew," and everything else came to a halt. From memory, he would pull together the ingredients from Indiana's secret and unwritten recipe and spend two days in the kitchen. On the first day, he would cook the chickens, hens, pork, beef, and wild game, then allow them to cool overnight so he could separate the meat from the bones. Early on the second day he would skim the broth and begin adding vegetables and seasonings. He would labor over the massive stockpot for hours, gently stirring, sniffing the thick aroma, always sampling his stew. Only Silas was allowed to taste his work in progress.

When he decided the stew was ready to eat, it would be served with hot cornbread (flat even then) and devoured as slowly as humanly possible, which wasn't very slow at all. As always, it was washed down with gallons of sweet tea.

Late in his life, after his cooking days were over, Silas at some unrecorded point passed along Indiana's recipe to Lib. Now, about twice a year, the family will clamor for the stew, and Lib will oblige with a hard day in the kitchen. Often, in the dead of winter, when Lib is visiting us in Virginia, on cue her grandchildren will begin whining about the absence of Brunswick stew in their lives. Like all good grandmothers, she will instantly succumb and start making lists of all the necessary ingredients. We freeze it by the gallon and enjoy until late spring.

Speaking of Virginia, if you have any interest in starting another civil war, or even a minor regional conflict, then go to North Carolina, sit at the table of a gifted cook, and announce at full volume that, according to someone's version of history, Brunswick stew actually originated in Brunswick County, Virginia! Not Brunswick County, North Carolina.

As soon as you say this, you might want to duck under the table. This stew is serious business in both states. Here is a serious recipe:

2	chickens (3 lbs. each), cut into 6 or 8 pieces	2	cups of lima beans
5	large tomatoes, peeled, seeded, chopped	2	cups of sliced okra
4	cups of fresh kernel corn	1	tablespoon of salt
4	medium potatoes, peeled, diced	1	tablespoon of ground black pepper
4	celery stalks	1	tablespoon of red pepper
2	large onions, thinly sliced	1	teaspoon of sugar

In a large stockpot, boil the chickens over high heat. Reduce the heat to medium low and simmer, partially covered, until the chicken is falling off the bones and the broth is thick. This should take 2-3 hours. Remove the chicken to a bowl and cool. Skim the broth. Add corn, celery, potatoes, onions, lima beans, and okra. Season with salt, pepper, and sugar. Bring to a simmer over medium heat. Reduce the heat to medium low and cook, stirring often, until the potatoes are tender, about 20 minutes.

Meanwhile, pull the chicken off the bones. Add the chicken to the vegetables and bring to a boil. Add tomatoes. Cover, reduce heat, and simmer for 3 hours. From time to time taste the stew for seasoning. Add more salt, pepper and sugar as desired.

Serve hot in warmed bowl with cornbread, flat or otherwise. Wash down with sugary iced tea.

This will render a delicious stew that will bring warmth to your family and keep everyone near the kitchen for many hours. And it might bear some resemblance to the one Indiana Jones prepared a hundred years ago.

I cannot say that it will be exactly like hers because Lib, my mother-in-law from North Carolina, would not give me her secret recipe.

Creole Crab Stew
Bread Sticks

SOUPS

BLACK BEAN SOUP

4   cloves garlic, minced
1   medium onion, chopped
1   tablespoon ground cumin
1   teaspoon crushed red pepper
3   tablespoons olive oil
3   16-ounce cans black beans, undrained, divided use

1   14.5-ounce can chicken broth
2   tablespoons lime juice
1   16-ounce jar salsa
2   tablespoons chopped cilantro
    Sour cream for garnish
    Fresh cilantro for garnish

In a large stock pot, cook garlic, onion, cumin and crushed red pepper in olive oil over medium heat until tender, about 5 minutes. Remove from heat. In blender, purée 2 cans black beans with chicken broth. Add to pot. Stir in remaining can of black beans. Add lime juice, salsa and cilantro. Heat to boiling, reduce heat, and simmer over low heat 30 minutes. Garnish with sour cream and tiny sprigs of cilantro.

10 cups

If you prefer to use dried beans instead of canned, use 1½ cups dried beans. Put beans in a stockpot and pour in water to cover beans plus 2 inches. Soak beans overnight; or bring to a boil for a few minutes, remove from heat, cover, and let soak about 1 hour. Proceed with directions in recipe.

TOMATO BISQUE

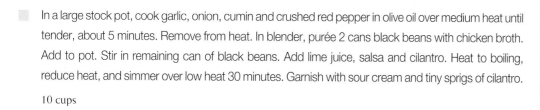

2-3 pounds peeled, fresh tomatoes (or two 10-ounce cans tomato purée)
    Salt and pepper to taste
1   cup diced tomatoes, drained
½   teaspoon onion juice

2   teaspoons lemon juice
¼   teaspoon sugar
½   cup sour cream
    Chopped chives or green onions for garnish

In a blender or food processor purée tomatoes in batches until smooth. Strain to remove seeds and season to taste with salt and pepper. Pour the tomato purée into a large saucepan and add the diced tomatoes. (If a smoother consistency is desired, omit the diced tomatoes and increase the amount of purée.) Add the onion juice, lemon juice and sugar. Simmer over low heat 20 minutes. Slowly stir in sour cream and heat through. Pour into bowls and garnish with chopped chives or green onions.

4 cups

To peel fresh tomatoes, make a small cut just through tomatoes' skins and drop them into boiling water for several seconds. Remove tomatoes and plunge in ice water. Cool and peel away skins.

CREAMY ARTICHOKE SOUP

5	tablespoons unsalted butter	2	cups half-and-half
1	bunch green onions with tops, chopped	½	cup dry white wine
8	ounces fresh mushrooms, sliced	1	14-ounce can artichoke hearts, drained and chopped
4	tablespoons flour	½	teaspoon salt
2	cups chicken broth		Cayenne pepper

In large saucepan over medium heat, melt butter and sauté onions and mushrooms until tender. Stir flour into mixture until well blended. Remove from heat and cool 2 minutes. Gradually stir in chicken broth, half-and-half and wine. Cook uncovered over medium heat until thickened, stirring often. Stir in artichoke hearts, salt and cayenne. Cook until heated through. Soup may thicken if cooked too long. Add extra broth and wine to maintain desired consistency.

Can add shrimp or crabmeat or a variety of different mushrooms.

8 servings

▪ Nations' Best Catering ▪

BUTCHIE'S FAVORITE CHILI

3	pounds ground beef	⅛	teaspoon cayenne pepper
3	large onions, chopped	½	teaspoon celery seed
2	green bell peppers, chopped	3	teaspoons cumin seed, crushed
4-6	ribs celery, chopped and boiled in water to soften	2	bay leaves
1	32-ounce can stewed tomatoes		Rice
1	10-ounce can tomatoes with green chilies		Shredded Cheddar for garnish
2	6-ounce cans tomato paste		Green onions for garnish
6	tablespoons chili powder		Sour cream for garnish

In a large skillet over medium-high heat brown meat. Drain off fat. Add remaining ingredients and cook 3-4 hours over low heat. Serve with rice, shredded Cheddar, green onions, and sour cream.

12 servings

PUMPKIN CURRY SOUP

An elegant soup for fall or winter

2	tablespoons unsalted butter	3	cups chicken broth, divided use
½	cup chopped onions	1	15-ounce can pumpkin
8	ounces fresh mushrooms, sliced	1	tablespoon honey
2	tablespoons flour	1	cup heavy cream
1	tablespoon curry powder		Sour cream and croutons for garnish

In a heavy saucepan over medium-high heat, melt butter and sauté onions until translucent. Add mushrooms and continue to cook 2-3 minutes. Sprinkle flour and curry powder over mixture and stir until well mixed. Add half of broth and cook until just heated. Remove from heat, let cool slightly, and purée the soup (in batches, if necessary). Return puréed mixture to pan and gradually add remainder of broth and the pumpkin. Cook over low heat, stirring often, 15 minutes. Add honey and cream and cook until heated. Serve soup warm with a dollop of sour cream and croutons.

6 cups

MUSHROOM BISQUE

This soup is particularly delicious with a little dash of white truffle oil poured into each individual bowl right on top of the soup. For a thicker soup, try omitting some of the chicken broth or milk.

4	tablespoons unsalted butter	1	cup milk
1	cup chopped onion	1	cup heavy cream
1	pound fresh mushrooms, chopped	½	teaspoon salt
4	tablespoons flour	⅛	teaspoon pepper
3	cups chicken stock		Cayenne pepper to taste
¼	cup chopped fresh parsley	3	tablespoons sherry

In stockpot over medium-high heat, melt butter and sauté onion until translucent. In a food processor chop mushrooms to a medium dice. Add to stockpot and sauté, stirring often. Sprinkle flour over mushroom mixture and cook, stirring, about 2 minutes. Add stock and parsley and continue stirring until well combined. Reduce heat to low and simmer about 20 minutes. Stir in milk, cream, salt, pepper, cayenne and sherry, cooking until heated through. Be careful not to boil.

6 servings

Location, Location, Location

When Sardis Dam was built in 1936-1940, the United States government bought land for about $7.50 per acre. Landowners were eager to sell their land for this premium price.

~Will Lewis, Jr.

ROASTED EGGPLANT SOUP

SOUP

2	large eggplants (12-14 ounces each), peeled	1	cup peeled, diced, seeded tomatoes (fresh or canned)
¼	cup olive oil, divided use	1	teaspoon dried marjoram
2	tablespoons unsalted butter	2	bay leaves
¼	cup minced shallots	4	cups chicken stock
½	cup minced carrots		Salt and freshly ground pepper to taste
1	tablespoon minced garlic	1	tablespoon lemon juice

YOGURT TOPPING

1	cup plain yogurt	2	tablespoons minced chives
	Grated zest of 1 lemon		Salt and freshly ground pepper to taste

Preheat oven to 375°. Cut eggplants into quarters and brush surfaces with 2 tablespoons of the olive oil. In a roasting pan, place eggplants and bake until soft, about 30 minutes. In a large saucepan, over medium heat, heat remaining olive oil and butter. Sauté shallots, carrots and garlic 2 minutes. Add tomatoes and simmer 5 minutes. Add marjoram, bay leaves, roasted eggplant and chicken stock. Bring to a simmer and cover. Reduce heat to maintain a simmer and cook 20 minutes. Remove bay leaves and transfer soup to a blender or food processor. Purée. If desired, at this point soup may be covered and refrigerated for serving the next day. Return to pan, heat slowly, and add salt, pepper and lemon juice.

For yogurt topping, in a small bowl, stir together yogurt, lemon zest, chives, salt and pepper. Garnish soup with yogurt topping.

8 cups

◀ **MENU**

DINNER PARTY AT AMMADELLE

Spinach-Oyster Soup

Herbed Green Beans

Company Squash

Horseradish Salad

Chargrilled Beef Tenderloin

Ice Box Rolls

Mocha Velvet Torte

And I can get used to walking a mile for two lard buckets full of water," she said. "I don't wants no propped-up porch. I wants a new porch…and a cook-stove and a well.

~William Faulkner

Go Down, Moses

BAKED POTATO SOUP

8	slices bacon	1½	teaspoons dried basil
1	cup yellow onion, diced	1	teaspoon salt
1½	teaspoons minced garlic	1	teaspoon coarsely ground pepper
⅔	cup flour	½	teaspoon Tabasco sauce
6	cups chicken broth, heated	1	cup grated Cheddar cheese (reserve some for garnish)
5	medium potatoes, baked, peeled and diced (4-5 cups)	½	cup sliced green onions (reserve some for garnish)
2	cups half-and-half		
¼	cup chopped, fresh parsley		

In a large saucepan over medium-high heat, cook bacon until crisp. Remove bacon from pan, cool, and crumble. Set aside for garnish. In the bacon drippings in saucepan, sauté onion over medium-high heat until translucent, about 3 minutes. Add minced garlic and sauté 3 minutes. Add flour, whisking until mixture just begins to turn golden. Add chicken broth gradually, whisking until liquid thickens. Add baked potatoes, half-and-half, parsley, basil, salt, pepper and Tabasco. Reduce heat and simmer 10 minutes. Do not allow soup to boil. Add grated cheese and green onions, reserving some for garnish. Heat soup until cheese melts completely. Garnish each serving with bacon, Cheddar and green onions.

14 cups

BRIE SOUP

½	cup unsalted butter	1	teaspoon dried thyme
½	cup chopped celery	1	bay leaf
½	cup chopped carrots	6	ounces Brie cheese
¼	cup chopped onion	½	cup heavy cream
½	cup flour		Salt and white pepper to taste
3	cups chicken broth		

In a stockpot over medium heat, melt butter and sauté celery, carrots and onion until tender. Add flour, stirring constantly, and cook 2 minutes. Gradually stir in chicken broth. Add thyme and bay leaf and simmer 5 minutes. Cut rind off Brie and cut cheese into chunks. Add to soup and stir until melted. Add cream, salt and white pepper to taste. Remove bay leaf. Serve hot.

5 cups

■ *Yocona River Inn* ■

Basic Chicken Stock

The key to a great soup is a homemade stock! It will keep in the refrigerator 3 days and up to 6 months in the freezer. Make a large pot of stock and freeze it in zip-top freezer bags. Just defrost as needed.

4 pounds chicken bones
(or bones from 2 chickens)

2 cups chopped
yellow onions

2 cups chopped carrots

½ cup white wine

6 quarts cold water

1 cup chopped celery

1 bay leaf

Fresh parsley

Fresh thyme

Peppercorns

Salt to taste

Preheat oven to 375°.
In a roasting pan large
enough to hold them in a
shallow layer, place the
bones, onions and carrots.

continued on next page

CORN AND POTATO CHOWDER

½ cup unsalted butter, room temperature, divided use	6 ears fresh corn or 2 cups frozen shoepeg corn
1 large onion, diced	1 tablespoon plus 1 teaspoon thyme
6 cups chicken stock	1 tablespoon salt
1 pound red potatoes, scrubbed and cubed	1 teaspoon pepper
	6 tablespoons flour

In a Dutch oven over medium-high heat, melt 2 tablespoons butter and sauté onion until translucent, about 3 minutes. Add chicken stock and potatoes. Reduce heat to medium and cook, covered, 25 minutes. If using fresh corn, cut kernels from cobs. Add corn, thyme, salt and pepper. Cook, covered, 30 minutes. In a small bowl stir together remaining 6 tablespoons butter and flour until no lumps remain. Add to hot soup and stir well. Before soup comes to a boil, lower heat to lowest setting and cook, covered, 15 minutes.

10 cups

CHEESY CHICKEN CHOWDER

3 cups chicken broth	¼ teaspoon pepper
2 cups peeled, diced potatoes	¼ cup unsalted butter
1 cup diced carrots	⅓ cup flour
1 cup diced celery	2 cups milk
½ cup diced onion	2 cups shredded Cheddar cheese
1½ teaspoons salt	2 cups boiled or smoked, diced chicken

In large saucepan over high heat, bring chicken broth to boil. Reduce heat and add potatoes, carrots, celery, onion, salt and pepper. Cover and simmer until vegetables are tender, about 15 minutes. In medium saucepan melt butter, add flour, and mix well. To saucepan, gradually stir in milk and cook over low heat until slightly thickened. Stir in cheese and cook until melted. Add cheese and flour mixture to broth along with the cooked chicken. Continue to cook over low heat until heated through.

12 cups

Basic Chicken Stock *continued*

Bake until bones are nicely browned, 45-60 minutes, stirring every 15 minutes. Transfer bones and vegetables to a large stockpot. Add the white wine to roasting pan and deglaze the pan by scraping the bits off the bottom. Add wine and bits to the stockpot. Add the water, celery, bay leaf, parsley, thyme, peppercorns and salt to the stockpot. Bring to a low simmer. Skim surface of stock as needed. Do not allow stock to boil and keep water level above bones, adding more water if needed. Simmer 3-4 hours. Strain through cheesecloth or a fine mesh strainer.

6 quarts

CREOLE CRAB STEW

2	large lemons	1	large sprig parsley
3	tablespoons unsalted butter	1	sprig marjoram
1	medium yellow onion, chopped	2	tablespoons chopped mint, divided use
2	cloves garlic, minced	1	tablespoon chopped tarragon
4	cups canned Italian tomatoes with juice, seeded and chopped	1	pound lump crabmeat, picked through
4	cups shellfish stock or fish stock		Salt to taste
1	bay leaf		Cayenne pepper to taste

Remove the zest from 1 lemon in 1 long strip, if possible, with a vegetable peeler and set aside. Juice the peeled lemon and thinly slice the remaining lemon. Set aside. In a deep skillet or Dutch oven, melt butter and sauté onion and garlic over medium heat until soft, about 4 minutes. Add the tomatoes with their juices and the stock and increase heat to medium-high until mixture boils. Turn heat down so that mixture is at a simmer and add the lemon zest strip, bay leaf, parsley sprig, marjoram sprig, 1 tablespoon chopped mint, chopped tarragon and 1½ tablespoons of the reserved lemon juice. Simmer, partially covered, 30-40 minutes. Add crabmeat and simmer gently about 10 minutes. Add salt, cayenne and more lemon juice if needed. Discard the bay leaf, parsley sprig and marjoram sprig. Stir in remaining tablespoon mint, spoon stew into bowls, and top each serving with a thin slice of lemon.

6-8 servings

Photo on page 38

SPINACH-OYSTER SOUP

¼	cup unsalted butter	1	10-ounce package frozen, chopped spinach, thawed and drained
½	medium onion, chopped	1	pint raw oysters, drained and chopped
2	cloves garlic, minced		Salt and black pepper to taste
½	cup flour		Cayenne pepper to taste
2½	cups half-and-half, heated		
1½	cups chicken stock		

In a large saucepan over medium heat, melt butter and sauté onion and garlic. Add flour and cook, stirring, 3 minutes. Add half-and-half and continue to cook, stirring, until smooth, 2-3 minutes. Remove from heat. In a blender pour chicken stock and add spinach. Blend well and add to saucepan. Add oysters and simmer until they begin to curl. Season with salt and peppers to taste and serve hot.

8 servings

Photo on page 42

SEAFOOD GUMBO

⅓ cup bacon grease or unsalted butter
⅓ cup flour
1½ cups finely chopped celery
1 large onion, chopped
2 cloves garlic, minced
1 16-ounce can whole tomatoes
1 16-ounce can tomato sauce
6 cups water
1 tablespoon salt
1 teaspoon pepper

3 bay leaves
1 teaspoon dried thyme
½ cup chopped parsley
1 pound frozen cut okra
2 pounds raw, peeled shrimp
1½ pounds crabmeat, picked through
1 pint raw oysters
1 teaspoon crushed red pepper
2 tablespoons Worcestershire sauce
  Hot cooked rice

In a large heavy skillet or Dutch oven over medium heat, melt bacon grease or butter. Add flour and cook, stirring constantly with wooden spoon for 10 minutes or until roux is the color of a penny. Add celery, onion and garlic. Cook until soft, stirring occasionally. In a blender process tomatoes. To the pot add blended tomatoes, tomato sauce, water, salt, pepper, bay leaves, thyme and parsley. Over medium heat, simmer for an hour, stirring enough to keep from sticking. Add okra and simmer 5 minutes. Add shrimp and crabmeat. Simmer 15 minutes. Add oysters, crushed red pepper and Worcestershire, and cook another 10 minutes. Remove bay leaves and serve over rice.

12-14 servings

CRAB AND CORN BISQUE

½ pound bacon, cut into small strips, divided use
4 tablespoons unsalted butter
1 white onion, diced
1 14.75-ounce can cream-style corn
3 11-ounce cans vacuum-packed crisp corn
2 14-ounce cans chicken broth

  Salt and pepper to taste
  Cayenne pepper to taste
  Creole seasoning to taste
  Garlic powder to taste
2 pounds crabmeat (preferably 1 pound each, lump and dark)
4 cups half-and-half

In a Dutch oven over medium heat, fry several bacon strips. Set aside for garnish. Add butter, onions and the remainder of the bacon strips, and cook until onions are translucent. Add corn and chicken broth and bring to slight boil. Cook over medium heat about 5 minutes. Add salt, pepper, cayenne, Creole seasoning and garlic powder. Cook 15 minutes, stirring often to prevent scorching. Turn heat to low and add crabmeat and half-and-half. Heat through. Garnish with reserved bacon.

12 cups

There are three basic types of roux: light or blond, medium or copper-colored, and dark. When making a roux, stir constantly to prevent burning. If black specks appear, it has burned and should be thrown out. Taking the roux off the heat just before reaching the desired color will prevent residual heat from cooking the roux too much.

47

Yocona River Inn

Basic Vegetable Stock

2 cups sliced yellow onions

2 cups sliced leeks

2 cups chopped carrots

Vegetable oil or unsalted butter

4 quarts cold water

1 cup chopped tomato

1 cup chopped celery

2-3 cloves garlic, whole

Bay leaf

Fresh parsley

Fresh thyme

Peppercorns

Salt to taste

In a large stockpot over medium heat, sauté the onions, leeks and carrots in just enough oil or butter to keep them from sticking. Sauté, stirring frequently, until the onions begin to brown. Remove pot from the heat. Add the water, tomato, celery,

continued on next page

FRENCH ONION SOUP

2	T-bones from steaks cooked on the grill
	Celery ribs and leaves for stock
	Whole carrots for stock
	Parsley sprigs for stock
1	teaspoon whole peppercorns
2	quarts water
1½	cups unsalted butter
2	yellow onions, thinly sliced
1	red onion, thinly sliced
1	white onion, thinly sliced
4-6	shallots, thinly sliced
1¾	cups flour
4	cups canned beef broth
1	tablespoon Worcestershire sauce
1½	teaspoons salt
1	teaspoon white pepper
2	tablespoons heavy cream
	Croutons
	Gruyère or Swiss cheese, grated

In a stockpot over high heat, boil bones, celery, carrots, parsley and whole peppercorns in 2 quarts water 15-20 minutes. Remove bones and strain liquid. (Discard bones and vegetables.) In a heavy saucepan over low heat, melt butter and add onions and shallots and sauté until tender. Stir in flour and cook 10 minutes, stirring constantly. Add bone stock and beef broth, Worcestershire sauce, salt and pepper. Bring to a boil. Simmer, covered, 15 minutes. Stir in cream. Serve in individual ovenproof ramekins. Garnish with croutons and grated cheese. Broil in oven until cheese is bubbly and begins to brown.

15 cups

Lafayette County Courthouse, 1870s

ORANGE CANTALOUPE SOUP

3 cups fresh orange juice

½ cup dry white wine

½ cup honey

1 teaspoon grated orange zest

1 cinnamon stick

¼ cup cornstarch

¼ cup fresh lemon juice

4-5 ripe flavorful cantaloupes, seeded, peeled, and cut into large chunks

¼ cup heavy cream or plain yogurt

Fresh mint leaves for garnish

In a medium enameled pot over high heat, bring the orange juice, wine, honey, orange zest and cinnamon stick to a boil. Reduce heat and let simmer. In a small bowl dissolve the cornstarch in lemon juice and whisk this mixture into the simmering liquid. Cook, whisking gently, until clear, smooth and thick. Remove from heat and take out the cinnamon stick. Refrigerate at least until room temperature. In a food processor, add cantaloupes to cream and process in batches. Stir purée into the juice mixture. Chill until very cold. Serve in chilled cups and garnish with mint.

8 servings

CHILLED STRAWBERRY SOUP

2 pints fresh strawberries (or one 16-ounce bag frozen strawberries)

2 cups heavy cream

½ cup orange juice

2 tablespoons lemon juice

½ cup sugar

⅛ teaspoon ground cardamom

½ cup water

Whipped cream for garnish

Wash and core strawberries. Reserve 3 strawberries for garnish. In a blender purée half the remaining strawberries. Add half the cream, orange juice, lemon juice and sugar to the blender and continue to purée. Add the remaining strawberries and whipping cream, ground cardamom, and water. Purée until mixture is smooth. Chill overnight or 8 hours. Serve with a dollop of whipped cream and garnish with slices of the reserved strawberries.

The thickness of the mixture can be adjusted by adding or reducing the amount of water.

4-6 servings

Basic Vegetable Stock *continued*

garlic, bay leaf, parsley, thyme, peppercorns and salt. Bring to a low simmer. Skim surface of stock as needed. Do not allow stock to boil. Keep water level above vegetables, adding more water if needed. Simmer 1 hour. Skim surface of the stock and strain through cheesecloth or a fine mesh strainer.

4 quarts

Artist Lee Harper Artwork, page 51

Originally from Meridian, Lee Harper has been a freelance painter and illustrator for ten years. She has lived in Oxford since 2001 along with her husband Andy, their son Ben, and cats Percy and Casey.

CUCUMBER SOUP

Author Lisa Howorth
Essay, page 52

Lisa resides in
Oxford with her
husband, Richard
Howorth, Oxford's
mayor. They own the
popular independent
bookstore, Square Books.
An expert on Southern
art, Lisa compiled and
edited *The South:*
A Treasury of Art and
Literature, which provides
a full range of Southern
artistic traditions. She is
the author, with Jennifer
Bryan, of *Yellow Dogs,*
Hushpuppies, and Bluetick
Hounds: The Official
"Encyclopedia of Southern
Culture" Quizbook.

4	cucumbers, peeled and sliced into ½-inch slices
2	shallots or 1 medium onion, finely chopped
7	cups chicken stock
4	tablespoons unsalted butter

2	tablespoons flour
	Salt and pepper to taste
3	egg yolks
¾	cup heavy cream, divided use
	Green food coloring, optional
1	tablespoon chopped mint or chives

In a large saucepan over medium heat, combine the cucumbers, shallots and stock. Simmer until the cucumbers are tender, 15-20 minutes. Pour mixture into a food processor or blender and purée. In a stockpot over medium-high heat, melt the butter and stir in flour. Cook until straw-colored. Gradually add puréed cucumber to flour mixture, stirring constantly. Bring to a boil. Season with salt and pepper to taste and simmer 2-3 minutes. In a small bowl mix egg yolks and ½ cup of the cream. Add a little hot soup to egg mixture, stirring constantly. Remove soup from the heat and gradually stir egg mixture into soup. Cool slightly. Gently reheat the soup until it thickens slightly. Do not boil. Add 1 or 2 drops food coloring, if desired. Refrigerate. In the bowl of an electric mixer, whip the remaining ¼ cup cream. Pour the chilled soup in bowls and stir a spoonful of whipped cream in each bowl. Sprinkle each serving with chopped mint or chives.

2½ quarts

Cows on the Oxford Square, 1930s

Square Books Jr. by Lee Harper ▶

MY GRANDMOTHERS' SOUPS

Lisa Howorth

Due Minestre Deliziose dalle Mia Nonne. (Two delicious soups from my grandmothers.) I know that there probably will be some recipes in this collection that are from the kitchens of real "Eyetalian Oxonians from Italy," but most of the good things I know how to cook are simple, peasant dishes that my grandmothers learned to cook on this side of the Atlantic. My father's mother, née Concettina Boccabella near Roseto, an Abruzzi town in the hills above the Adriatic, came to this country when she was about seven. (No one was ever sure about her age; she said she was born in 1902, my uncle Junior said 1904.) Nana remembers sausages hanging up in the barn to dry, and she remembers seeing the Statue of Liberty as she sailed into New York harbor. Her family settled in Washington, D.C., by accident; they were supposed to get off the train somewhere in Pennsylvania. They lived in the Italian ghetto on Capitol Hill behind Union Station. Because Nana was the oldest of thirteen children, she had to learn to cook from her mother, Philomena, who must have been unimaginably overworked and eternally nursing or pregnant. Nana was an excellent plain cook — nothing exotic or expensive, although she insisted all her life on "good" ingredients — good sausage, good cheese — that could only be purchased at her favorite "real Italian" store, Litteri's, in the market on Fifth Street, Northeast. She often made her own pasta using a broom handle, and the first time I took Richard (my husband and Oxford's mayor) to meet her, he was amazed to see pasta hanging to dry over the backs of the dining room chairs. Nana never went anywhere, including plane trips, without a shopping bag overflowing with a lemon pound cake, sacks of her knotty little chocolate chip cookies, cheese, and a couple quarts of her spaghetti sauce. She traveled with food the same way other people travel with flashlights, extra cash, or Lomotil — a survival kit.

In my family, this first soup has always been a favorite that we call "Scapellum Boose." Nana had never learned to read or write Italian before she came over, and afterward, she had little freedom to attend school, so her Italian and her English were both pretty corrupted and mongrelized — a sort of hillbilly Italian. She never could exactly explain what "Scapellum Boose" meant; and over the years I've asked "real Italians" how it might translate; never a clue. I've looked for the recipes in many Italian cookbooks and recently found a beef-based version in *Regional Foods of Southern Italy* by Marlena de Blasi (Viking, 1999). She calls the dish "Scrippelle 'mbusse," Abruzzese dialect for something to do with crêpes. Just as she wasn't sure about the recipe's name, Nana couldn't write it down or even tell me — I had to be shown. We brought her to Oxford one summer, and, after taking down and ironing and starching every curtain and darning every coverlet and sheet (Italians are as fanatic about their linens as they are about food), we got into the kitchen for a lesson. So here's scrippelle 'mbusse, and, as my Dad and Uncle Junior used to say, "There's no boose like it."

Have a rich chicken stock — at least 1½ quarts — prepared with bits of chicken and finely chopped carrots, parsley, and celery. To make the scrippelle or crêpes, beat 2 eggs in a bowl with a pinch of salt. Start adding flour — about ½ cup total — a little at a time. Continue adding flour and water (1 teaspoon at a time) until you have a very thin batter — it should pour in a thin stream. The thinner the batter is, the more delicate the crepe, which is what you want.

continued on next page

Rub a 9-inch skillet lightly with pork fat. Pour about 3 tablespoons of the batter onto skillet and roll skillet so batter spreads out. Cook both sides until just light golden-brown. Prick bubbles. Lightly pepper the crêpes and stack them as you make them. (Can be done hours before if necessary — but keep crêpes covered so they do not dry out.)

When ready to eat, take each crêpe and grate about 1 tablespoon Parmesan cheese over each and roll up. Place about 3 rolled crêpes in a wide, shallow soup bowl and ladle chicken broth and bits over. Sprinkle with a little more cheese and chopped parsley. This makes enough for 2 for a meal or 3 to 4 as a first course.

My maternal grandmother, Iris Kernodle, was born at The Hub in Alamance County, North Carolina, in 1904. Her father was a country doctor and, for reasons unknown, moved the family to D.C. when Dobba was a little girl. (He never practiced medicine again, and in the family we've always suspected something dark.) My grandmother met my grandfather in high school, and they married when she was only seventeen. My grandfather, Simone Del Vecchio, was an immigrant from Fiumedinisi, halfway between Messina and Taormina in Sicily. It's hard to imagine which family might have been more concerned about the match; my Sicilian great grandparents didn't speak much English and had high hopes of their only child going to the University of Pennsylvania on a track scholarship, and Dobba's southern Presbyterian family surely must have had reservations about my tiny, swarthy grandfather who, sometimes when visiting in North Carolina, was mistaken for an African American. At any rate, Dobba had to learn to cook all Daddy Sam's favorite recipes from Nonna, her Sicilian mother-in-law. This is one of my children's favorites, Padotoli Soup, or Meatball Soup, verbatim:

Ground beef — one pound. Mix with hands: 1 egg, salt, pepper, crushed garlic, a handful of bread crumbs, parsley, basil, oregano, and 1 tablespoon milk. Make into meat cakes (note: my grandmother could not bring herself to utter or write the word balls for any reason) the size of a Ping-Pong ball.

Use a 2 to 3 quart kettle. Fill with 1½ quarts cold water — salted. Add 1 bay leaf and raw cakes to water. Add 2 or 3 diced stalks celery. Simmer — do not boil.

When cakes float to top and when the broth looks right, taste it. There will be tiny particles of the meat cakes floating around so you might want to strain the broth. If you hate the color, add a little Kitchen Bouquet.

Slice 2 carrots and cook separately. Cook pasta — ditali, tubetti, or elbows — separately.

Ladle broth into soup bowls with a few cakes, carrots, and pasta. Sprinkle with grated Romano or Parmesan cheese. Also good over rice. Delicious, easy, and children love it.

Oxford Square, early 1960s

Photo by Martin J. Dain

Pear and Goat Cheese Salad

SALADS

CAESAR SALAD

4 anchovy fillets
3 garlic cloves
2 tablespoons extra virgin olive oil
1 teaspoon Worcestershire sauce
1 teaspoon Dijon mustard
¼ teaspoon hot pepper sauce
1⅓ cups mayonnaise

¼ cup plus 2 tablespoons freshly grated Parmesan cheese, divided use
2 tablespoons (or more) fresh lemon juice
Salt to taste
2 hearts of romaine, coarsely torn
2 cups croutons
Freshly ground black pepper

In a food processor, blend first 6 ingredients until smooth. Transfer to small bowl. Whisk in mayonnaise, 2 tablespoons Parmesan cheese and 2 tablespoons lemon juice. Season with salt and extra lemon juice, if desired. Place romaine in serving bowl. Add ¾ cup dressing and toss to coat. Sprinkle with croutons, remaining ¼ cup Parmesan cheese and pepper.

6 servings

SUSIE'S SALAD WITH HONEY MUSTARD VINAIGRETTE

VINAIGRETTE
2 tablespoons balsamic vinegar
3 tablespoons honey mustard
1 teaspoon coarse salt

¼ teaspoon freshly ground pepper
½ cup extra virgin olive oil

SALAD
Mixed greens
Toasted walnuts

Crumbled blue cheese
Dried cherries or cranberries

For vinaigrette, in a medium bowl, place the vinegar, honey mustard, salt and pepper. Whisk to combine. Slowly drizzle in olive oil, whisking constantly until emulsified.

For salad, in a serving bowl combine mixed greens, toasted walnuts, blue cheese and dried cherries or cranberries. Pour vinaigrette over salad and toss.

6-8 servings

Sensational Salad Dressing

A very light, crisp dressing

½ pound grated Romano cheese

2 cups canola oil

Juice of 2 lemons

4 cloves garlic, minced

Salt and pepper to taste

Fresh, chopped herbs, optional

Mix all ingredients well and refrigerate. Serve over mixed greens.

1 pint

Green Goddess Dressing

Great as a sandwich spread!

1½ cups mayonnaise

½ cup fresh parsley leaves

2 tablespoons chopped fresh chives

2 teaspoons champagne or white wine vinegar

1 teaspoon anchovy paste

1 teaspoon grated lemon zest

2 tablespoons fresh lemon juice

Process all ingredients in food processor until creamy. Refrigerate.

2 cups

LITTLE BLUE SALAD

SWEET AND SPICY PECANS

2	tablespoons sugar	1	cup pecans, soaked in warm water for 10 minutes, then drained
1	tablespoon chili powder		
⅓	teaspoon cayenne pepper		

BALSAMIC VINAIGRETTE

½	cup balsamic vinegar	2	small shallots, minced
3	tablespoons Dijon mustard	¼	teaspoon salt
3	tablespoons honey	¼	teaspoon pepper
2	cloves garlic, minced	1	cup olive oil

SALAD

¾	pound mixed salad greens	2	oranges, peeled and cut into slices
4	ounces blue cheese, crumbled	1	pint strawberries, quartered

For pecans, preheat oven to 350°. Mix sugar, chili powder and cayenne together. Add pecans, tossing to coat. Place on lightly greased baking sheet. Bake 350° 10 minutes, stirring once.

For vinaigrette, in a small bowl whisk together all vinaigrette ingredients.

For salad, in a serving bowl place salad greens, cheese, oranges and strawberries. Top with sweet and spicy pecans. Toss with balsamic vinaigrette.

6-8 servings.

ENDIVE SALAD

3	small to medium heads of endive, rinsed, dried, and chopped	⅓	cup crumbled Saga cheese
		¼	cup olive oil
1	14-ounce can hearts of palm, drained and chopped	2	teaspoons white wine vinegar
			Salt and pepper to taste

In a salad serving bowl, toss together endive, hearts of palm and cheese. Drizzle olive oil over salad. Sprinkle with vinegar, salt and pepper. Toss together lightly and serve.

4 servings

CRUNCHY APPLE WALNUT SALAD

DRESSING

¼ cup olive oil

2 tablespoons apple juice

2 tablespoons balsamic white vinegar

½ teaspoon Dijon mustard

¼ teaspoon salt

   Freshly ground pepper to taste

SALAD

2 Braeburn or Fuji apples, cut into bite-sized pieces

6 cups red leaf lettuce or other salad greens

¼ cup chopped walnuts

   Parmesan cheese, grated

▪ For dressing, in a jar, combine all dressing ingredients and shake well.

▪ For salad, in a serving bowl, combine apples, salad greens and walnuts. Pour dressing over salad and toss. Sprinkle with Parmesan cheese.

6-8 servings

"Our House" French Dressing

¾ cup sugar

1 teaspoon black pepper

1 teaspoon salt

1 teaspoon paprika

1 teaspoon onion salt

½ cup ketchup

¾ cup vinegar

½ teaspoon garlic salt

Combine all ingredients and shake well. Refrigerate. Serve over your favorite tossed green salad.

2 cups

HORSERADISH SALAD

An excellent accompaniment to beef

1 3-ounce package lemon gelatin

1 cup boiling water

⅔ cup prepared horseradish

½ teaspoon salt

1 cup heavy cream, whipped until soft peaks form

3 cups coleslaw

½ red bell pepper, chopped

½ green bell pepper, chopped

▪ In a mixing bowl dissolve gelatin in boiling water. Drain vinegar from the horseradish and add vinegar to gelatin. Allow mixture to cool and begin to set. (Can be put in the refrigerator and watched closely.) Add drained horseradish and salt. Fold in the whipped cream. Pour into oiled 1-quart ring mold and chill until set, about 8 hours. On a serving plate arrange 2½ cups coleslaw and sprinkle red and green peppers on top. Unmold gelatin onto slaw and put remaining ½ cup slaw in the center of the ring.

6 servings

Photo on page 42

In the years before 1860, Thomas Dudley Isom went to medical school, established a practice, married, and raised nine children. He practiced on the spot where the Downtown Grill now stands and helped Lafayette County through two terrible yellow fever epidemics. His daughter, Sarah McGehee Isom, was the first woman faculty member at the University of Mississippi or of any Southern university.

~Will Lewis, Jr.

CURRIED SPINACH SALAD

DRESSING

½ cup white vinegar
⅔ cup olive oil
1 tablespoon finely chopped chutney
1 teaspoon curry powder
1 teaspoon salt
1 teaspoon dry mustard
¼ teaspoon Tabasco sauce

SALAD

2 pounds fresh spinach leaves
2 Red Delicious apples, diced
⅔ cup dry roasted Spanish peanuts
½ cup raisins
⅓ cup thinly sliced green onions
2 tablespoons sesame seeds, toasted
1 cup grilled chicken, diced, optional

For dressing, in a jar, mix together all dressing ingredients and shake until fully combined.

For salad, in a serving bowl toss together all salad ingredients. Pour dressing over salad and toss thoroughly.

8-10 servings

CRUNCHY SLAW

The dressing for this Asian-inspired coleslaw is best made the day before.

DRESSING

½ cup sugar
½ cup vinegar
⅓ cup canola oil
1 chicken seasoning packet from ramen noodles
Freshly ground pepper to taste

SLAW

1 pound package chopped coleslaw mix
½ cup shelled sunflower seeds
⅓ cup toasted sliced almonds
   (or other nuts)
1 bunch green onions, chopped
1 package ramen noodles, broken into little pieces

For dressing, in a jar mix together all dressing ingredients and shake well. Refrigerate 24 hours.

For slaw, in a salad serving bowl toss together all slaw ingredients. Pour dressing over slaw just before serving and mix well.

6-8 servings

SWEET SLAW

Onion lovers, this one is for you.

DRESSING

1	cup vinegar	1	teaspoon prepared mustard
1	teaspoon celery seed	1	cup canola oil
½	teaspoon salt		

SLAW

1	large head green cabbage, shredded	¾	cup sugar
3	medium white onions, sliced thin		

For dressing, in a saucepan over high heat, stir together vinegar, celery seed, salt and mustard. Bring to a boil. Remove from heat and whisk in canola oil until well blended.

For slaw, in a large glass bowl, layer cabbage and onions, sprinkling sugar over layers. Pour dressing over slaw. Cover and refrigerate 3-4 hours. Toss gently before serving.

8-10 servings

Photo on page 129

> This Sweet Slaw recipe was from my great-aunt Patsy Forrester, and she always made it for family gatherings. It's a lighter slaw version than ones made with mayo—which makes it better for tailgating.
>
> ~Beth Doty

RED POTATO SALAD

DRESSING

¼	cup walnut oil	½	teaspoon sugar
1½	tablespoons white wine vinegar		Salt and pepper to taste
1	teaspoon Dijon mustard		

SALAD

2	pounds new red potatoes, halved	4	green onions, sliced diagonally
½	cup coarsely chopped walnuts	1	teaspoon dried dill

For dressing, in a jar mix together all dressing ingredients and shake well.

For salad, in a large pot of salted water boil potatoes just until tender, 8-10 minutes. Drain well and transfer to a serving bowl. Toss hot potatoes with dressing and set aside to cool, tossing occasionally. Add walnuts, green onions and dill. Toss again. Serve at room temperature.

6-8 servings

Photo on page 129

SHOUT HALLELUJAH POTATO SALAD

Winner of the Southern Foodways Symposium award in the potato salad competition

**Take the 6:10
to Holly Springs**

Until about 1940,
the travel outside the
county was by railroad.
The Depot, located near
the University, was the
center of much activity.

Weddings were
scheduled with
departing trains in mind
so that honeymooners
could leave town on
a convenient train.
Mr. and Mrs. Will Lewis,
Sr., were married at
9:30 a.m. and caught the
northbound for Chicago
after the reception.

~Will Lewis, Jr.

5	pounds petite gold potatoes	1⅛	cups mayonnaise
5	hard-boiled eggs, peeled and chopped	¼	cup yellow mustard
1	4-ounce jar diced pimientos	1-2	jalapeño peppers, seeded and minced
4	drops Louisiana Hot Sauce	½	cup chopped red onion
4	ribs celery, chopped	½	cup chopped green bell pepper
2	teaspoons celery salt	¼	cup chopped parsley
¼	cup seasoned rice wine vinegar		Salt and pepper to taste
1	cup sweet salad cube pickles		Paprika for garnish
1	tablespoon olive oil		

In a large pot of salted water over high heat, boil potatoes with skin on until tender, about 20 minutes. Drain in colander and peel off skins with fingers while holding under cold, running water. Cool potatoes, chop into small pieces, and transfer to a large mixing bowl. Add eggs. In a small bowl mix drained pimientos with hot sauce. Add to potato mixture. Add all remaining ingredients except paprika. Do not stir. Mix by hand, mashing some potatoes and leaving others in chunks. Add salt and pepper to taste, transfer to serving platter, and shape into mound with a spoon. Dust with paprika. Cover and refrigerate 3-4 hours.

20-25 servings

Oxford Depot, early 1930s

FARMERS' MARKET POTATO SALAD

DRESSING

4   green onions, chopped

2   tablespoons lemon juice

1   tablespoon minced fresh dill

1   garlic clove, minced

½   cup olive oil

¼   cup goat cheese, room temperature, cut into pieces

SALAD

1   pound new potatoes

½   pound fresh, young green beans

1   medium tomato, chopped

1   cucumber, peeled and chopped

½   cup kalamata olives, pitted

1   tablespoon drained capers

For dressing, in a jar combine all dressing ingredients and shake well.

For salad, in a large pot of salted water, boil the new potatoes just until tender, 10-12 minutes. Drain and let cool. Snap the stems off beans. Blanch them in a large pot of salted, boiling water 1-2 minutes. Drain immediately and put in ice water to cool quickly. Drain well when cold. Cut the potatoes into pieces and the beans in halves and transfer to a serving bowl. Add the tomatoes, cucumbers, olives and capers. Toss with dressing and refrigerate 3-4 hours.

4 servings

PEAR AND GOAT CHEESE SALAD

2   ripe pears

1   package herbed goat cheese

Chopped walnuts or pecans

Red leaf lettuce leaves

Balsamic vinegar

Cut pears in half lengthwise and scoop out seeds and core with spoon. Divide goat cheese into 4 equal balls. Roll cheese balls in chopped nuts. Place cheese balls in center of pears with pear lying peel-side down on bed of lettuce. Drizzle with vinegar and serve.

4 servings

Photo on page 54

...the land across which there came now no scream of panther but instead the long hooting of locomotives ... and all that remained of that old time were the Indian names on the little towns and usually pertaining to water — Aluschaskuna, Tillatoba, Homochitto, Yazoo ... the land had not retreated in minutes from the last spread of gravel but in years, decades, back toward what it had been when he first knew it: the road they now followed once more the ancient pathway of bear and deer....

~William Faulkner

Go Down, Moses

AVOCADO AND GRAPEFRUIT SALAD

**Auntie Mame's
Salad Dressing**

½ cup olive oil

½ cup canola oil

¼ cup apple cider vinegar

¼ cup balsamic vinegar

2 cloves garlic, peeled and halved

1 tablespoon Dijon mustard

1 teaspoon salt

1 dash cayenne pepper

1 dash paprika

In a large jar, combine all ingredients. Auntie Mame says, "Shake like h—!" Lasts 2 weeks in refrigerator.

1½ cups

DRESSING

2   tablespoons red wine vinegar

½   cup extra virgin olive oil

1   teaspoon Dijon mustard

Kosher salt
Freshly ground pepper

SALAD

2   Texas ruby red grapefruit

1   large avocado

Bibb lettuce

For dressing, in a jar combine all ingredients for dressing and shake well.

For salad, peel grapefruit and use knife to peel whole sections away from the membrane. Peel avocado and cut into 4 lengthwise sections. Arrange Bibb lettuce on a salad plate. Alternate grapefruit sections and avocado strips in a pinwheel fashion. Drizzle dressing over salad.

4 servings

BLACK BEAN AND RICE SALAD

4   cups chicken broth

2   bay leaves

2   cups raw rice

2   15-ounce cans black beans, rinsed and drained

2   red bell peppers, diced

1   green bell pepper, diced

1   bunch fresh cilantro, chopped

1   red onion, diced, optional

½   cup olive oil

3   tablespoons fresh lime juice

3   teaspoons ground cumin

2   tablespoons red wine vinegar

3   teaspoons chili powder

Salt and pepper to taste

Cilantro for garnish

In a casserole dish pour chicken broth and add bay leaves. Heat in the microwave 5 minutes on high power. Add rice, cover, and heat 20 minutes on 70% power. Stir cooked rice and let it rest 5 minutes. Transfer rice to a large bowl and add all other ingredients. Toss well. Garnish with cilantro sprig. Serve at room temperature.

12-14 servings

BROCCOLI SALAD

DRESSING

1½ tablespoons dried oregano

1 teaspoon garlic powder

1 teaspoon salt

¼ cup olive oil

⅜ cup white or red wine vinegar

1 tablespoon lemon juice

SALAD

2-3 small crowns fresh broccoli

½ cup corn from 1 medium cob, or canned or frozen

1 tablespoon salt

1 tablespoon pine nuts, toasted

For dressing, in a jar combine all dressing ingredients and shake well.

For salad, cut broccoli crowns into bite-sized pieces, including as much of the florets' thin stems as possible. In a covered medium pot, fill water to bottom of steamer or colander. Add about a tablespoon of salt to the water. Add broccoli and corn, cover, and steam until florets are tender and light green, about 5 minutes. (Canned corn, drained of liquid, may be used directly from can.) Be careful not to overcook or broccoli will fall apart in salad. Transfer colander to the sink and immerse in ice water until broccoli reaches room temperature. Drain well. In a large salad bowl, mix broccoli, corn and pine nuts. Pour dressing over broccoli and toss. Serve at room temperature or refrigerate 15-30 minutes before serving.

4 servings

Lafayette County Courthouse, late 1930s

Most Saturdays when I was a little boy, my dad would take me and my brother and sister to Grandma's house. We grew up in the restaurant business, so we were used to good food, yet Grandma's was still a treat. The moment I stepped through the door, my mouth watered. Some kind of well-seasoned chicken or beef was always cooking in a pan or in the oven. Everything Grandma made was well seasoned, and that's the key to this recipe. It's the strong flavors of oregano, salt, garlic and vinegar combined with the natural sweetness of the corn and cooked broccoli that make this simple salad so addictive. I relished eating my vegetables at Grandma's house, and I hope you will too.

~Tor Valenza

ASPARAGUS BUNDLES

These beautiful bundles resemble the yellow mimosa flowers of the Italian Riviera.

Jane's Vinaigrette

1 8-ounce jar Dijon mustard

1 cup vinegar

3 cups canola oil

1 tablespoon salt

2 teaspoons pepper

In a food processor add mustard, vinegar, salt and pepper. Process until well mixed. With motor running, slowly add oil through the food chute in a thin stream until dressing is emulsified. Refrigerate.

For a thinner dressing, use only 4 ounces of Dijon mustard.

1 quart

VINAIGRETTE

½ cup extra virgin olive oil

1 tablespoon Dijon mustard

1 teaspoon white pepper

1 teaspoon salt

1 teaspoon sugar

Zest of 1 lemon

1 tablespoon lemon juice

¼ cup balsamic vinegar

BUNDLES

1 pound asparagus, trimmed and blanched

4 slices prosciutto

Fresh chives to tie bundles

4 hard-boiled eggs, chilled

For the vinaigrette, in a mixing bowl whisk all vinaigrette ingredients together.

For bundles, coat blanched asparagus with vinaigrette. Make 4 bundles and wrap each with a slice of prosciutto. Tie each bundle with 2 strands of chives. Arrange bundles on individual serving plates. Press the yolk of 1 hard-boiled egg through a sieve over each bundle, forming golden flakes toward the tips. Sprinkle the remaining vinaigrette around the dish. Serve cold or at room temperature.

4 servings

Photo on page 108

COLD PASTA SALAD

12 ounces capellini or vermicelli

¾ cup olive oil

1 4-ounce jar chopped pimientos, drained

2 4-ounce cans black olives, sliced

6 green onions, chopped

1 yellow or red bell pepper, chopped

1 1-ounce package Hidden Valley ranch dressing mix

3 tablespoons mayonnaise

1 teaspoon freshly ground black pepper

3 tablespoons lemon juice

Greek seasoning to taste

In a large pot of salted water, boil pasta until *al dente*. Drain well, transfer to large bowl and toss with olive oil. Cool to room temperature. Add remaining ingredients and toss, mixing well.

For a heartier dish add slices of grilled chicken and blanched carrots.

10 servings

Photo on page 25

TOMATOES LUTÈCE

8	firm, ripe tomatoes, peeled	¼	teaspoon pepper
¼	cup chopped parsley	¼	cup olive oil
1	clove garlic, minced	2	tablespoons tarragon or cider vinegar
1	teaspoon salt	2	teaspoons prepared mustard
1	teaspoon sugar		Parsley or basil leaves, optional

Slice each tomato in 2-inch slices. In a small bowl blend together remaining ingredients. Pour over tomatoes and marinate several hours. For a special presentation, stack slices to reform the tomato shape. Or, serve slices on a platter. Garnish with parsley or basil leaves.

8 servings

TOMATO ASPIC

2	cups tomato juice		Tabasco sauce to taste
4	tablespoons vinegar	½	onion
1	tablespoon sugar	2	¼-ounce envelopes of unflavored gelatin
2	tablespoons lemon juice		Celery, olives or artichokes, optional
1-2	tablespoons Worcestershire sauce		

In a medium saucepan over high heat, pour tomato juice, vinegar, sugar, lemon juice, Worcestershire and Tabasco. Add onion and let come to a boil. Soak 2 envelopes of gelatin in ½ cup cold water. Remove onion from the juice mixture and stir in the gelatin mixture. Pour into salad mold. Refrigerate until set. May add celery, olives or artichokes before refrigerating, if desired.

1 salad mold

FRESH BABY TOMATO SALAD

2	pints grape tomatoes, sliced in half	2	tablespoons chopped cilantro
2	pints yellow pear tomatoes, sliced in half		Salt and pepper to taste
1	cup green onions, thinly sliced	½	cup extra virgin olive oil
½	cup goat's milk feta cheese, crumbled	4	tablespoons apple cider vinegar
		½	cup pine nuts, toasted

Mix all ingredients except pine nuts in a bowl until well combined. Add pine nuts just before serving.

8-10 servings

The recipe for Tomatoes Lutèce comes from my maternal grandmother, Ruth Pankratz. She passed it on to my mother, Gerry Pankratz Duvall, and to me and my sister, Ruth Ellen. My mother must have shared this recipe with many of her friends over the years; several of them have called me to make sure it will be included in *Square Table*. My mother served these tomatoes at small dinners, club meetings, and luncheons.

~Teresa Duvall Flautt

GREEK PASTA SALAD

DRESSING

2	tablespoons Greek seasoning	3	cloves garlic, minced
3	tablespoons lemon juice	½	cup olive oil

PASTA

1	can artichoke hearts, quartered and drained	8	ounces vermicelli, cooked *al dente*
1	small can black olives, drained and sliced	1	pound shrimp, cooked, peeled and cooled

For dressing, in a small bowl whisk all dressing ingredients.

For pasta, in a serving bowl toss together all pasta ingredients. Pour dressing over pasta mixture and toss well to coat. Refrigerate overnight.

6 servings

SHRIMP RÉMOULADE

RÉMOULADE SAUCE

1	bunch shallots, finely chopped	½	teaspoon freshly ground black pepper
2	small ribs celery, finely chopped	¼	teaspoon cayenne pepper
2	sprigs parsley, finely chopped	6	tablespoons white wine vinegar
3	tablespoons Creole mustard	5	teaspoons fresh lemon juice
5	teaspoons paprika	½	teaspoon dried basil
1¼	teaspoons salt	¾	cup olive oil

SHRIMP

1	cup coarsely chopped lettuce	1	pound fresh shrimp, boiled, peeled, and chilled

In a china or stainless steel bowl place shallots, celery and parsley. Add mustard, paprika, salt, pepper and cayenne. Blend with a wooden spoon. Add vinegar, lemon juice and basil. Blend again. Gradually add olive oil, stirring constantly. Cover the bowl with plastic wrap and refrigerate for at least 3 hours.

For shrimp, divide lettuce among 4 salad plates. Arrange boiled shrimp on top of lettuce and pour about ¼ cup rémoulade sauce over each portion.

4 servings

CORNBREAD SALAD

2	8.5-ounce boxes Jiffy cornbread mix, cooked
2	ribs celery, chopped
1	large green bell pepper, chopped
1	2-ounce jar chopped pimientos
1	cup chopped green onions with tops
½	cup pecans, chopped
1	large tomato, chopped
2	cups mayonnaise
	Salt and pepper to taste

Crumble cornbread into a large bowl. Add celery, green pepper, pimientos, green onions, pecans and tomatoes and toss gently. Stir in mayonnaise gently. Add salt and pepper to taste. Refrigerate overnight.

For a less sweet taste, substitute a self-rising cornmeal mix for the Jiffy mix.

6-8 servings

SPRING SALAD

DRESSING

⅓	cup vegetable oil
¼	cup red wine vinegar
¼	cup lemon juice
1	tablespoon sugar
1	teaspoon salt
½	teaspoon pepper
¼	teaspoon minced garlic

SALAD

1½	cups cooked chicken breast, cut in strips
1	cup sliced black olives
1	avocado, sliced in crescents
⅓	cup green bell pepper strips
¼	cup red onion, chopped
2-3	tablespoons pimiento slices
4	cups lettuce

For dressing, in a blender place all dressing ingredients and blend well.

For salad, in a large bowl toss together all salad ingredients. Add dressing and toss.

6 servings

Once there was —
Do you mark how the
wisteria, sun-impacted
on this wall here, distills
and penetrates this
room as though (light-
unimpeded) by secret
and attritive progress
from mote to mote of
obscurity's myriad
components? That
is the substance of
remembering — sense,
sight, smell: the muscles
with which we see and
hear and feel — not
mind, not thought:
there is no such thing
as memory... .

~William Faulkner
Absalom, Absalom!

Gorgonzola Dressing

*Delicious served as
a dip with fresh vegetables.*

16 ounces Gorgonzola
cheese

16 ounces sour cream

¼ cup mayonnaise

3 ounces cream cheese

Juice of ½ lemon

2 teaspoons olive oil

1 tablespoon
white wine vinegar

Salt and pepper to taste

Blend all ingredients
in food processor.
Refrigerate.

1 quart

MANDARIN CHICKEN SALAD

3	cups diced, cooked chicken breast	1	11-ounce can Mandarin oranges, drained
1	cup diced celery	2	ounces slivered almonds, toasted
2	tablespoons lemon juice		Green leaf lettuce
1	tablespoon minced onion		Orange slices and grape clusters for garnish
½	teaspoon salt		
⅓	cup mayonnaise		
1	cup seedless green grapes		

In a large mixing bowl toss together chicken, celery, lemon juice, onion and salt. Cover and refrigerate 3-4 hours. Add mayonnaise, grapes, oranges and almonds. Toss well. Serve on lettuce leaves. Garnish with additional orange slices and grape clusters.

5-6 servings

CHICKEN PASTA SALAD

PASTA
12 ounces vermicelli

MARINADE

1	teaspoon Accent seasoning	2	teaspoons seasoned salt
3	teaspoons lemon juice	4	tablespoons vegetable oil

SALAD

1	medium onion, chopped	1	small jar pimientos, drained
1	cup chopped celery	1	green or red bell pepper, chopped
1	4-ounce can green olives, sliced	4	chicken breasts, cooked and chopped
1	4-ounce can black olives, sliced	1	cup mayonnaise

For pasta, boil pasta in salted water until *al dente*. Drain well.

For marinade, in a small jar place Accent seasoning, lemon juice, seasoned salt and oil. Shake well. Pour over cooked vermicelli and let marinate overnight.

For salad, in a large serving bowl place marinated vermicelli. Add all salad ingredients and toss well. Refrigerate.

12 servings

CREOLE CRABMEAT SALAD

1   cup mayonnaise

1   tablespoon Creole mustard

1   tablespoon capers, drained

2   tablespoons Crescent City Grill cayenne and garlic sauce

2   teaspoons parsley

1   teaspoon Worcestershire sauce

1   teaspoon lemon juice, freshly squeezed

2   pounds jumbo lump crabmeat, picked through

Romaine

Combine the first 7 ingredients and mix thoroughly with a wire whisk. Gently fold crabmeat into dressing, making sure not to break up the crabmeat lumps. Serve on a bed of romaine lettuce.

5 servings

Artist Will Dunn Artwork, page 71

Will Dunn lives in Oxford and works at Lafayette Industries. He has studied under artists in Oxford and has participated in the University of Mississippi Creative Arts Program. He gathers inspiration for his vibrantly colorful work primarily from Impressionism and Expressionism.

RICE AND CHICKEN SALAD

Take this picnic-friendly salad to the Grove. It contains no mayonnaise.

1   teaspoon Dijon mustard

½   teaspoon salt

2   teaspoons red wine vinegar

6   tablespoons extra virgin olive oil

1   cup rice, cooked

½   cup diced Swiss cheese

¼   cup diced black olives

¼   cup diced green bell pepper

3   tablespoons diced dill pickles

2   large chicken breasts, boiled and cut into ½-inch cubes

In a mixing bowl stir together Dijon, salt, vinegar and olive oil. Stir in rice and coat well. Add cheese, olives, green peppers, pickles and chicken. Refrigerate 4-24 hours.

6 servings

Author Curtis Wilkie
Essay, page 72

During the 1960s Curtis Wilkie was a reporter for the *Clarksdale Press Register* and subsequently served as a national and foreign correspondent for the *Boston Globe* for 26 years. He has written for *Newsweek* and the *New Republic*, among others, and is coauthor, with Jim McDougal, of *Arkansas Mischief: The Birth of a National Scandal* (1998) and author of *Dixie: A Personal Odyssey through Events that Shaped the Modern South* (2001). Wilkie holds the Kelly Gene Cook Chair of Journalism at the University of Mississippi.

Yocona River Inn

LEMON CAPER VINAIGRETTE

½	cup fresh lemon juice	1	teaspoon apple cider vinegar
½	cup extra virgin olive oil	1	teaspoon black pepper
2	tablespoons capers	¼	teaspoon salt
2	cloves garlic, peeled	½-¾	cup vegetable oil

In a blender place all ingredients except vegetable oil. Blend well for 2 minutes. Adjust salt and pepper to taste. Taste for acidity. If it is too bland, add more lemon juice or vinegar, a teaspoon at a time. Add a little of the caper juice if desired. If it is too acidic, add water, a teaspoon at a time. (The vegetable oil will tone down all the flavors a bit.) Blend 2 minutes more. With the blender running, slowly pour ½ cup vegetable oil into the opening in top of blender. The dressing will begin to thicken. Add more oil to taste. More oil makes a thicker dressing, and the dressing will thicken some when it is chilled.

2 cups

Yocona River Inn

MOLASSES VINAIGRETTE

2	cups roughly chopped red onion	2	tablespoons apple cider vinegar
½	cup vegetable oil	2	teaspoons ground coriander
⅓	cup lemon juice	½	teaspoon salt
⅓	cup dark molasses	½	teaspoon black pepper

In a blender place all ingredients and blend for several minutes. The onion should be well puréed, but will still give some texture to the dressing. Turn off blender and adjust seasonings to taste. Purée an additional minute. Add more oil for a thicker dressing. (It will not thicken more when chilled.)

Good on a spinach salad with pecans and red onions.

2 cups

Construction²: Building Blocks of Oxford by Will Dunn ▶

FOOD

Curtis Wilkie

The first grand meal of my life occurred in Oxford, more than 50 years ago. Back then, Oxford was an unlikely setting for sumptuous food. The Square had the air of a farmer-go-to-market place, and the public eating establishments — none dared call themselves "restaurants" — had names that sounded like advertisements for acid reflux: Grundy's, Dirty Charlie's, the Bait Shop.

My feast took place at my grandparents' home on Van Buren, a couple of blocks down from the Square. It was either a Thanksgiving or Christmas, a time when my mother and I made the long expedition from south Mississippi to join her family for a holiday reunion. I would have been eight or nine years old and a stranger to anything richer than the red beans and rice that the school cafeteria in Summit produced as its specialty, no less than three times a week, it seemed.

I was in the midst of an unusual, though happy, childhood and oblivious to what might have been missing from our own dinner table. My mother was a widow, and we lived in dormitories on campuses where she studied and, later, taught. While she got her master's degree at Ole Miss after World War II, we stayed in Garland Hall, then a family dorm just up the hill from the university cafeteria. We took our meals there and I remember the 1940s era dance band that serenaded diners on Sunday evenings more clearly than the cuisine; I recall the trombones on "Sentimental Journey" but not a single meal.

In 1947, we moved to the Southwest Junior College campus where Mother took over duties as dean of women-registrar-English professor-psychology professor, and God knows what else. We lived in a one bedroom suite in the girls' dorm. Virtually all my meals were taken in the junior college cafeteria or the school lunchroom in town.

When Mother and I "ate in," our meals subsisted of such delicacies as "little pigs" (Vienna sausage out of a can), pork 'n' beans (canned), tuna (canned) — and when we were being very continental, spaghetti and meatballs (canned). She was a marvelous mother, but not much of a cook.

So when we gathered in Oxford for the holiday, I was stunned by the cornucopia of food on my grandparents' dining room table. The centerpiece, of course, was a roast turkey, surrounded by side dishes as colorful as a Christmas tree: a sweet potato casserole, green beans laced with slivers of almonds, homemade cranberry sauce, fresh rolls with the fragrance of a bakery, and a mysterious dessert called ambrosia that was said to be food of the gods. Not to mention Karo pecan pie.

As the bones piled up on Uncle Scott's plate, he declared that he was building a turkey graveyard. But I was the one who really gave way to gluttony. I had two or three helpings — the word we used for servings — and hand wrestled my cousin Bob Black for possession of the pulley bone. Then indigestion set in. My swollen tummy hurt. As I lay down on the living room sofa afterwards, I could overhear my relatives laughingly comparing my case to those emaciated survivors of World War II prison camps who were said to have eaten so much on their first day of freedom that they killed themselves.

Fast forward about 55 years. I lived to eat another day. Many, many days, and many, many wonderful meals.

After all those decades, I returned to Oxford and discovered it's a town where food has an honored spot in society. Downtown is filled with any number of real restaurants with interesting, sometimes exotic menus.

On Saturdays in season, the farmers' market off North Lamar beckons early in the morning if one wants to bag the luscious local tomatoes and other fresh vegetables before supplies run out.

Food is not only enjoyed here, it's formally celebrated each fall at a conference featuring prominent chefs and food writers from around the country. My neighbor John T Edge runs the festival for the Southern Foodways Alliance, and he turns an open lot on our street into a garden of culinary delights for the event's final night. At John T's invitation, I wander down and gorge myself on such regional treats as barbecued pork or fried chicken. Sometimes I overeat.

At least my feeding frenzies are no longer triggered by the sudden sight of good food. Today, in Oxford, it's always available.

Family with Red Wagon, Oxford Square   Connie Flake

Oxford native Connie Flake is an impressionist painter and painting instructor.

Polenta with
Pesto and Tomatoes
Plate by Cory Lewis

PASTA & GRAINS

HEARTY SPAGHETTI AND MEATBALLS

Al Dente

An Italian term that means literally "to the tooth." It is used to describe the ideal degree of doneness for cooked pasta—tender, but still firm to the bite. Cooking time will vary with the kind and size of pasta; fresh pasta may take only 3-5 minutes to reach *al dente* stage, while dried can take up to 10 minutes.

SAUCE

1	tablespoon olive oil	1½	6-ounce cans tomato paste, divided use
1	large green bell pepper, chopped	1	tablespoon chopped, fresh oregano
1	large onion, chopped	1	tablespoon chopped, fresh parsley
1	tablespoon minced garlic	1	tablespoon sugar
½	cup chicken broth	1	teaspoon salt
4	8-ounce cans tomato sauce	1	teaspoon black pepper
1	14.5-ounce can diced tomatoes	2	bay leaves

MEATBALLS

1½	pounds ground sirloin	2	teaspoons chopped, fresh oregano
1	medium green bell pepper, finely diced	¼	cup grated Parmesan cheese
1	medium onion, finely diced	1	teaspoon salt
2	teaspoons minced garlic	½	teaspoon black pepper
10	saltine crackers, finely crushed		Cooked spaghetti
2	teaspoons chopped parsley		

For the sauce, in a large skillet over medium-low heat, heat oil and sauté bell pepper, onion and garlic 5 minutes. Add chicken broth and simmer 10 minutes. Add tomato sauce, diced tomatoes, 6 ounces tomato paste, oregano, parsley, sugar, salt, pepper and bay leaves. Stir well. Cover and lower heat to simmer, stirring occasionally.

To make the meatballs, in a large mixing bowl, mix sirloin, bell pepper, onion, garlic, cracker crumbs, parsley, oregano, cheese, salt and pepper. Form into balls a bit larger than a golf ball and brown over medium-low heat, turning often, 30-45 minutes. (The browner the exterior, the less likely they will be to break up in the sauce.) Transfer meatballs to paper towels to drain off any excess fat.

Stir remaining 3 ounces tomato paste into sauce. Add meatballs, stir gently, cover, and allow to simmer at least 30 more minutes, stirring occasionally. Serve over spaghetti.

6-8 servings

Pasta Water

Cook pasta in a
large pot with plenty of
generously salted water.
Before draining pasta,
save a few tablespoons
of pasta water to add to
hot cooked pasta and
other ingredients. The
additional pasta water
stretches the sauce
and ensures a creamy
mouthful. Do not rinse
cooked pasta. Simply
pour it into a colander
and shake well to
drain water.

SHRIMP SPAGHETTI

½	cup unsalted butter	1½	teaspoons black pepper
1	pound fresh mushrooms, sliced	1	tablespoon parsley flakes
3	pounds large, raw, peeled shrimp	1	tablespoon lemon juice
1	teaspoon salt	1	tablespoon Worcestershire sauce
½	teaspoon dried basil	½	cup unsalted butter, melted
½	teaspoon dried thyme	12	ounces spaghetti
¼	teaspoon garlic powder	8	ounces Parmesan cheese

Preheat oven to 350°. In a large skillet over medium-high heat, melt butter and sauté mushrooms. Add shrimp and sauté just until pink. Place shrimp mixture in a 3-quart casserole and sprinkle with salt, basil, thyme, garlic powder, pepper, parsley, lemon juice, Worcestershire and butter. Bake uncovered 25 minutes, stirring occasionally. While shrimp is cooking, boil spaghetti until *al dente* and drain. Stir the Parmesan into hot spaghetti. Add spaghetti mixture to casserole and stir to combine. Return to oven and bake 5-10 minutes until heated.

6 servings

CREAMY ARTICHOKE AND MUSHROOM PENNE

12	ounces penne pasta	1	cup heavy cream
½	small onion, chopped	2	tablespoons capers
1	clove garlic, minced	¼	teaspoon salt
3	tablespoons unsalted butter, melted	¼	teaspoon pepper
8	ounces fresh mushrooms	½	cup freshly grated Parmesan cheese
1	15-ounce can artichoke hearts, drained and chopped	2	tablespoons chopped fresh parsley

Boil pasta in salted water until *al dente*. Drain well. In a medium skillet over medium-high heat, sauté onion and garlic in butter until tender. Add mushrooms and sauté 5 minutes. Add artichokes and cook until thoroughly heated, about 2 minutes. Remove vegetables from skillet and keep warm. To skillet add cream and bring to a boil. Cook, stirring constantly, until cream is reduced by half. Add artichoke mixture, capers, salt and pepper. Stir until combined. Toss pasta and cream mixture together. Sprinkle with Parmesan cheese and parsley.

6 servings

L & M's Kitchen and Salumeria

BUCATINI ALL'AMATRICIANA

12 ounces bucatini (long, tubular pasta), or spaghetti

3 thin slices guanciale (cured pork jowl), chopped

½ red onion, diced

2 cloves garlic, thinly sliced

¼ cup olive oil

1 cup tomato sauce

¼ cup Parmigiano-Reggiano cheese

Chopped parsley

Salt and pepper to taste

Crushed red pepper to taste

Boil pasta in salted water until *al dente*. In a large skillet over medium heat, render fat from guanciale with red onion and garlic in olive oil until onion is translucent and guanciale is crisp. Add tomato sauce and bring to a boil. Add cooked pasta and toss to coat noodles. Stir in Parmesan cheese and chopped parsley. Add salt, pepper and crushed red pepper to taste.

4 servings

FUSILLI ISABELLA

Gemelli Pasta with Cream Rosemary Sauce

1 pound pasta (gemelli or fusilli)

½ cup unsalted butter

½ 6-ounce can Italian-style tomato paste

¼ cup port wine, bourbon or vodka

2 cups heavy cream

Fresh ground black pepper and salt to taste

⅛ teaspoon cayenne pepper

2-3 sprigs fresh rosemary, chopped

2 cups grated Parmesan cheese

Shavings of Parmesan for garnish

Boil pasta in salted water until *al dente*. Drain well. In a large skillet over medium heat, place butter and stir in tomato paste with a wooden spoon or heatproof spatula until well combined. Add wine, bourbon or vodka and cook until alcohol evaporates, 3-5 minutes. Add cream, pepper, salt, cayenne and rosemary. Cook 5-10 minutes, stirring constantly, so that mixture does not stick to the bottom of the pan. Remove from heat and add the cooked, drained pasta to the skillet. Toss. Add grated Parmesan cheese and toss again. Sprinkle cheese shavings on top.

4 servings

Pasta Sauce

1 small onion, chopped

1 green bell pepper, chopped

2 tablespoons olive oil

4 cloves garlic, minced

4 cups Italian plum tomatoes

2 6-ounce cans tomato paste

2 tablespoons minced parsley

1 teaspoon dried oregano

1 tablespoon salt

1 teaspoon black pepper

1 cup red wine

In a large skillet over medium-high heat, sauté onion and pepper in olive oil until tender. Stir in garlic, tomatoes, tomato paste, parsley, oregano, salt and pepper. Simmer for 2 hours. Stir in wine.

8-10 servings

ITALIAN LASAGNA

Gemelli with Four Cheeses

2 ounces fontina cheese, cut into thin strips

2 ounces Gorgonzola cheese, crumbled

2 ounces Swiss cheese, cut into thin strips

½ cup heavy cream

1¼ pounds gemelli pasta

Salt and freshly ground pepper

½ cup freshly grated Parmesan cheese

In a saucepan over low heat, place fontina, Gorgonzola, Swiss cheese and cream. Cook until cheeses have almost completely melted, about 5 minutes. Stir well and keep warm. Boil pasta in salted water until *al dente*; drain. Spoon pasta onto warm plates. Spoon cheese sauce over pasta, season to taste with salt and pepper, and sprinkle Parmesan cheese on top.

6 servings

MEAT LAYER

1	onion, chopped
2-3	cloves garlic, minced
1	tablespoon olive oil
1	pound lean ground beef
1	pound hot sausage
½	teaspoon salt

½	teaspoon pepper
8	ounces cream cheese, room temperature
1	26-ounce jar tomato and basil sauce
1	teaspoon chopped, fresh oregano
2	teaspoons chopped, fresh basil

PASTA LAYER

	Salt
8	lasagna noodles

1	cup sour cream

CHEESE LAYER

8	ounces crumbled feta cheese
1	15-ounce container ricotta cheese

2	cups finely grated Parmesan cheese, divided use
	Fresh basil for garnish

For meat layer, preheat oven to 350°. In a large skillet over medium heat, sauté onions and garlic in olive oil until translucent. Add ground beef and sausage. Break up meat and cook until browned. Drain fat. Add salt, pepper, cream cheese, tomato sauce, oregano and basil. Reduce heat to low and simmer while preparing noodles.

For pasta, bring a large pot of salted water to boil. Add lasagna noodles and cook just until tender. Drain noodles and mix with sour cream to keep them from sticking.

For cheese layer, in a heatproof bowl, stir together feta, ricotta and 1½ cups Parmesan. Microwave on high until mixture is of spreading consistency, 20-30 seconds.

To assemble, arrange 4 noodles in the bottom of a greased 9 x 13-inch casserole. Top with half of meat mixture, and half of cheese mixture. Repeat all layers. Bake uncovered on center oven rack until bubbling at the edges, 40-50 minutes. If necessary, cover towards the end of baking time to prevent excess browning. Sprinkle with remaining ½ cup Parmesan cheese and garnish with fresh basil.

6-8 servings

Yocona River Inn

ROASTED MARINARA SAUCE

4-5	cups chopped, fresh tomatoes (or canned tomatoes with juice)	½	teaspoon dried basil
1	bell pepper, coarsely chopped	½	teaspoon dried thyme
1	medium yellow onion, coarsely chopped	½	teaspoon dried oregano
½	cup coarsely chopped green onions	½	teaspoon salt
4-6	whole cloves garlic	1	teaspoon black pepper
		½	cup red or white wine

Preheat oven to 375°. In a large mixing bowl, combine all ingredients and stir well. Pour into a large roasting pan. Cover with foil and bake in the top half of oven 15 minutes. Remove from oven and carefully lift off foil. Stir well. If there is not enough liquid to cover the bottom of the pan, add more wine, tomato juice or water. Replace the foil and return pan to oven for 15 minutes. Repeat stirring process. Repeat this process at least 2 more times, for a minimum cooking time of 1 hour. The marinara is done when the onion and pepper are soft enough to purée. Remove from oven and cool. Strain through a sieve and reserve the liquid for another use. (It makes great soup stock.) Purée tomato sauce. If sauce is too thin, it can be reduced on the stove. Marinara will keep for a week in the refrigerator. It freezes well.

4 cups

The Flaky Baker

PASTA À LA VODKA

16	ounces spaghetti	¾	cup vodka
1	small onion, finely diced	1	teaspoon crushed red pepper
2	tablespoons olive oil	1	cup heavy cream
3	cloves garlic, minced		Salt and pepper to taste
1	26-ounce jar pasta sauce		Fresh basil, chopped
1	14-ounce can tomatoes, crushed or puréed		Freshly grated Parmesan cheese

Boil pasta in salted water until *al dente*. Drain. In a large saucepan over medium heat, sauté onion in olive oil 3 minutes. Add garlic and sauté 1 minute. Add pasta sauce, tomatoes, vodka and red pepper. Cook 15 minutes, stirring occasionally. Remove from heat and stir in cream. Return to heat to warm cream, but do not boil. Add salt and pepper to taste. Add pasta to sauce and toss. Top with basil and Parmesan.

4-6 servings

Fresh Egg Pasta

Whether you make it by hand or use a machine, you can have fresh pasta ready to cook in minutes.

2 cups flour, plus extra for board and sprinkling

3 eggs

Heap 2 cups flour on pastry board. Make a well in center and break eggs into well. Using a fork, lightly beat the eggs. With a circular motion, gradually incorporate the flour. Continue until all flour is incorporated. Using the palm and heel of your hand, knead the dough until elastic and soft, at least 5 minutes. Pasta can be rolled out with a rolling pin and cut into strips with a sharp knife or rolled through a hand-cranked machine.

1 pound fresh pasta to serve 6

FETTUCCINI WITH MUSHROOMS

To clean fresh mushrooms, wipe them with a damp paper towel, or immerse them quickly in cold water, shaking loose any dirt particles. Dry them thoroughly with a towel.

1   ounce dried porcini mushrooms
3   tablespoons unsalted butter, divided use
4   shallots, finely chopped
    Salt
1   clove garlic, minced
1   tablespoon fresh marjoram
2   teaspoons tomato paste

1   pound mixed fresh mushrooms, chopped
¼   teaspoon freshly ground black pepper
2   tablespoons flour
1   cup beef broth
½   cup dry white wine
1½ pounds fresh fettuccini (or 1 pound dried)
    Parmigiano-Reggiano cheese, freshly grated

In a small bowl place dried porcini mushrooms and cover with boiling water. Let soak about 30 minutes. Remove mushrooms, chop, and set aside. Line a mesh sieve with a wet paper towel and strain the mushroom liquid through it. Set aside. In a large sauté pan over medium heat, melt 1 tablespoon butter and sauté shallots with 1 pinch of salt until shallots are soft, about 5 minutes. Stir in garlic and marjoram and sauté 1 minute. Stir in tomato paste and chopped porcini mushrooms and sauté 5 minutes, stirring frequently. Add fresh mushrooms, and sauté 5 minutes, continuing to stir. Add 1 pinch of salt and ¼ teaspoon freshly ground pepper. Reduce heat to low and cook 5 minutes. Set aside. In a large saucepan over high heat melt remaining 2 tablespoons butter. Whisk in flour until well combined and cook 1 minute. Add beef broth, whisking constantly until blended. Add white wine and reserved mushroom liquid to taste. (Too much will be overpowering.) Cook over high heat for 15 minutes, whisking occasionally. Stir in reserved mushroom mixture and simmer over very low heat 10 minutes. While sauce simmers, cook pasta in boiling salted water until *al dente*. Drain pasta, reserving 1 cup of pasta water. Pour half of pasta into a serving bowl and toss with half of mushroom sauce. Cover with remaining pasta and mix in remaining sauce. If pasta seems too dry, add a few tablespoons of pasta water. Sprinkle with Parmesan.

6 servings

Federal Building, late 1800s, currently City Hall

PASTA AL BROCCOLETTI E POMODORI SECCHI

Pasta with Broccoli and Sun-Dried Tomatoes

1	pound pasta of choice	1	pound blanched broccoli florets, drained
½	cup extra virgin olive oil		
4	cloves garlic, peeled and gently crushed	⅔	cup julienned oil-cured sun-dried tomatoes
2	teaspoons crushed red pepper	¼	cup pine nuts
	Freshly ground black pepper	½	cup grated Romano cheese
3	tablespoons water		Salt to taste

Boil pasta in salted water until *al dente*. Reserve 1 cup of the cooking water before draining pasta. In a large skillet over very low heat, heat oil and add garlic, crushed red pepper and black pepper. When garlic is tender, flatten it with a fork or spoon to make a paste. Add 3 tablespoons water and stir until combined. Add broccoli florets and sun-dried tomatoes. Cover and simmer just until broccoli is tender. Remove cover and set aside. Add cooked pasta and reserved cup of cooking water to skillet. Add pine nuts, cheese and salt; toss.

4 servings

PEPPERONI SPAGHETTI CAKES

¼	pound spaghetti, broken into pieces	2	cloves garlic, minced
⅓	cup finely chopped pepperoni		Salt and pepper to taste
⅓	cup chopped red bell pepper	1	large egg, lightly beaten
¼	cup grated Parmesan cheese	1	teaspoon olive oil, divided use
½	cup chopped green onions		Sour cream

Boil spaghetti in salted water until *al dente*. Drain. In a large mixing bowl, toss together the pepperoni, bell pepper, Parmesan cheese, green onions, garlic, salt and pepper. Add the cooked spaghetti and toss. Add the beaten egg and mix well. In a medium nonstick skillet over medium heat, heat ½ teaspoon olive oil until hot, but not smoking. Add half the spaghetti mixture, pressing it with the back of a spoon and cooking until the underside is golden, about 3 minutes. Turn and repeat on the other side. Transfer cake to a plate and top with sour cream. Repeat with the other half of spaghetti mixture. Serve immediately.

2 servings

Blanching

To blanch vegetables, bring a pot of lightly salted water to a boil and add about 2 teaspoons baking soda. Drop vegetables in water and let them cook for 1-2 minutes. Drain vegetables in a colander and immediately pour ice water over them to stop the cooking process. Blanching tenderizes vegetables to prepare them for sautéing, or for marinating and chilling. The baking soda intensifies the vegetables' color.

Pesto

2 cups fresh basil leaves

5 cloves garlic

¾ teaspoon salt

¼ cup pine nuts
or walnuts, toasted

½ cup olive oil

¾ cup Parmigiano-
Reggiano cheese, grated

Pepper to taste

In a food processor
pulse basil, garlic, salt
and pine nuts until well
combined. With motor
running, pour olive oil
through the food chute in
a slow, thin stream until
mixture is combined. Add
cheese and process until
combined. Pesto will keep
1 week in the refrigerator.
It makes an excellent
sauce for pasta, pizza
and chicken.

1½ cups

BRAVO BAKED LINGUINE

2	pounds lean ground beef	12	ounces linguine
2	cloves garlic, minced	16	ounces sour cream
1	28-ounce can crushed tomatoes	8	ounces cream cheese, room temperature
1	8-ounce can tomato sauce	2	bunches green onions, chopped
1	6-ounce can tomato paste	1	cup shredded Cheddar cheese
1	teaspoon salt	½	cup grated Parmesan cheese
2	teaspoons sugar		

In Dutch oven over medium-high heat, brown beef with garlic. Drain fat and return beef to Dutch oven. Stir in tomatoes, tomato sauce, tomato paste, salt and sugar. Simmer 30 minutes. Preheat oven to 350°. Boil linguine in salted water until *al dente*. Drain well. Arrange pasta in a lightly greased 9 x 13-inch baking dish. In a small bowl stir together the sour cream, cream cheese and green onions. Spread cream cheese mixture over pasta and top with meat sauce. Bake 20-25 minutes. Sprinkle with cheeses and bake 5 minutes. Let stand 5 minutes before serving.

8 servings

CAJUN SHRIMP AND PASTA

8	ounces linguine	2	pounds medium, raw, peeled shrimp
½	cup unsalted butter	1	10-ounce can diced tomatoes with green chilies, drained
⅓	cup flour	1	tablespoon Creole seasoning
1	bunch green onions, chopped	1	tablespoon chopped, fresh parsley
1	small onion, minced	¼	teaspoon pepper
½	green bell pepper, minced	⅛	teaspoon salt
4	cloves garlic, minced	½	teaspoon hot sauce, optional
2	celery ribs, minced		Chopped, fresh parsley for garnish
1	chicken bouillon cube		
2	cups heavy cream		

Boil linguine in salted water until *al dente*. Drain and keep warm. In a Dutch oven over medium heat, melt butter and stir in flour. Cook, stirring constantly for 2 minutes. Add green onions, onion, bell pepper, garlic and celery. Sauté until tender, about 5 minutes. Add bouillon cube, cream, shrimp, tomatoes with chilies, Creole seasoning, parsley, pepper and salt. Cook until thickened, about 10 minutes. Stir in hot sauce, if desired. Serve over linguine and garnish with parsley.

6-8 servings

ANGEL HAIR FLAN

3 ounces angel hair pasta
3 eggs
1 cup heavy cream
1 teaspoon salt

Freshly ground black pepper
½ teaspoon nutmeg
1 cup Parmesan cheese, divided use

Wild Rice with Pecans

1 cup chopped pecans

4 tablespoons
unsalted butter

3 ribs celery, chopped

3-4 cups cooked wild rice

1 teaspoon garlic salt

2-3 tablespoons chopped,
fresh parsley

Preheat oven to 350°. Boil pasta in salted water until *al dente*. Drain. Spray mini muffin tins with cooking spray. Put pasta in muffin cups filling ¾ full. In a mixing bowl, combine eggs, cream, salt, pepper, nutmeg and ⅔ cup Parmesan cheese. Top the pasta with cheese mixture, dividing it evenly among muffin cups. Sprinkle with remaining ⅓ cup Parmesan. Bake until set, 10-15 minutes.
Can also be made in a 10-inch pie pan.

24 flan

In a large skillet over medium-high heat, lightly sauté pecans in butter. Add celery and sauté just until it begins to soften, about 3 minutes. Add wild rice, garlic salt and parsley. Cook, stirring occasionally, until rice is heated through.

6-8 servings

SAUTÉED RICE AND VEGETABLES

4 tablespoons unsalted butter, divided use
½ cup slivered almonds
2 tablespoons olive oil
1 medium Vidalia onion, chopped
½ medium red or green bell pepper, chopped

1 cup long-grain rice
1⅔ cups chicken stock, hot
½ cup chopped, fresh parsley
¼ cup chopped, fresh basil
Salt and pepper to taste

In a large skillet over medium-high heat, melt 2 tablespoons butter. Add almonds and sauté, stirring often, until golden brown. Remove almonds from pan and set aside. Add olive oil to skillet and heat until hot, but not smoking. Add onions and peppers and cook until soft, about 5 minutes. Reduce heat to low, add rice, and stir until combined. Add hot chicken stock and increase heat to high for 1 minute, stirring constantly. Reduce heat to simmer and cover. Cook approximately 15 minutes, stirring occasionally, until liquid is almost absorbed. Stir in remaining 2 tablespoons butter, chopped parsley, basil, salt, pepper and almonds.

Add to this versatile dish blanched and chopped fresh asparagus, green peas or grated Parmesan cheese.

4 servings

BACON FRIED RICE

6	slices bacon	½	teaspoon crushed red pepper
1	green bell pepper, chopped	3	cups cooked rice
½	cup sliced fresh mushrooms	2	large eggs, beaten
3	green onions, chopped	¼	cup soy sauce
1	large clove garlic, minced		

In a large skillet or wok over high heat, cook bacon until crisp. Remove bacon, crumble, and set aside. To bacon drippings, add bell pepper, mushrooms, onions, garlic and red pepper. Stir-fry 5 minutes. Add rice and heat thoroughly. Push rice mixture to sides of pan, forming a well in the center. Pour beaten eggs into well and cook until eggs are set. Stir rice mixture into eggs. Stir in soy sauce and crumbled bacon.

4 servings

SPINACH AND ONION COUSCOUS

1	medium onion, minced	1	5.8-ounce box plain couscous
1	clove garlic, minced	¾	cup freshly grated Parmesan cheese
2	tablespoons olive oil	2	tablespoons lemon juice
1⅔	cups chicken broth	½	teaspoon salt
1	10-ounce package frozen spinach, thawed	½	teaspoon pepper
		½	cup chopped, toasted pecans

In a large saucepan sauté onion and garlic in olive oil until tender. Add chicken broth and spinach. Bring to a boil. Stir in couscous, cover, and remove from heat. Let stand until liquid is absorbed, about 5 minutes. Stir in cheese, lemon juice, salt, pepper and pecans. Serve immediately.

6-8 servings

Nations' Best Catering

BARKSDALE-ISOM HOUSE CHEESE GRITS

2	cups chicken stock	4	eggs, beaten
1	cup water	½	cup milk
2	cups quick grits	2	tablespoons crushed garlic
1	pound sharp Cheddar cheese, shredded	1	tablespoon chopped basil
			Salt and pepper to taste
½	cup unsalted butter, melted	4	bunches green onions, chopped

Preheat oven to 350°. In a stockpot bring chicken stock and water to a boil. Stir in grits, cover, reduce heat, and simmer 5 minutes. Remove from heat and add cheese and butter, stirring until cheese is completely melted. In a small bowl, beat eggs and milk together and add to grits, stirring until well combined. Stir in garlic and basil. Add salt and pepper to taste. Add green onions. Pour into a greased casserole dish and bake until bubbling, about 45 minutes.

Add ham, shrimp, or sausage for a more substantial dish.

12 servings

JALAPEÑO-STILTON CHEESE GRITS

1½	quarts water	2	jalapeños, seeded and diced
4	tablespoons unsalted butter	1½	teaspoons salt
1	cup diced red onion	3	cups quick grits
¼	cup minced garlic	8	eggs, beaten
1	cup heavy cream	1	pound Stilton cheese, crumbled
1	yellow bell pepper, seeded and diced		

Preheat oven to 350°. In a stockpot over high heat bring water, butter, onion, garlic, cream, peppers and salt to a simmer. Add the grits, stirring constantly until they are soft and creamy, about 3 minutes. Set aside to cool. In a large mixing bowl, whisk eggs and cheese. Stir into grits. Grease a 12 x 12-inch casserole dish and dust with flour. Pour in grits and bake until firm, 40-45 minutes.

Substitute Monterey Jack, Gouda, Edam or Gorgonzola for the Stilton.

12 servings

Artist Jere Allen
Artwork, page 87

Recently retired from the faculty at the University of Mississippi, Jere Allen is an internationally known artist whose work is best described as figurative. He is included in *Who's Who in American Art* and studied on a Group Studies Fulbright Grant in Costa Rica. He received the 1993 Visual Art Award of the Mississippi Institute of Arts and Letters, and an Individual Artist Fellowship from the Mississippi Arts Commission. His exhibitions include a one person show at the Contemporary Art Center of Peoria, and "Art for Art Sake" in New Orleans. He also exhibited in *Outward Bound: American Art on the Brink of the 21st Century*, an exhibition currently traveling throughout Asia. His resume includes a number of solo exhibits at galleries in Washington, D.C.; Germany; Beverly Hills, California; and New Orleans. His work has been shown in 35 states and was included in the Smithsonian Institution Traveling Exhibition Service.

Author Julia Reed
Essay, page 88

Julia grew up in
Greenville, Mississippi.
She is senior writer at
Vogue and a contributing
editor at *Newsweek*.
She also writes for
the *New York Times*
Magazine, among other
publications. Reed
divides her time between
New Orleans and
New York City. Her
celebrated book of essays
Queen of the Turtle Derby
and *Other Southern*
Phenomena was
published in 2004.

Ajax Diner

CHEESE GRITS

8	cups water	2	tablespoons kosher salt
2	cups quick grits	1½	tablespoons Tabasco sauce
4	ounces unsalted butter	½	teaspoon garlic powder
1	cup grated Cheddar cheese	½	cup Parmesan cheese

In a large saucepan, bring water to a boil, and whisk grits in slowly. When grits return to boil, turn heat down to medium and continue to whisk grits until it thickens. Remove from heat and let sit for 10 minutes. Add butter, cheese, salt, Tabasco, garlic powder and Parmesan cheese. Whisk until cheese is melted and the consistency is uniform.

12 servings

POLENTA WITH PESTO AND TOMATOES

3	cups water		Pesto
1¼	teaspoons salt	1	14.5-ounce can Italian style diced tomatoes (or 2 cups chopped fresh tomatoes)
1	cup cornmeal		
4	tablespoons unsalted butter		Grated Parmesan cheese for garnish
¾	cup freshly grated Parmesan cheese		

Spray an 8-inch square pan with cooking spray. In a medium saucepan over medium-high heat, bring water, salt and cornmeal to a boil, whisking out lumps. Reduce heat to medium and stir constantly with a wooden spoon until polenta is thick, shiny, and pulls away from the sides of the pan, 10-20 minutes. Remove from heat and stir in butter and cheese. Spread evenly in prepared pan. Refrigerate until set, about 30 minutes. (At this point polenta can be wrapped well and frozen.)

Preheat oven to 350°, or preheat oven broiler. Drain tomatoes well. Unmold polenta and cut into any desired size or shape, larger pieces for a side dish, or small squares for appetizer servings. Larger pieces can be grilled, if desired. Top polenta shapes with a spoonful of pesto, a few tomatoes and a sprinkle of Parmesan cheese. Heat 3-5 minutes under oven broiler or 20 minutes in a 350° oven.

9 servings

Photo on page 74

208 by Jere Allen ▶

V. D. DINNER

Julia Reed

My mother is a really good cook and probably the best entertainer I know. I was the only child in my class who had parties thrown for every holiday, even St. Patrick's Day, and she has given countless rehearsal dinners for the children of her friends, including one for which she and her friend Bossy made, from scratch, over a hundred pieces of Chicken Kiev. That one was a triumph—and a huge pain—but by far her most famous menu is one Bossy has dubbed the "V.D. Dinner."

In this case, thankfully, "V.D." does not stand for venereal disease but for visiting dignitary. When I was growing up, my father dragged a lot of them, mostly Republicans and political columnists, through town. It was the late 1960s and early-to-mid 1970s; he and his friend Hodding Carter III were on their then-noble quest to "build a two-party system in the South." That was their mantra, and to that end, they dragged folks through the Delta who had previously seen no percentage in showing up, given the fact that our one-party had been run by the likes of Ross Barnett and Jim Eastland, and far, far worse. One month Hodding would turn up with the Soviet ambassador and the next Daddy would show up with Elliott Richardson or Ronald Reagan. We'd have Roy Reed from the *New York Times*, followed by Robert Novak and Roland Evans. And on and on.

The problem was that my father, at least, brought all of them through with maybe a day's notice to my mother, and a request for not just a dinner, but a dinner for, say, 25 or 50. Finally she quit threatening to kill him and got comfortable with a menu she kept always in reserve. It consisted of rare beef tenderloin with bordelaise or béarnaise sauce; wild rice with mushrooms; scalloped oysters; spinach and artichoke casserole; and homemade yeast rolls, followed by her justifiably famous charlotte russe or a sinfully rich chocolate mousse.

I think everybody should have a "V.D." menu. We may not all have future presidents dropping by, but everybody entertains to impress, after all. In Julia Child's *Menu Cookbook*, she includes a menu for "entertaining the boss," that includes, not surprisingly, tenderloin and chocolate mousse. When I first moved to Washington, I was so desperate to prove myself to my colleagues in journalism, most of whom were older and far more experienced than I was, that at one of my very first dinner parties I whipped out the V.D. dinner. It was summer, so I think I had white corn soufflé instead of wild rice, and I decided to get swanky and improve on the spinach-and-artichoke casserole by braising fresh artichoke bottoms and filling them with creamed fresh spinach. It was a big success—a party I still remember vividly more than 20 years later—but I needn't have bothered with the spinach. Last year, I published the original casserole, which uses canned artichoke hearts, frozen spinach, and Philadelphia cream cheese in the *New York Times Magazine*—almost as a joke—and it was included in Harper Collins's annual "Best Recipes of the Year."

My mother has always told me just to serve food that tastes good, and I have finally learned to listen. And the V.D. dinner, after all these years, still tastes really good. So good that after William F. Buckley, Jr., came down with his wife Pat, a noted Manhattan hostess, she wrote my mother for the recipe for the scalloped oysters. The party for the Buckleys was an especially spiffy V.D. dinner. Mrs. Buckley wore a black Bill Blass sheath and her husband played the piano into the wee hours accompanied by Dick Goodwin, a British friend of ours who farmed cotton in the Delta and played a mean xylophone. When I was finally made to go to bed, Bossy's sexy niece was dancing on the table.

I was glad it worked out. I could tell Mrs. Buckley had her doubts about being dragged to Mississippi. On the ride in from the airport, we passed a shopping center where a stretch limo was parked with a big blinking sign in front of it that read: "SEE JFK'S DEATHCAR!" She, quite rightly, pronounced it "barbaric" and probably had visions of some Klukkers and the ghost of Bilbo running around out there in the darkness. But the swell time at the V.D. dinner erased all that, and, in the end, her memories were of some fine Gulf oysters layered with cream between some crushed Ritz crackers.

It may sound a tad old-fashioned, but the V.D. dinner never failed to wow the dignitaries. In a chapter from *Mrs. Whaley Entertains* entitled "A Serious Admonition that I'm Totally Positive About," she says "Don't serve your guests dishes you haven't made successfully two or three times—and quite lately. When the special evening comes, you need to be comfortable with the food you are serving and with the way it is being served."

Northeast Corner   Jeffrey Allen

Allen studied painting at the Cortona Program in Italy. He shares a studio in Oxford with his father, painter Jere Allen.

Jack's Catfish
Bronze Catfish by Bill Beckwith

F I S H & S E A F O O D

BAKED SHRIMP

5	pounds headless raw shrimp in shells
1	24-ounce bottle ketchup
⅔	cup Worcestershire sauce
2	tablespoons prepared horseradish

	Juice of 1 lemon
1	teaspoon salt
1	teaspoon pepper

Preheat oven to 325°. In a large baking dish arrange shrimp. In a mixing bowl stir together ketchup, Worcestershire, horseradish, lemon juice, salt and pepper. Pour over shrimp. Bake uncovered, stirring every 15 minutes, until shrimp separate from their shells, about 45 minutes.

5 servings

MARINATED SHRIMP

2	cups unsalted butter, melted
⅓	cup Worcestershire sauce
2½	tablespoons black pepper
2	teaspoons salt
2	lemons, thinly sliced

½	teaspoon Tabasco sauce
½	teaspoon dried rosemary
1	tablespoon sugar
5	pounds raw shrimp in shells
	French bread

Preheat oven to 400°. In a mixing bowl, stir together butter, Worcestershire, pepper, salt, lemons, Tabasco, rosemary and sugar. Pour over shrimp and bake 45-60 minutes. Serve with French bread to dip in the sauce.

5 servings

Soon now they would enter the Delta. The sensation was familiar to him. It had been renewed like this each last week in November for more than fifty years — the last hill, at the foot of which the rich unbroken alluvial flatness began as the sea began at the base of its cliffs, dissolving away beneath the unhurried November rain as the sea itself would dissolve away.

~ William Faulkner

Go Down, Moses

SHRIMP CREOLE FOR A CROWD

¼ cup vegetable oil or bacon drippings
¼ cup flour
1¼ cups chopped onion (1 large onion)
1 cup chopped green onions
1 cup chopped celery
1 cup chopped green bell pepper (1 whole)
2 cloves garlic, minced
1 16-ounce can chopped tomatoes, with juice
1 8-ounce can tomato sauce
1 6-ounce can tomato paste
1 cup water
1½ teaspoons salt
1 teaspoon black pepper
¼ teaspoon cayenne pepper
2-3 bay leaves
1 tablespoon lemon juice
1 teaspoon Worcestershire sauce
⅛ teaspoon Tabasco sauce
5 pounds raw, jumbo shrimp, peeled
Saffron rice, cooked
Fresh parsley for garnish

In a Dutch oven over medium-high heat, heat oil or bacon drippings. Add the flour and stir constantly to make a peanut butter-colored roux. Add the onions, green onions, celery and green peppers; cook 15 minutes. Add the remaining ingredients except for shrimp, rice, and parsley. Simmer 1 hour. Mixture will be thick. Add shrimp and let simmer 10-15 minutes. Serve over saffron rice and garnish with parsley.

The sauce may be divided into 4 portions and frozen for later use. Each portion serves 6-8. Add 1-2 pounds shrimp per ¼ recipe of sauce and simmer until shrimp is cooked, about 10 minutes.

14 cups

Our little burg has not escaped national notice. *USA Today* named Oxford as one of the "Best 100 Small Towns in America," and "a thriving New South Arts Mecca." Norm Crampton listed Oxford in his book *One Hundred Best Small Towns in America,* and *National Geographic Explorer* called us "sophisticated little Oxford."

Oxford Square, late 1920s

SHRIMP SCAMPI

½ cup unsalted butter

2 teaspoons Worcestershire sauce

¼ cup sherry

2 tablespoons fresh lemon juice

1 tablespoon sugar

1 clove garlic, minced

½ teaspoon salt

1 pound raw shrimp, shelled and deveined

¼ cup minced parsley

Hot cooked rice or pasta

Parmesan cheese

Preheat oven broiler. In a saucepan over low heat, melt butter. Add Worcestershire sauce, sherry, lemon juice, sugar, garlic and salt. Mix well. In a baking dish arrange shrimp in a single layer. Pour sauce over shrimp. Broil 8 inches from broiler element for 8 minutes. Remove from oven and let stand 15 minutes. Sprinkle with parsley. Broil again for 8 minutes. Serve over hot, cooked rice. Sprinkle with Parmesan cheese.

4 servings

Though shrimp is high in cholesterol, it is low in fat and is a good source of protein, iron, and vitamins.

ITALIAN SHRIMP

4 tablespoons unsalted butter

5 tablespoons olive oil

½ cup Italian vinaigrette salad dressing

6 cloves garlic, minced

1 teaspoon hot pepper sauce

¼ cup Worcestershire sauce

8 bay leaves

2 teaspoons paprika

1 teaspoon dried oregano

1 teaspoon dried rosemary

1 teaspoon dried thyme

1 teaspoon black pepper

1 teaspoon salt

2 pounds raw, large shrimp, unpeeled

¼ cup dry white wine

French bread

In a heavy skillet over medium heat, melt butter and add olive oil, salad dressing, garlic, hot pepper sauce, Worcestershire, bay leaves, paprika, oregano, rosemary, thyme, pepper and salt. Cook until sauce begins to boil. Add shrimp and cook 15 minutes. Add wine and cook 10 minutes. Serve shrimp with sauce and crusty French bread for dipping.

4-6 servings

RICE AND SHRIMP SUPREME

3⅓ cups chicken broth

2 teaspoons salt, divided use

1 cup uncooked rice

1 cup pine nuts

4 tablespoons unsalted butter, divided use

½ red bell pepper, chopped

½ yellow bell pepper, chopped

1 medium onion, diced

1 bunch green onions, finely chopped

3 cloves garlic, minced

1 pound mushrooms, sliced

1 pound raw, shrimp, peeled and deveined

¼ teaspoon Old Bay seafood seasoning

½ teaspoon lemon pepper

1 tablespoon chopped, fresh parsley

⅓ cup mayonnaise

⅓ cup white wine

TOPPING

1 cup fresh breadcrumbs

¼ cup chopped, fresh parsley

½ cup unsalted butter, melted

In a saucepan over high heat, bring chicken broth and 1 teaspoon salt to a boil. Add rice, reduce heat, cover, and simmer 15 minutes. Preheat oven to 350°. In a dry skillet over medium heat, toast pine nuts until they begin to brown. Set aside to cool. In the same skillet melt 1 tablespoon butter and sauté peppers, onions, green onions and garlic until soft. Remove vegetables from skillet and set aside. To skillet add 3 tablespoons butter and sauté mushrooms until most of liquid is evaporated. To mushrooms add shrimp, seafood seasoning, lemon pepper and 1 teaspoon salt. Cook until shrimp begin to turn pink, but are not done. In a large mixing bowl combine cooked rice and any remaining chicken broth, shrimp mixture and reserved vegetable mixture. Add parsley, mayonnaise, toasted pine nuts and wine. Gently stir until combined. Transfer to a lightly greased casserole dish.

For topping, in a bowl toss together breadcrumbs, parsley and butter. Sprinkle on top of casserole. Bake until heated through, 20-30 minutes.

6-8 servings

COCONUT PRAWNS
WITH SWEET DIPPING SAUCE

PRAWNS

2	cups flour, divided use
4	ounces sweetened, flaked coconut
1	12-ounce can beer
½	teaspoon baking powder
½	teaspoon paprika
½	teaspoon curry powder

¼	teaspoon salt
¼	teaspoon cayenne pepper
2	pounds raw, freshwater prawns with tails, peeled
	Vegetable oil for frying

SWEET DIPPING SAUCE

1	10-ounce jar orange marmalade
3	tablespoons prepared horseradish

3	tablespoons Creole mustard

In a shallow bowl place ½ cup flour. In another shallow bowl place coconut. In a large mixing bowl, combine 1½ cups flour, beer, baking powder, paprika, curry powder, salt and cayenne. Dredge prawns in flour, then dip into the beer batter. Roll in coconut. In a heavy skillet over high heat, pour vegetable oil deep enough to completely cover prawns. Heat oil to 350°. Put coated prawns in hot oil and fry until coconut is golden brown. Remove from skillet and drain on paper towels.

For dipping sauce, in a bowl combine the marmalade, horseradish and mustard. Mix well and serve hot or cold.

4-6 servings

Sons of the Soil

Some of Oxford's most famous citizens wanted to be known as farmers. Before the Civil War, L. Q. C. Lamar owned an 1,100 acre farm he called Solitude, which was located on the river near Abbeville.

While serving as a Senator and Cabinet member, he bought another farm at Taylor. William Faulkner had a farm, Greenfield, located off Highway 30. All were "working farms," but apparently none made a profit.

~Will Lewis, Jr.

Oxford Square, early 1960s

Photo by Martin J. Dain

The trout hung, delicate and motionless among the wavering shadows. Three boys with fishing poles came onto the bridge and leaned on the rail and looked down at the trout. They knew the fish. He was a neighborhood character.

~ William Faulkner

The Sound and the Fury

■ *City Grocery* ■

SHRIMP AND GRITS

GRITS

1	cup quick grits	1	teaspoon cayenne pepper
4	tablespoons unsalted butter	1½	tablespoons paprika
¾	cup extra-sharp, white Cheddar cheese	1	tablespoon Tabasco sauce
½	cup grated Parmesan cheese		Salt and pepper to taste

SHRIMP

2	cups chopped, smoked bacon	3	teaspoons minced garlic
3	tablespoons olive oil	3	cups sliced mushrooms
1½	pounds raw, 26-30-count shrimp, peeled	2	tablespoons lemon juice
	Salt and pepper to taste	3	tablespoons white wine
		2	cups sliced green onions

■ For grits, cook grits according to package instructions. Whisk in butter, Cheddar, Parmesan, cayenne, paprika and Tabasco. Mix thoroughly and season with salt and pepper to taste.

■ For shrimp, in a skillet over medium-high heat, cook bacon until it begins to brown. Remove from heat and reserve bacon and drippings. Heat a large skillet until very hot. Add olive oil and 2 tablespoons of reserved bacon grease. As oils begin to smoke, toss in shrimp to cover bottom of pan. Before stirring, season with salt and pepper. Stir until shrimp begin to turn pink all over. Let the pan return to its original hot temperature. Stir in minced garlic and bacon bits. Be careful not to burn the garlic. Toss in mushrooms and quickly coat with oil. Add lemon juice and wine. Stir until everything is well coated, about 30 seconds. Toss in green onions and stir about 20 seconds. Serve over grits.

4 servings

Oxford Square, about 1900

JAMBALAYA

1	pound smoked sausage, sliced	2½	teaspoons Tabasco sauce
3	tablespoons canola oil	¼	cup Worcestershire sauce
2	medium yellow onions, chopped	½	teaspoon dried thyme
2	green bell peppers, chopped	¾	teaspoon chili powder
4	ribs celery, chopped	3	tablespoons chopped parsley
3	cloves garlic, minced	6	green onions, chopped
1	28-ounce can chopped tomatoes		Salt and pepper to taste
3½	cups chicken broth	2	cups raw rice
2	chicken breasts, boiled and chopped	1	pound raw shrimp, shelled

In a large Dutch oven over high heat, fry sausage until lightly browned. Remove sausage, drain on paper towels, and set aside. To the pan add oil, onions, peppers, celery and garlic. Cook over medium heat until the vegetables are wilted and onions are translucent. Add tomatoes, chicken broth, chicken, fried sausage, Tabasco, Worcestershire, thyme and chili powder. Simmer, uncovered, 30-60 minutes. Add parsley, green onions, salt, pepper and rice. Cover and simmer until rice has absorbed the liquid, about 30 minutes. Stir in shrimp and cook until the shrimp turn pink, 3-5 minutes.

12 servings

JACK'S CATFISH

1	cup flour		Black pepper
1	teaspoon black pepper		Creole seasoning
1	teaspoon garlic powder	6	green onions, chopped
8	6-8 ounce catfish fillets	½	cup chopped fresh parsley
½	cup vegetable oil		Lemon slices
	Dried parsley flakes	⅓	cup fresh lemon juice
	Garlic powder	⅓	cup white wine

Preheat oven to 350°. In a sack, mix flour, black pepper and garlic powder. Put fillets in sack and shake gently to coat. In a skillet over high heat, heat oil and quickly brown both sides of fillets. While fillets are browning sprinkle them with parsley, garlic powder, pepper and Creole seasoning. Transfer fillets to a lightly greased baking dish. Sprinkle with green onions and fresh parsley; garnish with lemon slices. Pour lemon juice over fillets. Remove any excess grease from skillet and deglaze pan with white wine. Pour this mixture over the fish and bake 30 minutes.

8 servings

Photo on page 90

The tradition of Mississippi cuisine in all its variety and eccentricity still largely emanates from the private home or the strange, colorful places like Lusco's and Doe's. In Lafayette County, which some know as Yoknapatawpha, several miles from Ole Miss campus I have found two such institutions which make me forget the martini business lunches in Manhattan. Both of these Lafayette County establishments are grocery stores. One of them, in Abbeville near the Tallahatchie River, [and] the other is in the hamlet of Taylor.... At the back of the store are several long tables and the specialty is catfish, possibly the best I ever had.

~Willie Morris

"A Cook's Tour"

Baked Catfish Fillets

½ cup Worcestershire sauce

¼ cup soy sauce

2 tablespoons lemon pepper

2 catfish fillets

In a small bowl stir together Worcestershire, soy sauce and lemon pepper. Put catfish in a zip-top plastic bag, pour marinade over fish, and refrigerate 1 hour. Drain marinade and bake catfish in a lightly greased baking dish 6-8 minutes at 475°.

◾ *Ajax Diner* ◾

CATFISH AND BLACK-EYED PEA CAKES

CAKES

3	cups cooked black-eyed peas, drained
2	catfish fillets (9-12 ounces each), baked and flaked
⅓	cup minced jalapeños
½	yellow onion, minced
1	egg, beaten
2	tablespoons red wine vinegar
1	tablespoon dry mustard
2	cups breadcrumbs

⅓	cup Creole mustard
1	teaspoon kosher salt
	Flour for dusting
1	cup heavy cream
1	cup half-and-half
1	egg, beaten
2	cups breadcrumbs
3	tablespoons unsalted butter

JALAPEÑO TARTAR SAUCE

4	cups mayonnaise
½	cup chopped, pickled jalapeños
4	tablespoons pickled jalapeño juice
¼	cup apple cider vinegar
	Juice of 1 lemon

1½	teaspoons Tabasco sauce
1½	teaspoons ground cumin
2	teaspoons kosher salt
1	teaspoon white pepper

In a large mixing bowl, place half the black-eyed peas and mash them well. Add the rest of the peas whole, the flaked catfish, jalapeños, onions, egg, vinegar, dry mustard, breadcrumbs, Creole mustard and salt. Combine thoroughly. (At this point, mixture may be stored in an airtight container in the refrigerator and made into patties as needed.) Mold with hands into 2-inch patties, using about ⅓ cup of mixture per patty. Dust patties lightly with flour. In a mixing bowl combine cream, half-and-half and egg. Stir until combined. Coat patties completely with cream mixture. Pour breadcrumbs into a shallow bowl and dredge coated patties in crumbs, making sure they are completely covered. Reshape the cakes so that they are uniform. In a large skillet over medium-high heat, melt butter and heat until bubbling. Fry cakes, being careful not to crowd the pan, until golden brown, 4-5 minutes on each side.

For tartar sauce, in a small bowl combine all ingredients and mix well. Serve catfish cakes with sauce.

about 24 cakes
5 cups tartar sauce

CATFISH CAKES

2½-3	pounds catfish fillets, baked and flaked	2	cups cracker crumbs
2	eggs, beaten	2-3	dashes Tabasco sauce
¾	cup mayonnaise	⅔	cup flour
¼	cup half-and-half	1½	teaspoons salt
2	tablespoons Dijon mustard	½	teaspoon white pepper
4½	teaspoons Worcestershire sauce		Unsalted butter for frying
2½	teaspoons Old Bay seafood seasoning		Lemon slices
			Tartar sauce

Line a cookie sheet with waxed paper. In a large bowl combine the catfish, eggs, mayonnaise, half-and-half, mustard, Worcestershire sauce, seafood seasoning, cracker crumbs and Tabasco. Blend well. By hand, form mixture into 3-4-inch patties. Place them on lined cookie sheet and refrigerate 30 minutes. Preheat oven to 200°. Line another cookie sheet with a brown paper bag or paper towels. In a shallow bowl mix the flour, salt and pepper. Dredge both sides of each catfish cake in the seasoned flour. Heat a large skillet and melt enough butter to completely cover the bottom, about 3 tablespoons. When the butter is very hot, add a few catfish cakes to the skillet. Do not crowd the pan. Cook until golden brown, 4-5 minutes on each side. Transfer cakes to the brown paper-lined cookie sheet and keep warm in oven. Wipe skillet lightly with a paper towel. Add more butter and continue frying remaining cakes. Serve with lemon slices and tartar sauce.

twelve 4-inch catfish cakes

Tartar Sauce

1 medium kosher pickle, grated

1 medium onion, grated

1 teaspoon capers, chopped

1 teaspoon chopped chives

1 cup mayonnaise

4 dashes Tabasco sauce

3 dashes Worcestershire sauce

Cayenne pepper to taste

Combine ingredients and refrigerate at least 3 hours.

COMPANY CATFISH

2	eggs, beaten	6	tablespoons unsalted butter, divided use
½	cup flour		Salt, pepper and paprika to taste
½	cup Parmesan cheese	½	cup sliced almonds
6	6-8 ounce catfish fillets		

Preheat oven to 400°. In a shallow bowl lightly beat eggs. In another shallow bowl stir together the flour and Parmesan cheese. Dip the fillets into egg and then the flour/cheese mixture. In a large skillet over medium-high heat, melt 4 tablespoons butter and lightly brown the fillets. Place them in a baking dish and sprinkle with salt, pepper and paprika. Bake until the fillets are flaky, about 15 minutes. Drizzle with 2 tablespoons melted butter and sprinkle almonds on top.

6 servings

Bouré

Salmon with Dijon Caper Sauce

1 cup Dijon

¾ cup mayonnaise

2 tablespoons red wine vinegar

1 teaspoon lemon juice

2 tablespoons capers, minced

6 (6-ounce) salmon fillets

Olive oil

Chili powder

Salt and pepper to taste

1 cup breadcrumbs

Whisk first 5 ingredients together and let stand at room temperature 30 minutes. Brush salmon fillets with olive oil and season with chili powder, salt and pepper. Roll in breadcrumbs. Bake at 325°. about 15 minutes. Serve with Dijon Caper Sauce.

WALNUT-CRUSTED SALMON

SALMON

1	cup finely chopped walnuts		Salt and pepper to taste
⅔	cup fresh breadcrumbs	4	teaspoons mayonnaise
2	tablespoons unsalted butter, melted	4	6-ounce salmon fillets, skinned
2	tablespoons chopped parsley		

SAUCE

1	cup plain yogurt	½	English cucumber, grated
1	small clove garlic, minced		Salt and pepper to taste

Preheat oven to 425°. In a mixing bowl combine nuts, breadcrumbs, butter, parsley, salt and pepper. Season salmon with additional salt and pepper, and place in a greased baking dish. Spread 1 teaspoon mayonnaise on each fillet. Top with crumb mixture and press into fish. Bake until fish is flaky, 10-15 minutes.

In a small bowl combine the yogurt, garlic and cucumber. Season with salt and pepper. Serve salmon with sauce.

4 servings

SALMON IN DILL PEPPERONCINI SAUCE

4	6-ounce salmon fillets, skinned	1	cup heavy cream
1	tablespoon olive oil	2	tablespoons finely chopped parsley
1	tablespoon unsalted butter	2	tablespoons finely chopped dill
1	shallot, finely chopped		Salt and white pepper to taste
¼	cup seeded, minced pepperoncini peppers		Lemon slices

In a skillet over medium-high heat, sauté salmon fillets in olive oil, turning once, about 7 minutes. Transfer to plate and keep warm. In skillet melt butter and sauté shallots and peppers until soft. Add cream and simmer until thick, 7-10 minutes. Add parsley and dill. Season with salt and white pepper to taste. Serve over salmon. Garnish with lemon slices.

■ Yocona River Inn ■

PAN-ROASTED SALMON WITH MAPLE GLAZE

1 cup maple syrup	1 tablespoon chopped garlic
¼ cup lemon juice	1 teaspoon crushed red pepper
2 tablespoons soy sauce	6-8 salmon fillets, individually portioned
1 tablespoon minced or grated gingerroot	Salt and pepper to taste
	Canola oil

In a small saucepan over high heat, combine the syrup, lemon juice, soy sauce, gingerroot, garlic and red pepper. Bring to a boil and lower heat to maintain a gentle simmer. Reduce the glaze by ⅓, or to about 1 cup in volume. Position an oven rack in the top third of the oven and preheat to 450°. While the glaze reduces, rinse salmon in cold water and pat dry. Season with salt and pepper, and refrigerate until glaze is finished. Spoon a little reduced glaze on each piece of fish. Use a brush to distribute glaze over the entire fillet. Let fillets rest at room temperature for 5-10 minutes. In a nonstick sauté pan over medium-high heat, add enough oil to cover the bottom. Do not let the oil smoke. Gently lay the salmon fillets in the pan, flesh side down. Sauté until the glaze has browned on the fish, about 2 minutes. Remove pan from heat and flip the salmon. Brush the tops of fillets liberally with glaze. Transfer to a greased baking dish and roast until just done, 4-6 minutes, or when the fish flakes easily. Place fish on a serving plate and brush again with the remaining glaze.

6-8 servings

Mango-Papaya Salsa

1 cup diced fresh mango

1 cup diced fresh papaya

2 tablespoons fresh lime juice

1-2 tablespoons chopped, fresh cilantro leaves

1 tablespoon finely chopped, fresh jalapeño peppers

¼ teaspoon salt

Combine all ingredients. Serve as a dip for chips or as an accompaniment to grilled fish, meat or quesadillas.

2 cups salsa

GRILLED SALMON FILLETS

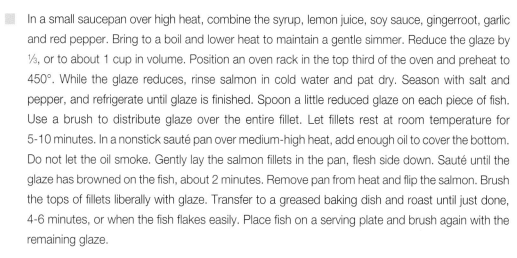

Olive oil	1 tablespoon fresh dill
6 6-ounce salmon fillets	1½ teaspoons fresh lime juice
¼ cup mayonnaise	1½ teaspoons brown sugar
¼ cup whole grain mustard	

Rub olive oil on skin side of salmon fillets. In a small bowl mix together the mayonnaise, mustard, dill, lime juice and brown sugar. Spread on the meat side of fillets. Place on grill over medium-hot coals, skin side down. Cover grill and cook 25 minutes without turning.

6 servings

PECAN CRUNCH GROUPER

4	6-8 ounce grouper fillets	2	tablespoons unsalted butter, melted
¼	cup fresh lemon juice	1½	tablespoons honey
¼	teaspoon salt	¼	cup soft breadcrumbs
¼	teaspoon freshly ground black pepper	¼	cup finely chopped pecans
2	tablespoons Dijon mustard	2	teaspoons chopped, fresh parsley

Preheat oven to 450°. Sprinkle fillets with lemon juice, salt and pepper. Arrange in a greased 9 x 13-inch baking dish. In a small bowl, combine mustard, butter and honey. Brush on fillets. In another small bowl mix breadcrumbs, pecans and parsley. Spoon over fillets. Bake until fish flakes easily with a fork, about 10 minutes.

4 servings

FILLETS WITH PARMESAN SAUCE

6	6-ounce fish fillets (snapper, grouper or trigger)	¼	cup unsalted butter, room temperature
2	tablespoons fresh lemon juice	3	tablespoons mayonnaise
	Unsalted butter, melted	3	tablespoons chopped green onions
½	cup grated Parmesan cheese	¼	teaspoon salt
		⅛	teaspoon Tabasco sauce

Preheat oven broiler. Skin fillets and baste with lemon juice. Let rest 10 minutes. Baste with melted butter. Place on a well-greased broiler pan and broil 4 inches from heat for 4-5 minutes. Turn fish over and broil until fish flakes. In a small bowl combine Parmesan cheese, butter, mayonnaise, green onions, salt and Tabasco. Remove fish from the broiler and spread half of cheese mixture on fish. Return to broiler until the fish browns. Transfer to plates and use remaining cheese mixture for additional spread.

6 servings

PANÉED REDFISH

FISH

6	redfish fillets, skinned		2	tablespoons unsalted butter
	Lemon pepper			Juice of 2 lemons
	Garlic salt		¼	cup Worcestershire sauce
	Flour			Cajun seasoning

SAUCE

2	tablespoons unsalted butter		1	cup heavy cream
½	onion, chopped		½	cup vermouth
1	14-ounce can artichoke hearts, drained and chopped		½	pound raw shrimp, shelled and chopped
2	tablespoons flour		1	bunch asparagus

Preheat oven broiler. Sprinkle fillets with lemon pepper and garlic salt. Dredge in flour. In a large iron skillet over medium-high heat, sauté fillets in butter for 2½ minutes on each side. Sprinkle lemon juice, Worcestershire and Cajun seasoning on fillets. Broil in oven 5 minutes.

For sauce, in a saucepan over medium-high heat, melt butter; sauté onions and artichokes until onions are clear. Stirring constantly, blend in flour. Slowly add cream and vermouth. Stir until smooth and thickened. Add shrimp and cook until shrimp are pink. Boil asparagus in salted water, just until tender, 3-5 minutes. To serve, place fish on serving platter and arrange asparagus on top. Cover with sauce and serve hot.

6 servings

Artist Priscilla Hamric Artwork, page 105

Painter Priscilla Hamric has been a medical technologist at Baptist Health Care since 1990. Hamric is also a senior in the University of Mississippi's BFA program with an emphasis in painting. She lives in Oxford with her husband, Ed Koen, and their two teenagers.

Photo by Martin J. Dain

South side of the Square, early 1960s

Author Jim Dees
Essay, page 106

Longtime resident of Oxford and Taylor, Jim Dees is the host for *Thacker Mountain Radio*, a literature and music program on Oxford's Bullseye 95.5 and Mississippi's public radio stations. He has written for the *Oxford Eagle* and is former editor of *Oxford Town,* for which he still contributes a weekly column. Most recently, he edited the collection *They Write Among Us: New Stories and Essays from the Best of Oxford Writers.*

CRAWFISH FETTUCCINI

2	tablespoons unsalted butter		1	cup heavy cream
1	medium yellow onion, chopped		1	tablespoon paprika
1	medium green bell pepper, chopped		4	Roma tomatoes, diced
1-3	cloves garlic, minced			Cajun seasoning to taste
1	pound crawfish tails, cooked		½	pound fettuccini, cooked *al dente*

In a medium skillet over medium heat, melt butter and add onion and bell pepper. Sauté until onions are clear. Add garlic and crawfish tails. Sauté 3-5 minutes. Add cream and paprika. Reduce sauce to about half. Add tomatoes and cook just enough to heat. Season to taste with Cajun seasoning. Serve over cooked fettuccini.

4-6 servings

CRAWFISH DELICACY

½	cup vegetable oil		4	green onions, chopped
1	small onion, chopped		¼	cup chopped fresh parsley
½	small green bell pepper, chopped		3	cups hot water
1	rib celery, chopped		½	teaspoon salt
2	pounds frozen, cooked, peeled crawfish tails, thawed		¼	teaspoon cayenne pepper
3	tablespoons flour		¼	teaspoon black pepper
1	1.5-ounce envelope beef stew seasoning mix		¼	teaspoon garlic salt
				Hot, cooked rice

In a large saucepan over medium-high heat, heat oil and sauté onions, bell peppers and celery. Stir in remaining ingredients except rice and bring to a boil. Reduce heat and simmer, stirring occasionally for 30 minutes. Serve over hot, cooked rice.

6-8 servings

Courthouse Clock by Priscilla Hamric ▶

priscilla Hamric ©2004

OUT to LUNCH
EAT or WE BOTH STARVE

Jim Dees

There are times when the skyscrapers, subways, and metropolitan roar of Oxford become deafening and one is compelled to, as Twain wrote, "light out for the territory." One popular source of solace is located seven miles south of town, downhill from the Thacker fire tower. Here one finds Taylor, Mississippi (pop. 330), home to Taylor Grocery, a catfish/steak house where all the locals are on a first name basis...with all the dogs on the front porch. Taylor Grocery offers nourishment and history. The room is in a 100-year-old wooden building, the walls a dizzying collage of the signatures of satisfied customers. ("We died for their fins," reads one.) Among numerous artifacts, hanging from the ceiling is a "Redneck Windchime," which consists of two empty beer cans and two empty bean cans.

Though the nighttime catfish is legendary, the Grocery began serving lunch on a trial basis in 2002 and it has become the most popular lunch secret in Oxford. Despite having only an hour to eat and the plethora of fine lunch spots in Oxford, dozens of Oxonians make the winding, curvy drive to Taylor every day.

"The food is better than my grandmother's," one patron told me. "Now that's really saying something. But don't quote me."

Such heresy is the creation of Pat Chrestman, the lunch cook at Taylor, as well as a walking history of Oxford food.

"I started at Kreme Kup on University Avenue selling those 19-cent hamburgers," she says. "Then I worked at Smitty's on the Square. I opened, closed, waited, cooked — whatever Miss Louise (Smith) needed. After that I was manager at James Food Center. We baked a lot of bread for various businesses. I remember Ron used to come in and get our bread to serve at the Hoka."

Chrestman then joined forces with Lynn Hewlett at Dixie Creek on West Jackson Avenue and began serving the tenderest pork barbecue sandwiches and ribs. Hewlett then hired her at Taylor to begin a plate lunch business, and the two embarked on serving the classic "meat and three" plus sweet tea, all for only five dollars. Be forewarned, when they say "sweet tea," this elixir will curl your tongue.

The menu is not for the faint-hearted or denizens of South Beach: beef tips and rice, meat loaf, fried chicken, pork tenderloin, and, of course, hold on to your carbs, chicken fried steak and hamburger steak. Then there are the fearless vegetables: real mashed potatoes and gravy, creme corn, green beans, English peas (Give me strength), broccoli-and-cheese casserole, a truly fearsome Rotel cabbage, and, of course, daily, like oxygen itself, fried okra.

The clientele are addicted, many come five days a week: lawyers and sheriff's deputies, city street workers with their names on their shirts, bankers with their guts under theirs. Car salesmen, house painters with splattered clothes, dirty roofers, gigantic football players (extra meat) and, on the second Tuesday of every month, the Red Hat Club. The club consists of 30 to 40 mature ladies who come to lunch brightly dressed and laugh and compare their fine red hats. When Pat tried to put them all together in a private room, the Red Hats demurred.

"We want to be where we can see the men," said one.

Taylor was a railroad town at the turn of the 20th century, founded by John Taylor in 1832 following his purchase of the land from the Chickasaws. According to the current owners, Lynn and Debbie Hewlett, Taylor Grocery was thought to have been built in 1899 and served the small community as a dry goods store until 1930, when it was refashioned as a general store. The store evolved into a catfish restaurant in the late 1970s. Taking over for original owners, Jerry and Evie Wilson, Mary Katherine Hudson ran the restaurant for 18 years and, as Hewlett says, "really made Taylor a name for catfish."

Hewlett has taken the Church of Cat even further. The dinner crowds are huge now and there are more brown bags than at a Saints game. Hewlett directs traffic and sips and dips: his favorite place to spit is near the "Don't spit on the porch" sign. At night, three-hour waits are encouraged and the hordes join Hewlett on the porch and enjoy the slower pace while sitting on old church pews. All manner of media have reported on the charms of Taylor Grocery from *Field and Stream* to the Food Channel. As a result, tiny Taylor now attracts true international riffraff like Jimmy Buffet and Trent Lott.

But lunch will remain the true reflection of Taylor, a country comfort for the tranquility-challenged. Just don't step on the dogs on your way in.

Pat agreed to give me her Rotel recipe because nobody can make it like hers anyway:

TAYLOR'S ROTEL CABBAGE

1 medium-sized head of bell pepper	1 smidgen of granulated garlic
1 medium-sized chopped onion	1 pinch of salt, pinch of black pepper
1 stick of butter	1 medium-sized head of cabbage
1 smidgen of sugar	1 can of original Rotel
1 smidgen of cayenne pepper	

DIRECTIONS:

Let all your smidgens and pinches come to a boil. Add chopped cabbage and let cook until cabbage is soft. Add Rotel and bring to boil. Let cool.

Serves 4-8.

Teriyaki Cornish Hens
Asparagus Bundles

POULTRY

TERIYAKI CORNISH HENS

1   6-ounce package long-grain and wild rice mix

1½ tablespoons cornstarch

¼   cup plus 2 tablespoons water

2   tablespoons unsalted butter

¾   cup teriyaki sauce

2   tablespoons lemon juice

3   tablespoons sugar

⅛   teaspoon pepper

⅛   teaspoon ground ginger

4   1-1½ pound Cornish hens

    Pepper for sprinkling

Prepare rice according to package directions. Set aside. Preheat oven to 375°. Combine cornstarch and water, stirring well. Set aside. In a medium skillet over medium-high heat, melt butter and stir in teriyaki, lemon juice, sugar, ⅛ teaspoon pepper and ginger. Gradually stir in the cornstarch mixture. Cook, stirring constantly, until smooth and bubbly, 1-2 minutes. Set sauce aside. Remove giblets from hens. Rinse hens with cold water and pat dry. Sprinkle with pepper. Stuff hens with prepared rice and close the cavities. Secure with wooden toothpicks and truss. Place hens, breast side up, in a shallow pan. Bake 30 minutes. Then baste with sauce every 10 minutes for an additional 40 minutes.

4 servings

Photo on page 108

TUSCAN CHICKEN

6   chicken breast halves

    Flour for dusting

3   tablespoons olive oil, divided use

2   cups chickpeas, drained

1   onion, coarsely chopped

3   cloves garlic, minced

4   ripe tomatoes, coarsley chopped

1   teaspoon cinnamon

2   tablespoons thyme

    Salt and pepper to taste

½   cup black olives

Preheat oven to 350°. Lightly dust chicken breasts with flour. In a heavy large skillet over high heat, brown chicken in 2 tablespoons olive oil. Arrange chicken in a lightly greased 9 x 13-inch baking dish. Scatter drained chickpeas over chicken. To same skillet add 1 tablespoon olive oil and sauté onion and garlic. Add tomatoes, cinnamon and thyme. Simmer 10 minutes. Pour over chicken. Season with salt and pepper and scatter black olives around chicken. Bake uncovered at 350° until juices run clear, 30-45 minutes.

6 servings

Cornish hens originated in Cornwall, England. When purchasing hens, look for the smaller ones because they are the most tender and flavorful.

CHICKEN CURRY

3	tablespoons unsalted butter	½	teaspoon lemon juice
¼	cup minced onion		Hot, cooked rice
2	tablespoons curry powder		Chopped peanuts
3	tablespoons flour		Flaked coconut
¾	teaspoon salt		Raisins
¾	teaspoon sugar		Chopped pineapple
⅛	teaspoon ground ginger		Crumbled bacon
1	cup chicken broth		Chopped fresh mint or basil
1	cup milk		Chopped green onions
2-3	cups diced, cooked chicken		

In a heavy saucepan over low heat, melt butter and sauté onion with curry. Blend in flour, salt, sugar and ginger. Cook over low heat, stirring frequently, until mixture is smooth and bubbly. Remove from heat. Add chicken broth and milk, stirring constantly. Bring to boil and continue stirring 1 minute. Add chicken and lemon juice and heat thoroughly. Spoon chicken curry over rice and pass condiments.

4 servings

MARINATED CHICKEN BREASTS

This tender chicken can be prepared ahead. Just save the last hour of cooking until ready to serve.

8	boneless, skinless chicken breast halves		Flour
⅔	cup fresh lemon juice	½	cup unsalted butter
1	teaspoon salt	1	cup sliced mushrooms
½	teaspoon pepper	½	cup water or chicken broth

Marinate chicken in lemon juice, salt and pepper for 1 hour in refrigerator. Preheat oven to 275°. In a shallow bowl place flour. Remove chicken breasts from marinade and dredge in flour. In a heavy large skillet over medium heat, melt butter and brown chicken breasts lightly on both sides. Transfer chicken to a greased 9 x 13-inch baking dish and pour skillet drippings over chicken. Cook covered, 1 hour. Add mushrooms and ½ cup water or broth. Cook uncovered 1 hour.

8 servings

Always marinate poultry in the refrigerator, and discard the marinade or boil it for at least five minutes before brushing it on cooked poultry.

Cooked poultry should not be kept at room temperature for more than two hours. Leftovers should be reheated to 165° (steaming hot) to kill bacteria.

CRANBERRY CHUTNEY CHICKEN

CRANBERRY CHUTNEY

1   16-ounce can whole-berry cranberry sauce

Zest of 1 lemon

½   cup raisins

½   teaspoon dried ginger mixed with 2 teaspoons water

1   teaspoon Dijon mustard

1   green apple, peeled and chopped

1   large onion, chopped

¼   cup chopped, green bell pepper

½   cup cider vinegar

½   cup packed brown sugar

1   teaspoon salt

5   cloves garlic, minced

CURRIED CHICKEN

8   boneless, skinless chicken breasts

Salt and pepper to taste

5   tablespoons olive oil, divided use

3   tablespoons flour

1   tablespoon curry powder

½   cup chicken broth, hot

1¼   cups plain yogurt

Hot cooked rice

For chutney, in a small saucepan, combine all chutney ingredients. Simmer, stirring frequently, until thickened, about 1 hour. Cool and refrigerate.

For chicken, season with salt and pepper and sauté in a heavy large skillet over medium-high heat in 4 tablespoons olive oil until firm but not browned. Remove chicken. Add 1 tablespoon olive oil to skillet and blend in flour. Cook 3 minutes, stirring constantly. Add curry and blend. Add hot chicken broth and stir until smooth. Add yogurt and cook until thickened. Blend in chutney and mix well. Return chicken to pan. Cover and cook over low heat 15 minutes. Serve over rice.

8 servings

Mule Auction on the Oxford Square, 1901

On June 13, 1836, Thomas Dudley Isom was present on the front lawn of the current First Presbyterian Church when his uncle and two others purchased from Indian Princess Hoka for $800 the land where the Square and the University are now located. Nine days later, on June 22, the County Board accepted his donation of the land for the Square and laid out a town designated "Oxford." Many accounts give Isom credit for naming Oxford after the British village in hopes of attracting a university.

~Will Lewis, Jr.

Try this chicken version of the Veal Country Captain that John Currence, chef and owner of City Grocery, made at the James Beard House—to rave reviews.

■ *City Grocery* ■
COUNTRY CAPTAIN CHICKEN

8	boneless, skin-on chicken breasts	1½	tablespoons Madras curry powder
	Salt and pepper	3-4	tablespoons crushed red pepper
¼	cup unsalted butter	2	cups veal stock (or unsalted beef bouillon)
3	tablespoons bacon fat, divided use		
2	tablespoons garlic purée	6	cups canned crushed tomatoes with juice
2	yellow onions, sliced		
2	green bell peppers, julienned	¾	cup dried currants
4	tomatoes, chopped	2	tablespoons olive oil
1	tablespoon dry thyme	6	tablespoons Burgundy wine
		½	cup unsalted butter, chilled, cubed

■ Season chicken breasts with salt and pepper and set aside. In a Dutch oven over medium-high heat, melt butter and 2 tablespoons bacon fat. Sauté garlic and onion until translucent but not browned. Add bell peppers and sauté until tender. Stir in fresh tomatoes, thyme, curry powder and crushed red pepper and bring to a simmer. Stir in veal stock, crushed tomatoes and currants and bring to a boil. Reduce heat to medium-low and simmer 45 minutes.

■ Preheat oven to 350°. Heat 2 large sauté pans until hot. Add 1 tablespoon olive oil and ½ tablespoon bacon fat to each pan and swirl to coat the bottom of the pans. Carefully place 4 chicken breasts in each pan. Brown on 1 side, turn and brown slightly on the other side. Add 3 tablespoons wine to each pan and swirl briefly to deglaze. Divide the tomato mixture in half and pour in each pan. Place pans in oven for 15 minutes. Remove pans and transfer chicken breasts to individual serving plates. Whisk 4 tablespoons butter into each pan and season to taste with salt and pepper. Top each breast with tomato mixture.

8 servings

Leon Holley Garage, 1920s

TENDER GRILLED CHICKEN

1	cup canola or olive oil	2	teaspoons onion powder
½	cup fresh lemon juice	½	teaspoon thyme
1	teaspoon salt	1	clove garlic, crushed
1	teaspoon paprika	8-10	boneless chicken breasts, skinned
2	teaspoons dried basil		

Combine all ingredients in a heavy plastic bag. Marinate overnight in the refrigerator. Preheat oven to 300°. Bake chicken in marinade for 30 minutes on a large baking dish. Preheat a charcoal or gas grill. Transfer chicken to the grill and cook until tender, or until internal temperature reaches 180°.

8-10 servings

HOMEMADE CHICKEN PIE

2	pie crusts		Kosher salt to taste
6	tablespoons unsalted butter, divided use		Freshly ground pepper
4	tablespoons flour	3	cups cooked chicken, cut into 1-inch pieces
1	cup chicken broth		
1	cup milk		

Preheat oven to 400°. Line a quiche pan with one pie crust. In a large skillet over medium-high heat, melt butter and stir in flour. Cook, stirring, until smooth and bubbly, about 2 minutes. Add chicken broth and milk. Stir until smooth and season with salt and pepper. Place chicken in pie shell. Cover with the white sauce and dot with remaining 2 tablespoons butter. Cover with second crust and seal edges. Make slits in top to release steam. Cover edges of crust with foil to keep them from becoming too brown. Bake for 10 minutes. Reduce heat to 350° and continue cooking until crust is golden brown, about 30 minutes.

4-6 servings

The table was set in the kitchen where it always was and Molly stood at the stove drawing the biscuit out as she always stood, but Lucas was not there and there was just one chair, one plate, his glass of milk beside it, the platter heaped with untouched chicken....

~William Faulkner

Go Down, Moses

113

Roasted Garlic Purée

Remove outer skin from garlic bulb but do not separate cloves. Place garlic in a baking dish and add enough olive oil to cover garlic. Cover with foil and bake at 350° until very tender, about 45 minutes. Remove garlic from olive oil and cool several minutes. Squeeze pulp out of bulbs. Purée in a food processor.

■ Bouré ■

BACON AND PROVOLONE STUFFED CHICKEN BREASTS WITH ROASTED GARLIC GRAVY

STUFFED CHICKEN BREASTS

3	cups cooked crumbled bacon	6	6-ounce boneless, skinless chicken breast halves
½	cup chopped, fresh basil		Olive oil
1½	cups diced provolone cheese		Salt and pepper

ROASTED GARLIC GRAVY

¼	cup unsalted butter	2	cups heavy cream
¼	cup flour	1½	cups roasted garlic purée
3½	cups chicken broth		Salt and white pepper to taste

For chicken, preheat grill or oven to 350°. In a mixing bowl stir together bacon, basil and cheese. In the thickest part of chicken breast insert the tip of a chef's knife. Being careful not to cut all the way through the breast, cut from one side of breast to the other, making a pocket for stuffing. Carefully add small amounts of bacon mixture at a time, being careful not to overstuff or tear chicken breast. Brush breasts with olive oil and sprinkle with salt and pepper. Grill or bake until internal temperature reaches 160°.

For gravy, in a medium saucepan over medium-high heat, melt butter. Add flour and stir. Reduce heat to low and cook until roux is blond. Add chicken broth and stir until thick. Add cream and roasted garlic purée. Simmer 2-3 minutes. Add salt and pepper to taste. Serve gravy over chicken breasts.

6 servings

North Lamar, 1926

CHICKEN IN PUFF PASTRY

1½ cups cooked, chopped chicken
8 ounces Pepper Jack cheese, cubed
¼ red bell pepper, chopped
¼ cup chopped green onions

⅓ cup mayonnaise
Salt and pepper to taste
1 16-ounce package frozen puff pastry
1 egg, beaten

Preheat oven to 375°. In a large mixing bowl, stir together chicken, cheese, bell pepper, green onions, mayonnaise, salt and pepper. Roll out 1 sheet of puff pastry on a floured work surface. Place half of chicken mixture in the center of pastry. Fold 2 sides of pastry over the chicken filling, overlapping the sides. Moisten and seal seams. With a sharp knife, score top of pastry. Transfer to a parchment-lined or lightly greased cookie sheet. Brush with egg. Repeat with remaining filling and pastry sheet. Cook until golden brown, 20-30 minutes. Let rest 10 minutes before slicing.

6 servings

Then they were busy in the yard in the dusk, smelling the cooking chicken, until Molly called Henry and then a little later himself, the voice as it had always been, peaceful and steadfast: "Come and eat your supper."

~William Faulkner

Go Down, Moses

CAPTIVATING CHICKEN

4 boneless, skinless chicken breast halves
¼ cup flour
Salt, white pepper, black pepper to taste
3 tablespoons unsalted butter
1 teaspoon minced garlic
½ cup chicken broth

¼ cup white wine
1 tablespoon fresh lemon juice
⅓ cup half-and-half
¼ pound sliced, sautéed mushrooms
1 tablespoon chopped parsley
½ teaspoon dried basil
½ cup grated Swiss cheese
Angel hair pasta, cooked *al dente*

Cut chicken breasts lengthwise into ¾-inch strips. In a bag place flour, salt and peppers. Shake to combine. Add chicken strips and shake to coat with flour. In a heavy large skillet over medium-high heat, melt butter and add chicken, turning to brown all sides. Add garlic and sauté 1 minute. Add broth, wine and lemon juice. Simmer until chicken is completely cooked, about 15 minutes. Pour in half-and-half and stir well. Stir in mushrooms, parsley, basil and cheese. Season to taste with salt and pepper. Serve over pasta.

4 servings

CHICKEN BUNDLES
WITH CHEESE SAUCE

To prepare chicken for use in this recipe, place breasts in a stockpot and cover with cold water. Add one onion with skin, roughly chopped; two ribs celery with leaves; one unpeeled carrot, roughly chopped; two bay leaves; and a few whole peppercorns. Bring to a boil, reduce to simmer and cook, covered, 30 to 45 minutes. Remove chicken. Strain broth and reserve for another use.

CHICKEN

2 8-ounce packages refrigerated crescent rolls

16 ounces cream cheese, room temperature

2 tablespoons unsalted butter, room temperature

Chopped chives, green onions, or green chilies, optional

4 chicken breasts, cooked and cubed

2 tablespoons unsalted butter, melted

½ cup seasoned breadcrumbs

CHEESE SAUCE

2 tablespoons unsalted butter

2 tablespoons flour

⅛ teaspoon salt

1 cup milk

½ cup shredded Cheddar cheese

1 tablespoon finely chopped onion

½ teaspoon Worcestershire sauce

Pepper

Preheat oven to 350°. On a floured work surface, divide the crescent roll dough into 8 rectangles, pinching the diagonal seams together. (Two triangles pinched together at the dotted line make a rectangle.) Flatten dough slightly with a rolling pin. In a mixing bowl stir together cream cheese, butter and any optional ingredients. Stir in cooked chicken. Place ⅛ of chicken mixture on 1 side of each dough rectangle. Fold in half to form a package and pinch to seal seams. Brush with melted butter and roll in breadcrumbs. Place in a lightly greased shallow baking dish and bake until golden brown, about 30 minutes.

For cheese sauce, melt butter in a 1-quart saucepan over low heat. Stir in flour and salt. Add milk. Cook and stir continuously until thick and bubbly. Add cheese, onion, Worcestershire and pepper. Cook until cheese is melted. Serve sauce over chicken bundles.

8 servings

CHICKEN CORDON BLEU

12 skinless, boneless chicken breast halves
12 small slices Swiss cheese
12 small slices cooked ham
½ cup flour
½ teaspoon salt
⅛ teaspoon pepper
½ teaspoon paprika
½ cup vegetable oil
½ cup sherry
1 teaspoon chicken bouillon
1 tablespoon cornstarch
1 cup heavy cream

Cover chicken breasts with plastic wrap and pound flat with a meat mallet. Place 1 slice of cheese and 1 slice of ham on each breast. Fold breast over ham and cheese and secure with toothpick. In a shallow bowl mix flour, salt, pepper and paprika. Dredge chicken in flour mixture and set aside. In a large skillet over medium-high heat, heat oil. Add chicken breasts and brown on all sides. Remove from skillet and set aside. To skillet add sherry and bouillon. Reduce heat to low and add chicken breasts. Simmer, uncovered, until chicken is fully cooked, about 20 minutes. Remove chicken from skillet and take out toothpicks. In a small bowl mix cornstarch and cream until smooth. Add to skillet and stir until thickened. Serve sauce over chicken breasts.

12 servings

I remember her own fried chicken, which she would soak overnight in buttermilk and make for me late at night…and we would sit on the front porch and gorge ourselves on the nocturnal feast and talk….

~Willie Morris

"A Cook's Tour"

GLAZED CHICKEN AND PEARS

1 16-ounce can pear halves in heavy syrup
½ cup white wine
2 teaspoons cornstarch
½ teaspoon dry mustard
¼ teaspoon salt
¼ teaspoon pepper
¼ teaspoon grated lemon zest
2 tablespoons fresh lemon juice
2 teaspoons soy sauce
    Salt and pepper for sprinkling
4 boneless chicken breast halves, trimmed
2 tablespoons oil

Drain pears, reserving liquid. Set aside. Whisk together pear liquid and enough wine to make 1 cup. Add cornstarch, mustard, salt, pepper, lemon zest, lemon juice and soy sauce. Set aside. Lightly salt and pepper each side of chicken and brown in oil over medium-high heat for 2-3 minutes on each side. Remove to platter. Add pear liquid and scrape pan sides and bottom. Return chicken to pan, add pears, cover, and simmer 15 minutes.

4 servings

Artist Paula Temple
Artwork, page 121

Paula Temple has lived in Oxford since 1985 and is a Professor of Art at the University of Mississippi. She has also worked as a graphic designer and exhibiting artist in Charleston, S.C.; Santa Rosa, Calif.; Miami, Fla., and the Eastern Caribbean with the Peace Corps; and served as an Artist-in-Residence in Cortona, Italy. Her active exhibition record includes solo exhibitions at the American Embassy in Bridgetown, Barbados, Louisiana Museum of Arts and Sciences, and the University of the West Indies, St. Georges, Grenada. She was included in the

SAUTÉED CHICKEN OVER WILTED SPINACH WITH KUMQUAT SAUCE

3	kumquats (or 2 clementines)	3	tablespoons white wine vinegar
1	large shallot	⅛	teaspoon crushed red pepper
2	boneless chicken breast halves	1	tablespoon chopped, fresh parsley
	Salt and pepper		Salt to taste
1	tablespoon unsalted butter	4	cups packed spinach leaves (about 1 bunch)
2	tablespoons sugar		
⅓	cup water		

Cut kumquats crosswise into thin slices and discard seeds. Thinly slice shallot. Cover chicken breasts with plastic wrap and pound flat with a meat mallet. Sprinkle with salt and pepper. In a medium skillet over medium-high heat, melt butter. Add chicken to skillet and sauté until golden, about 5 minutes. Turn chicken, reduce heat to medium, and cook just until done, about 5 minutes. Transfer chicken to a plate, cover, and keep warm. To skillet add shallots and cook, stirring frequently, about 1 minute. Sprinkle sugar over shallots and cook undisturbed until sugar is melted and golden. Immediately stir in kumquats, water, vinegar and crushed red pepper. Simmer 1 minute. Stir in parsley. If sauce is too thin, simmer until thickened to desired consistency. Transfer ⅔ of sauce to a small bowl. Add spinach to the remaining sauce and salt to taste; turn spinach with tongs until just wilted. Divide spinach between 2 plates and top with chicken. Spoon sauce over chicken.

2 servings

FAIRY BELL'S FRIED CHICKEN

3-4	pounds chicken pieces, or 1 chicken, cut up	1	cup buttermilk
	Salt	2	cups flour
2	eggs		Salt and pepper
			Vegetable oil

Rinse chicken and place in a large baking dish. Cover with water and sprinkle with salt. Refrigerate overnight. Drain, rinse, and pat dry. In a shallow bowl beat eggs with buttermilk. In a separate shallow bowl, combine flour with salt and pepper to taste. Drain chicken pieces and dredge in egg mixture, then flour mixture. In a heavy large skillet over high heat, pour enough oil to cover chicken. Heat until flour sprinkled in the pan causes grease to splatter. Turn heat to medium. Add chicken and fry chicken, uncovered, until brown on one side, 5-8 minutes. Turn chicken to brown the other side. Larger pieces will take longer. Remove and drain on paper towels.

4-6 servings

Photo on page 25

CHICKEN CAKES WITH CREOLE SAUCE

CHICKEN CAKES

2	teaspoons unsalted butter		1	egg, lightly beaten
½	medium red bell pepper, diced		2	tablespoons mayonnaise
4	green onions, thinly sliced		1	tablespoon Creole mustard
1	clove garlic, minced		2	teaspoons Creole seasoning
3	cups chopped, cooked chicken		4	tablespoons vegetable oil, divided use
1	cup soft breadcrumbs			

CREOLE SAUCE

1	cup mayonnaise		1	tablespoon chopped fresh Italian parsley
3	green onions, sliced		¼	teaspoon cayenne pepper
2	tablespoons Creole mustard			Parsley sprigs for garnish
2	cloves garlic, minced			

In a large nonstick skillet over medium-high heat, melt butter and add bell pepper, green onions and garlic. Sauté until vegetables are tender, 3-4 minutes. Transfer to a large mixing bowl and add chicken, breadcrumbs, egg, mayonnaise, mustard and Creole seasoning. Shape chicken mix into eight 3½-inch patties. In same skillet over medium heat, heat 2 tablespoons oil. Fry 4 patties at a time until golden brown, about 3 minutes on each side. Drain on paper towels. Repeat with remaining 2 tablespoons oil and 4 patties.

For sauce, combine all sauce ingredients except garnish in a food processor and pulse until well blended. Serve cakes with Creole sauce and garnish with fresh parsley.

8 servings

Centennial Exhibition "Artists Who Teach" in Washington, D.C. Her work appears in Best of Watercolor, Portrait Inspirations and Best of Watercolor 3, and her award-winning painting "Light, Grace and Spirit" for the American Cancer Society toured the country, and the artist was featured on the Rosie O'Donnell Show in New York. Her awards include the Mississippi Institute of Arts and Letters Award and the Mississippi Arts Commission Fellowship.

Lyric Theatre, early 1940s

Ritz Theatre, early 1940s

119

CHICKEN ENCHILADAS

Author Larry Brown
Essay, page 122

Celebrated novelist
and short-story writer
Larry Brown was
captain of the Oxford
Fire Department before
retiring to write full-time
in 1990. Brown's five
novels, two story
collections, and two
books of essays, all
center upon his native
Mississippi. His work
gained widespread
critical acclaim and
attracted a vast audience
of devoted readers.
Translated into
numerous languages,
his writing twice won
the Southern Book
Critics' Circle Award.
Brown died November
24, 2004. He is
missed by all.

FILLING

2-3 chicken breast halves, cooked and
    shredded
2   green onions, chopped
¼ cup chopped, fresh cilantro

½ teaspoon dried oregano
½ teaspoon salt
¼ teaspoon pepper

SAUCE

2   tablespoons vegetable oil
3   cloves garlic, minced
2   tablespoons chili powder
3   tablespoons flour

1   tablespoon ground cumin
⅛ teaspoon cinnamon
2½ cups chicken broth, hot
½ cup canned tomato sauce

TORTILLAS

    Vegetable oil
10 6-inch corn tortillas
½ cup grated Cheddar cheese

½ cup grated Monterey Jack cheese
    Cilantro sprigs

For filling, in a large bowl toss together all filling ingredients.

For sauce, in a large skillet over medium-high heat, heat oil and sauté garlic 1 minute, stirring constantly. Add chili powder, flour, cumin and cinnamon and cook 1 minute, stirring constantly with a wooden spoon. Mixture will be dry like a roux. Whisk in hot chicken broth until mixture is smooth and thickened, about 2 minutes. Whisk in tomato sauce and simmer 2 minutes. Keep warm.

For tortillas, preheat oven to 400°. Grease a 9 x 13-inch baking dish and set aside. Heat a griddle or skillet over high heat and barely coat surface with oil.

To assemble, grasp 1 tortilla with tongs and heat on griddle about 30 seconds on each side. Transfer to warm plate and repeat with remaining tortillas. Grasp 1 heated tortilla with tongs and dip into warm sauce, coating both sides. Set coated tortillas aside in prepared baking dish. Spoon ¹⁄₁₀ of filling onto center of 1 tortilla. Roll up and place seam side down in baking dish. Repeat with remaining tortillas and filling. Pour remaining sauce over tortillas and sprinkle with cheese. Bake on center oven rack until heated through and cheese is melted, 15-20 minutes. Garnish with cilantro.

6-8 servings

Faulkner's Alley by Paula Temple ▷

LB'S CHICKEN STEW

Larry Brown

You get up early in the morning, about six. It's October, cool, the leaves on the maple are turning yellow. Some honkers may be howling down the early morning sky. Your two black iron pots are already sitting in the front yard on their little sawed-off pieces of two-inch-galvanized-pipe legs, which raises their bellies off the ground just enough to let you shove a little firewood up under there, and also leaves room for a good bed of coals to build up later. You've made sure they're fairly level. The pots are freshly washed and the woodpile is piled. All you have to do at this point is light the wood and bring the water hose and have some coffee. It's too early for beer just yet. You'll have plenty of time for beer later. This day'll probably run about 20 hours.

You put about 20 gallons of water in each pot and now is a good time to get some breakfast, while you can't do anything else but wait for the water to boil. It'll take a while, so you've got time for pancakes and bacon if you want them. Nobody else in the house is up yet. Nobody else has to do anything yet.

After breakfast you take all the chickens and hens and dump them into the sink and cut them out of their plastic bags and open them up, get the little paper packets out of there, chunk everything that's inside them but the livers. Five whole hens or chickens go into each pot after the water gets to boiling. The idea now is to keep the fire really hot and make those pots rise to a rapid boil. You have to leave the chickens in until they're completely disintegrated. It'll be ten o'clock or so by then. Chicken parts and bones and skins will be rolling in a yellow foaming broth. Once that happens, you pull the wood back from the fire and just let the coals keep the broth hot.

It'll be past lunchtime by the time you pick through all the meat, all the bones, all the skin, all the inedible parts like the joints at the end of the drumsticks, the cartilage in the backbones, that weird-ass wedge-shaped tail part, who wants to eat that? All the meat and about half the skin goes into some clean trays. All the other stuff goes in the garbage. You might be having a beer after all this work. But it'll still be after four before anybody arrives. It's getting close to time for most of the work to start.

If you've got invited helper friends, they'll be there by then. Make sure you have plenty of lawn chairs in the yard. Music is good at this time, guitar playing not so good with those greasy fingers. But don't despair. There'll be plenty of time for finger picking later.

If you've got somebody to help you in the kitchen, she'll be working on slicing about 10 or 15 pounds of potatoes and cutting them into chunks, peeling and dicing 4 or 5 big white onions, slicing up 4 or 5 packs of carrots, and it's a lot easier to just get whole frozen okra to dump in later, 4 or 5 or 6 or 7 boxes of that, too. The rest of the stuff is in cans: whole peeled tomatoes, lima beans, kernel corn, English peas. All those cans have to be opened and brought outside, along with everything else. By now the meat is back in and you've built the fires back up but not as high as you had them when you were cooking the meat right off the bone. Just dump everything in, halving it between the two pots. If you have people who can't eat onions, like my mama, who taught me how to make this, you can leave one pot onion-free. It's pretty crucial to have enough tomatoes. You want it red. If it's not red you've got to get some more tomatoes. If it's not red, it's not chicken stew.

So you let everything cook for a while. You put some Cajun seasoning in it. Tony Chachere's is good. Everything will be cooking together, and it'll be getting on up in the afternoon a little. A few guests might start arriving early, but you'll hopefully have all the coolers full of beer by then.

All this time, while all this has been going on, or ever since you dumped the meat and skin back in, somebody has to have been standing there stirring both pots with a long-handled wooden paddle to keep it from sticking. This is very important and requires the full-time services of an invited helper friend who can be paid with beer and cornbread or crackers and a few bowls of steaming stew and perhaps a few quarts of it to take home. You wish you could extend this last courtesy to each and every guest, but that would require buying about 200 Ball fruit jars and then giving them all away. Not to mention having to fill them all up.

So along about now everything should be smoking. Invited helpers have set up the tables and chairs, and have spread tablecloths to hold the crackers and plates of cornbread and cakes and cookies and pies the guests will be bringing to the feast. You might want to run inside and change clothes now, while you still have a chance.

Back in the yard in clean duds, a few people have gathered around the pots to witness the transformation. All day long it's been a thin and chunky boiling red combination of vegetables and meat, well, fruit too if you want to count the tomatoes, but along in here at a point in time that's hard to define, but easy to see, the ingredients in the pot somehow come together and maybe meld their molecules or something and they go from being 40 gallons of chicken soup to 40 gallons of chicken stew. It thickens. When it thickens, it's done. A few taste tests are in order, and you have to be careful not to burn your lips and tongue, because it is very hot when it comes out of that iron. If it needs any more seasoning, now's the time to do it. You can pull most of the fire back, and just leave a few coals under it. But somebody has to keep stirring.

The sun's hanging low in the sky when the first of the cars and pickups and vans and SUV's start coming up the driveway. Soon the yard will fill with 200 people, and guitars will be hauled out, and friends will laugh and talk and visit, and, most importantly, eat together.

Larry completed this essay for Square Table *just days before his death on November 24, 2004.*

Mid-Town Shopping Center, about 1970

Southern Pork Roast

MEAT & GAME

CHARGRILLED BEEF TENDERLOIN

5-6 pounds beef tenderloin
Olive oil
4 cloves garlic, minced

Coarsely ground black pepper
Charcoal and lighter fluid

Clean the tenderloin with a sharp fillet knife to remove membrane. Coat with olive oil, garlic and pepper. Refrigerate at least 2 hours. Place 5 pounds of charcoal in grill. Soak the coals with lighter fluid and light with a match, making sure all areas are lit. Let the fire burn for 30-45 minutes, or until all briquettes are red. Spread out the charcoal. Place tenderloin directly over the coals. Turn after 12½ minutes. Cook a total of 25 minutes to achieve a rare to medium-rare result at the thickest part. The ends will be medium to well done. Slice to serve.

8-10 servings

BEEF FILLETS WITH BLUE CHEESE-PORTOBELLO SAUCE

6 6-ounce beef tenderloin fillets
2 teaspoons chopped fresh tarragon
½ teaspoon pepper
5 tablespoons unsalted butter, divided use

8 ounces portobello mushroom caps, sliced
⅓ cup dry red wine
½ cup sour cream
3 ounces blue cheese, crumbled, divided use

Sauce for Beef Tenderloin

8 ounces sour cream

1 tablespoon tarragon vinegar

¼ teaspoon salt

⅛ teaspoon white pepper

2 tablespoons prepared horseradish

¼ teaspoon Tabasco sauce

¼ teaspoon chopped, fresh chives

Mix all ingredients in a bowl and refrigerate until serving time.

1 cup

Rub fillets with chopped tarragon and pepper. In a large skillet over medium-high heat, melt 2 tablespoons butter. Add fillets and cook 5-10 minutes on each side or until desired temperature is reached. Remove from skillet and keep warm. In same skillet melt remaining 3 tablespoons butter. Add sliced mushrooms. Sauté until tender, about 4 minutes. Add wine and cook 1-2 minutes, stirring to loosen particles from bottom of skillet. Stir in sour cream. Sprinkle in 2 ounces cheese and stir until melted. Serve sauce over fillets with remaining cheese sprinkled on top.

6 servings

Twelve years ago
I decided I wanted
Oxford for my home
when I was having coffee
at the Hoka, a café in a
warehouse with a tin
roof. A violent rainstorm
came up. The sound of it
thrashing on the tin
moved something deep
within me, a memory of
another storm, my pals
and me in a barn
sleeping on hay when
I was a boy: That tin roof
was the margin against
everything dangerous.

~Barry Hannah

High Lonesome

SABBATH BRISKET

Begin preparation the day before serving.

3-4 pounds beef brisket, trimmed of fat	1 pound potatoes, cut into 1-inch cubes
1 tablespoon kosher salt	Paprika
Pepper to taste	1 pound carrots, peeled and cut into 1-inch pieces
1 large onion, sliced	
½ cup water	

Rub the brisket with salt and refrigerate 2-3 hours. Preheat oven to 350°. Rinse salt from meat, pat dry, and sprinkle with pepper. Line a roasting pan with foil and arrange half the onion slices on the foil. Place meat on top and add remaining onion slices. Pour water into the pan, but not on top of the meat. Cover tightly with heavy-duty aluminum foil, and cook 2½-3 hours. Cool and refrigerate overnight. Two hours before serving, preheat oven to 350°. Uncover and remove meat; discard any congealed fat. Cut meat against the grain into thin slices at an angle. Place back into pan. Re-cover and bake 1 hour. Sprinkle potatoes with paprika. Add the potatoes and carrots to baking dish. Cook until potatoes are fork-tender, about 1 hour. Serve juice alongside meat.

6-8 servings

MISSY'S POT ROAST

4-5 pounds beef pot roast	3 cloves garlic, minced
2 teaspoons salt	2 tablespoons packed brown sugar
¼ teaspoon pepper	½ teaspoon dry mustard
2 tablespoons unsalted butter	¼ cup lemon juice
½ cup water	¼ cup vinegar
1 cup tomato juice	¼ cup ketchup
3 medium onions, chopped	1 tablespoon Worcestershire sauce

Rub surface of roast with salt and pepper. In large Dutch oven over medium-high heat, melt butter and brown roast on all sides. Add water, tomato juice, onions and garlic. Preheat oven to 375°. Bake roast, covered 1½ hours. In a small bowl mix brown sugar, mustard, lemon juice, vinegar, ketchup and Worcestershire and add to the pan. Reduce heat to 250° and bake 2-3 hours.

Leftover sauce and meat make an excellent soup base.

8 servings

BEEF BOURGUIGNONNE

1 tablespoon olive oil

8 ounces bacon, diced

2½ pounds beef chuck, cut into 1-inch cubes

Kosher salt and freshly ground pepper to taste

1 pound carrots, peeled and sliced diagonally into 1-inch chunks

2 yellow onions, sliced

2 cloves garlic, minced

½ cup Cognac

1 750-ml bottle dry red wine

2 cups beef broth

1 tablespoon tomato paste

1 teaspoon fresh thyme leaves, or ½ teaspoon dried

Salt and pepper to taste

4 tablespoons unsalted butter, room temperature, divided use

3 tablespoons flour

1 pound frozen whole onions

1 pound fresh mushrooms, stems discarded, caps thickly sliced

Rice, pasta or toasted garlic bread

Chopped, fresh parsley for garnish

"Bourguignonne"
is a French term
meaning "as prepared
in Burgundy."

In a large Dutch oven over medium heat, place olive oil and bacon. Cook, stirring frequently, until bacon is lightly browned, about 10 minutes. Remove bacon and set aside. Pat beef cubes dry with paper towels, sprinkle with salt and pepper, and add to hot bacon grease in Dutch oven, a single layer at a time. Sear 3-5 minutes, turning to brown on all sides. Set beef aside. Add carrots and onions to Dutch oven and cook until onions are lightly browned, 10-15 minutes. Add the garlic and cook for 1 minute. Add the Cognac, stand back, and ignite with a match to burn off the alcohol. Preheat oven to 250°. Return bacon and beef to Dutch oven. Add wine plus enough beef broth to almost cover meat. Add the tomato paste and thyme. Stir and season to taste with salt and pepper. Bring to a simmer, cover pot with a tight-fitting lid and bake until the meat and vegetables are very tender when pierced with a fork, about 1 hour, 15 minutes. Return to range-top over medium heat. In a small bowl combine 2 tablespoons butter and the flour with a fork. Stir flour mixture into beef mixture. Stir in frozen onions. In a medium skillet, over medium heat, sauté the mushrooms in 2 tablespoons butter until lightly browned, about 10 minutes. Add mushrooms to beef mixture. Increase heat under Dutch oven until beef mixture comes to a boil. Lower heat and simmer 15 minutes. Adjust seasonings. Serve over rice, pasta or garlic toast. Garnish with parsley.

12 servings

Cognac is a type
of brandy that originated
in Cognac, France.

127

GRILLADES AND GRITS

Then he could smell the
smoke, and food, the hot
fierce food, and he began
to say over and over to
himself *I have not eaten
since I have not eaten since*
trying to remember
how many days it had
been since Friday....

~William Faulkner

Light in August

4	pounds beef rounds, ½-inch thick
½	cup bacon drippings, divided use
½	cup flour
1	cup chopped onions
2	cups chopped green onions
¾	cup chopped celery
1½	cups chopped green bell peppers
2	cloves garlic, minced
1	28-ounce can diced tomatoes
½	teaspoon tarragon
⅔	teaspoon thyme
1	cup water
1	cup red wine
½	teaspoon black pepper
2	bay leaves
½	teaspoon Tabasco sauce
2	tablespoons Worcestershire sauce
	Salt to taste
3	tablespoons chopped parsley
1	recipe Ajax Diner Cheese Grits, page 86

Trim fat from meat and pound with a meat mallet or rolling pin to tenderize. Cut into 2-inch pieces. In a Dutch oven brown meat well in 4 tablespoons bacon grease. Remove meat and keep warm. To Dutch oven add 4 tablespoons bacon grease and flour. Stir and cook to make a dark brown roux, about 5 minutes. Add onions, green onions, celery, green pepper, garlic and sauté until limp, about 8 minutes. Add tomatoes, tarragon, thyme, water and wine. Stir until well combined. Return meat to Dutch oven and add pepper, bay leaves, Tabasco, Worcestershire, and salt to taste (beginning with 1 teaspoon). Lower heat and simmer at least 2 hours. Stir in parsley and cool. Refrigerate overnight. Reheat thoroughly, remove bay leaves, add wine or tomato juice if too dry, and adjust seasonings. Serve over cheese grits.

10 servings

MENU ▶

SUPPER AT ROWAN OAK

Smoked Ham
Red Potato Salad
Sweet Slaw
Sweet Onion Pie
Buttermilk Biscuits
Pecan Squares

Salsa Verde

10 tomatillos,
husked and washed

1 teaspoon garlic purée

1 teaspoon honey

2 green onions, sliced

1 tablespoon red onion,
diced

1 tablespoon jalapeños

3-4 tablespoons
chopped cilantro

1-2 teaspoons kosher salt

1-2 teaspoons pepper

Place all ingredients
in a food processor and
process until well blended,
but not smooth. Season to
taste with salt and pepper.
If salsa is too acidic,
add more honey.

▪ *Ajax Diner* ▪

TAMALE PIE

1	yellow onion, diced	1½	tablespoons kosher salt
1	tablespoon garlic purée	1	tablespoon black pepper
¼	cup unsalted butter	1	teaspoon cayenne pepper
2	cups chopped green chilies	2	tomatoes, seeded and chopped
2	cups corn, canned or frozen	1	recipe Ajax Cheese Grits, page 86
3	cups smoked, pulled pork meat		Sliced pepper Jack cheese
2½	tablespoons chili powder		Salsa Verde
1½	tablespoons ground cumin		

Preheat oven to 375°. In a medium skillet over medium heat, sauté the onions and garlic in butter until onions are tender. Add green chilies, corn and meat. Cook 5 minutes. Stir in chili powder, cumin, salt, pepper and cayenne. Mix well. Remove pan from heat and add tomatoes. In the bottom of a well-buttered, deep baking dish, spread half of the cheese grits and let cool until firm. Layer all of the meat mixture over grits. Spread remaining cheese grits over the meat as evenly and smoothly as possible. Bake uncovered 45 minutes. Top with cheese slices and bake until melted, about 10 minutes. Let sit for at least 1 hour before cutting. Top with Salsa Verde.

9 servings

SMOKED HAM

*Friends in need are instantly comforted when they see
Caroline and Cooper McIntosh arrive at their doorsteps with one of their famous smoked hams.*

4	Cook's Hams or other precooked ham, shank or butt halves	8-16	tablespoons coarse ground pepper
2	pounds light brown sugar	3	tablespoons ground cloves
		64	ounces sorghum molasses

Remove hams from plastic, rinse, and put on large pans. Mix brown sugar, pepper and cloves together. Pour sorghum molasses over hams, spreading with hands to cover. Press brown sugar mixture into molasses, making sure to cover the ham. If sugar slides off, scoop it off the pan and press on ham again. Remove hams from pans. Place 2 hams on lower rack and 2 on upper rack of a meat smoker. With lid closed, smoke on hot fire with water pan until the hams reach 140°-150°, 2-4 hours in smoker. Replace molasses, seasonings, water, charcoal, hickory chips or wood as needed. Cook with lid closed.

*Hams with a high water content, at least 23%, and
low salt are best.*

4 hams

Photo on page 129

GRILLED PORK TENDERLOIN

½ cup canola oil	1 clove garlic, crushed
⅓ cup soy sauce	1 tablespoon chopped, fresh parsley
¼ cup red wine vinegar	1 tablespoon dry mustard
3 tablespoons lemon juice	1½ teaspoons pepper
2 tablespoons Worcestershire sauce	1½ pounds pork tenderloin

In a small bowl combine all ingredients except pork. Mix well. Add pork, turning to coat. Seal pork and marinade in zip-top bag. Refrigerate 4-24 hours. Remove pork and reserve marinade. Grill over medium-hot coals until internal temperature reaches 160°, about 16 minutes, turning once. Let stand 5-10 minutes before slicing. In a small saucepan over high heat boil marinade for 2 minutes. Pour over sliced meat. Serve warm or at room temperature.

6 servings

PORK SCALOPPINE WITH TOMATO AND BASIL

2½ pounds pork tenderloin, sliced into 1-inch thick scallops	2-3 pounds ripe tomatoes, cored, peeled, seeded, and diced
Salt and freshly ground pepper for sprinkling	2 tablespoons unsalted butter
Flour for dredging	1 teaspoon crushed red pepper
¼ cup olive oil	Salt and pepper to taste
6 cloves garlic, crushed	10-12 fresh basil leaves, chopped

Place the pork scallops between plastic wrap and pound with a meat mallet or small iron skillet to a thickness of about ¼-inch. Pat dry and season with salt and pepper. Coat scallops with flour, shaking off any excess. In a large, nonstick skillet over medium heat, heat olive oil and add as many of the pork scallops as will fit in a single layer. Turn pork to brown on both sides. Remove pork and drain on paper towels. Repeat with remaining pork scallops. To same skillet add the garlic and cook until lightly browned. Pour off any excess oil and add tomatoes, butter and crushed red pepper. Season lightly with salt and pepper and bring to a simmer. Add pork to the sauce and simmer until sauce is slightly thickened, about 5 minutes. Stir half the basil into the skillet and cook for 1 minute. Garnish with remaining basil.

6 servings

Red Onion Confit

Serve over grilled pork chops.

2 red or Vidalia onions, sliced

3 tablespoons unsalted butter

2 tablespoons brown sugar

¼ cup dry red wine

2 tablespoons red wine vinegar

Salt and pepper to taste

In a large skillet over low heat, slowly cook the onions in butter until softened and translucent, 5-10 minutes. Stir in brown sugar and continue cooking over low heat until onions begin to caramelize. Remove pan from heat and stir in red wine and red wine vinegar. Return pan to heat and stir well. Simmer on low until most of the liquid has evaporated. The sauce should be thick and caramel-like. Add salt and pepper.

6 servings

SOUTHERN PORK ROAST

1 5 to 6-pound pork loin	1 teaspoon garlic salt
1 teaspoon onion salt	½ teaspoon pepper

SAUCE

1 onion, finely chopped	1 cup water
4 tablespoons unsalted butter	2 tablespoons balsamic vinegar
1 10-ounce jar plum jam or jelly	⅓ cup soy sauce
⅓ cup packed brown sugar	

For roast, preheat oven to 325°. Rub pork loin with salts and pepper and place in a roasting pan. Bake 2½ hours. Remove from oven, baste with half of sauce, and continue cooking until internal temperature reaches 160°, 30-60 minutes. Serve the remaining sauce with pork.

For sauce, in a heavy medium skillet over medium-high heat, sauté the onion in butter until translucent. Add jelly, brown sugar, water, balsamic vinegar and soy sauce. Bring to a boil, reduce heat, and simmer 2-3 minutes.

12 servings

Photo on page 124

ESCALOPES DE VEAU

2 pounds veal, cut in thin slices	½ cup dry, white wine
½ cup chopped onion	¼ cup Italian breadcrumbs
1 tablespoon unsalted butter	2 tablespoons unsalted butter, melted
1 teaspoon salt	½ cup grated Swiss cheese
½ teaspoon pepper	Fettuccine
¼ cup beef broth	

Preheat oven to 350°. Place veal slices between layers of plastic wrap and pound with a meat mallet or small iron skillet until ¼-⅛-inch thick. In a heavy large skillet over medium-high heat, sauté onion in butter until golden. Place onions in a greased casserole dish. Add veal, salt, pepper, broth and wine. Top with breadcrumbs and drizzle with melted butter. Sprinkle with cheese. Bake uncovered 1 hour. Serve over fettuccine.

4 servings

VEAL PICCATA

1½ pounds veal scallops, thinly sliced

½ cup flour

4 tablespoons unsalted butter, divided use

2 tablespoons olive oil

Salt and pepper

3 tablespoons lemon juice

½ cup dry, white wine

½ cup veal or chicken broth

2 tablespoons finely chopped parsley

Lemon, peeled and thinly sliced for garnish

Place veal between 2 sheets of plastic wrap and pound with a meat mallet or small iron skillet until ¼-inch thick. Dredge in flour and shake off excess. In large skillet over medium-high heat, heat 2 tablespoons butter and olive oil. Brown meat about 2 minutes per side. Sprinkle with salt and pepper. Transfer to platter and keep warm. To skillet add lemon juice, wine and broth. Heat to boiling and boil for 2-3 minutes, stirring to loosen browned particles. Add parsley and remaining 2 tablespoons butter. Return meat to skillet and heat through. Garnish with lemon slices.

May substitute chicken for veal.

4 servings

VEAL WITH MARSALA

2 tablespoons olive oil

2 tablespoons unsalted butter, divided use

2 cups flour

1 tablespoon salt

Freshly ground black pepper

1 pound veal from top round, pounded to ¼-inch thick

½ cup Marsala wine

1 cup mushrooms, sliced

Angel hair pasta

In a large skillet over medium-high heat, put oil and 1 tablespoon butter. In a shallow bowl combine flour, salt, and pepper. Dredge veal in flour mixture. Brown quickly in skillet. Remove from pan. Increase heat to high. Add remaining butter, wine, and mushrooms. Reduce liquid to sauce consistency. Add veal and reduce heat to low. Serve with angel hair pasta.

4 servings

At first they had come in wagons: the guns, the bedding, the dogs, the food, the whiskey, the keen heart-lifting anticipation of hunting…. There had been bear then. A man shot a doe or a fawn as quickly as he did a buck, and in the afternoons they shot wild turkey…. But that time was gone now … the territory in which game still existed drawing yearly inward as his life was drawing inward, until now he was the last of those who had once made the journey in wagons….

~William Faulkner

Go Down, Moses

BUTTERFLIED LAMB ON THE GRILL

½	cup packed fresh cilantro	¼	teaspoon freshly ground black pepper
3	large cloves garlic	2-5	pounds leg of lamb, trimmed, boned, and flattened
5	tablespoons extra virgin olive oil, divided use		Salt and pepper to taste
3	tablespoons balsamic vinegar		

In a food processor place cilantro, garlic, 3 tablespoons olive oil, vinegar and ¼ teaspoon pepper. Pulse until finely chopped. Cut 1-inch-deep slits over surface of lamb and pound lightly for uniform thickness. Spoon cilantro mixture into slits, pressing to penetrate meat. Cover and refrigerate overnight. Preheat grill. Rub lamb with remaining 2 tablespoons oil. Season with salt and pepper. Grill until meat thermometer registers 125° for medium-rare. Let stand 5 minutes before slicing.

10 servings

MUFFULETTA

3	cloves garlic, chopped	2	tablespoons chopped, fresh parsley
1	cup Spanish olives, chopped	2	tablespoons white wine vinegar
1	cup black olives, chopped	1	loaf crusty Italian bread
½	cup chopped roasted red peppers (1 pepper)	⅓	pound Genoa salami, thinly sliced
3-4	pickled pepperoncini peppers, seeds removed, chopped	½	pound provolone cheese, thinly sliced
1	cup extra virgin olive oil	½	pound Swiss cheese, thinly sliced
		⅓	pound prosciutto ham, thinly sliced
			Potato chips

Combine garlic, olives, peppers, olive oil, parsley and vinegar. Refrigerate and let rest overnight or 24 hours. Cut bread in half horizontally. Drizzle olive oil from olive salad on bottom half. Layer salami, provolone, Swiss and prosciutto on bottom half of bread, topping with olive salad. Add top half of bread. Slice, and serve with potato chips.

4-6 servings

SAUSAGE AND ONION PIZZA

A pizza stone and wooden paddle are the secret to success.

3 cloves garlic, minced
2 tablespoons extra virgin olive oil
½ pound hot sausage
1 16-ounce can tomatoes, chopped
1 Pizza Dough recipe
Cornmeal

1 onion, thinly sliced and separated into rings
2 tablespoons chopped basil
1 cup grated fontina cheese
1 cup grated mozzarella cheese
Kosher salt

Thirty minutes before baking, place a pizza stone on the bottom rack of the oven and preheat oven to 500°. In a small bowl, combine the garlic and olive oil and let stand for 30 minutes. In a large skillet brown sausage. Drain and set aside. In a saucepan over medium heat, boil tomatoes until reduced to just the meat of the tomatoes.

Place half of the Pizza Dough recipe on a floured cloth and roll out to a 10-inch circle. Roll dough over the rolling pin and transfer to a wooden paddle that has been dusted with cornmeal. Brush the dough to within ½-inch of the edge with half of the garlic-infused oil. Spread half of the cooked tomatoes over pizza, followed by half the sausage, half the onions, half the basil and half the cheeses. Sprinkle pizza stone with Kosher salt and slide pizza onto the stone. Cook until lightly browned, 8-10 minutes. Repeat the process to make second pizza.

two 10-inch pizzas

IT'S THE LIMIT

6 quail or doves
Jane's Krazy Mixed Up Seasoning
Pepper
Flour
3 tablespoons oil
¾ cup water

1 can beef consommé
2 tablespoons fresh lemon juice
1 teaspoon Worcestershire sauce
1 teaspoon flour
½ cup white wine
Fresh parsley for garnish

Preheat oven to 325°. Season birds with seasoning mix and pepper. Dredge in flour and brown slightly in a large skillet in hot oil. Add water, consommé, lemon juice, Worcestershire and 1 teaspoon flour. Cook over low heat for 5-8 minutes to thicken. Pour wine over birds and simmer for 10-12 minutes. Put in oven for 1 hour or until tender. Garnish with parsley.

May be cooked ahead, refrigerated, and reheated at 300°.

4-6 servings

Pizza Dough

¼ cup warm water
1 envelope dry active yeast
2 cups flour, divided use
½ cup lukewarm water
2 tablespoons olive oil
1 tablespoon milk
½ teaspoon kosher salt

In a small bowl combine warm water, yeast and ¼ cup of the flour. Let stand 20 minutes. Pour yeast mixture into the bowl of an electric mixer. Add remaining 1¾ cups flour, ½ cup lukewarm water, olive oil, milk and salt. Mix until well combined. Put dough hook on mixer and knead dough 8 minutes, (or knead by hand on a floured cloth). Place dough in a greased bowl and turn to coat with shortening. Cover with a towel and let rise in a warm place until doubled in volume, about 1 hour. Place dough on a floured cloth and cut in half.
Dough for
two 10-inch pizzas

TERIYAKI DUCK

1 cup soy sauce	4 cloves garlic, peeled and crushed
1 cup sugar	2 tablespoons bourbon
1 piece fresh ginger, about 3 inches, peeled and sliced	1 3-pound duck

Cook soy sauce and sugar in a small saucepan over medium-low heat until sugar dissolves, about 2 minutes. Stir in ginger, garlic and bourbon; cook 30 minutes. Remove ginger and garlic. Pour sauce into a small mixing bowl. Preheat oven to 350°. Rinse duck and pat dry. Thoroughly prick skin without piercing the flesh. Place on a rack in a shallow pan, breast side up. Tuck wings under the back and tie legs together with kitchen string for even cooking. With a pastry brush, coat duck with sauce both inside and out. Place rack in a baking pan and roast for 1-1½ hours, or 20 minutes per pound, basting every 15 minutes. Baste more frequently for a darker skin. Do not overcook. For best results, use a meat thermometer inserted in the meatiest part of the duck. Duck is done when internal temperature reads 180°. To test for doneness without a thermometer, make sure a fork can be easily inserted and that when the meat is pricked, juices run clear.

The sauce is also great for chicken and makes a great marinade for pork chops and short ribs.

2-4 servings

SMOTHERED DOVES

12 doves	½ cup chopped, green onions
Salt and pepper to taste	1½ cups water
Flour	1 cup dry sherry
½ cup vegetable oil	¼ cup chopped parsley

Preheat oven to 400°. Sprinkle doves with salt and pepper; dust lightly with flour. In a heavy roasting pan in the oven, brown doves in oil. Remove doves and add onions and water to roasting pan. Heat and stir until onions are translucent. Return doves to roaster, cover, and reduce heat to 350°. Cook until tender, about 1 hour, basting every 15 minutes. Halfway through cooking, add sherry. Remove doves and keep warm. Into pan drippings, add chopped parsley with a little flour to make a gravy.

8-12 servings

Artist Vivian Neill
Artwork, page 138

Painter Vivian Pigott Neill began her life as an artist doing realistic pencil drawings. Following a 25-year interlude during which she co-owned Hal and Mal's restaurant in Jackson, Vivian and her daughter, Mallory moved to Oxford where she then finished a degree in fine arts from Ole Miss. Time spent together at the dining table is a prominent theme in her figurative work. She and her husband Walter Neill, a metal sculptor, share Neill Studios near the Yocona community in Lafayette County.

SMOKED QUAIL STUFFED WITH GOAT CHEESE AND OYSTER-MUSHROOM POLENTA

MARINADE

½ cup orange juice	2 teaspoons paprika
½ cup lime juice	Salt and cayenne pepper
½ cup olive oil	4 semi boneless quail
1 tablespoon minced garlic	

GRILLING

Charcoal	1½ cups hickory chips

STUFFING

1 yellow onion, chopped	1½ cups heavy cream
2 tablespoons extra virgin olive oil	1 cup polenta
2 teaspoons minced garlic	½ cup goat cheese
2 ounces oyster mushrooms, chopped	Salt and pepper to taste
1½ cups chicken stock	

For marinade, combine all ingredients for marinade in a heavy plastic bag. Marinate quail for at least 2 hours.

For grilling, light a small pile of charcoal on grill and soak 1½ cups hickory chips in water. After coals have turned grey, put drained chips on fire and allow to burn for 5 minutes. Put quail on indirect heat for approximately 5-10 minutes, or until they have cooked halfway. It is important to cook quail partially so they will remain pliable for stuffing.

For stuffing, in a Dutch oven over medium-high heat, sauté onion in olive oil until translucent. Add garlic and mushrooms. Sauté just enough for the mushrooms to absorb the oil. Add stock and cream. Bring to a boil. Whisk in polenta, and return to a boil. Turn heat to low and stir continuously with a wooden spoon until polenta is done, 20-30 minutes. Stir in cheese and season with salt and pepper to taste.

For assembly, preheat oven to 350°. After polenta has cooled enough to handle, place quail breast side up and stuff generously with polenta, being careful not to break the delicate skin on the backside of the quail. When ready to serve, bake 5-7 minutes.

2-4 servings

Author Barry Hannah
Essay, page 139

Essay, page 139

Barry is the author of 11 works of fiction, including his first novel, *Geronimo Rex* (1972), which was awarded the William Faulkner Prize and nominated for the National Book Award; *Airships* (1978), a collection of stories widely regarded as a contemporary classic; *Ray* (1980), nominated for the American Book Award; and *High Lonesome* (1996), nominated for the Pulitzer Prize in Fiction. He received the 2003 PEN/Malamud Award honoring excellence in the art of the short story. He is writer in residence and director of the MFA program in creative writing at the University of Mississippi.

WONDERFUL DREAMS

Barry Hannah

When Barry Hannah saw a friend recently at City Grocery, one of Oxford's finest restaurants, he had a "guilt-flash" about not having written something for *Square Table* yet. So, he sat down and wrote about an evening at City (as the locals fondly call said restaurant) because he felt strongly about "the cause for the electric [Powerhouse] theater" that he "deeply supports." His memory of an evening at City:

I could never come across with much about food, only a recurring extended image of blurred yet distinct, and many, dinners in City Grocery, soft shell crabs and the sage and gourmand of our age, Jim Harrison, which meant I could listen and come away wiser and dreamier, because the soft shell crab done up properly always gives me wonderful dreams. To my eternal regret, I never got to eat soft shell crabs with pal Larry Brown. Larry was a curator of oysters (Seattle, '95 with him). Did anybody know that?

That's it. The face and wisdom of good Michigander Jim Harrison. Through the heavenly steam of a crab plate.

Nancy Moore

Artist Nancy Moore is an adjunct faculty member in art education at Ole Miss. She travels throughout Mississippi showing teachers how to use art to teach other subjects.

Girls at the Grocery by Vivian Neill

Roasted Sweet Potatoes

VEGETABLES

CARCIOFINI TRIFOLATI

Hearts of Artichokes Sautéed

⅓ cup extra virgin olive oil

1 tablespoon unsalted butter

2 15-ounce cans artichoke hearts, whole or halved, and drained

¼ cup white wine

3 cloves garlic, minced

1 tablespoon dried marjoram

⅓ cup chopped Italian parsley

Salt and pepper to taste

½ cup grated Parmigiano-Reggiano cheese, optional

Heat a large skillet over medium heat. Add olive oil and butter. Add remaining ingredients except Parmesan and stir. Cover, reduce heat to medium-low, and cook gently about 10 minutes. Remove the cover and let the liquid evaporate to desired consistency. Sprinkle with Parmesan, if desired. Serve hot or at room temperature.

6 servings

ASPARAGUS STIR-FRY

1½ pounds fresh asparagus

1 tablespoon peanut oil

¾ cup chicken broth, divided use

1 tablespoon cornstarch

1 teaspoon sugar

2 tablespoons soy sauce

½ cup cashews, coarsely chopped and toasted

2 teaspoons fresh mint, chopped

Snap off tough ends of asparagus. Remove scales with a knife or vegetable peeler. Diagonally cut into 1-inch pieces. In a large skillet over medium-high heat, stir-fry asparagus in peanut oil. Add ¼ cup chicken broth, cover skillet, and cook until crisp-tender, about 4 minutes. In a small bowl combine remaining ½ cup chicken broth, cornstarch, sugar and soy sauce. Stir until smooth and add to asparagus mixture, stirring constantly. Bring to a boil and boil for 1 minute, stirring constantly. Sprinkle with cashews and mint.

6 servings

L & M's Kitchen and Salumeria

Grilled Asparagus

1 bunch fresh asparagus

2-3 tablespoons extra virgin olive oil

Kosher salt and crushed black pepper to taste

Blanch asparagus in boiling, salted water for 2 minutes. Shock asparagus in ice bath for 2 minutes. Remove and allow asparagus to dry. Coat with olive oil and season generously with salt and pepper. Grill over open flame for 1-2 minutes, turning often.

4 servings

Cabbage, like citrus fruit, is a very high source of vitaman C. It is also high in fiber, other vitamins, minerals, and antioxidants.

ZESTY CARROT CASSEROLE

8	large carrots, peeled and sliced	1	teaspoon lemon juice
¼	cup water		Salt and pepper to taste
¼	cup mayonnaise	½	cup plain breadcrumbs
2	tablespoons grated onion	3	tablespoons unsalted butter, melted
2	tablespoons prepared horseradish		

Preheat oven to 350°. Microwave carrots on high power in ¼ cup water until crisp tender, about 5 minutes. Drain, reserving ¼ cup liquid. Spray a large casserole dish with cooking spray and arrange carrots in the dish. In a small bowl, mix mayonnaise, the reserved liquid, onion, horseradish, lemon juice, salt and pepper. Spoon over carrots. Top with breadcrumbs and drizzle with butter. Bake until heated through, 15-20 minutes.

6-8 servings

RED CABBAGE CASSEROLE

This simple dish makes a wonderful accompaniment to beef or pork.

1	medium red cabbage, shredded	¼	cup water
1	small onion, chopped	2	tablespoons firmly packed dark brown sugar
3	medium apples, peeled, cored and chopped		Freshly ground black pepper to taste
¼	cup red wine vinegar	2	tablespoons unsalted butter

Preheat oven to 300°. In a large bowl, combine all ingredients except butter. Place in a large buttered casserole. Dot with butter. Cover and bake 2 hours.

6 servings

MENU

FARMERS' MARKET BOUNTY ON THE SQUARE

Creole Butter Beans
Hearty Eggplant
Green Tomato Casserole
Green Beans Vinaigrette
Stewed Tomatoes and Okra

During the Christmas holidays of 2002, my wife, Meredith, and I were living in New York City. We decided to take the week between Christmas and New Year's Eve to rediscover our native Mississippi. We loosely planned a road trip throughout the Mississippi Delta. About six hours into our trip, we realized there was little happening in the Delta during the holidays. No green vegetation, no open restaurants—the locals were taking holidays of their own. Consequently, we shortened our journey and decided to take a detour to Oxford.

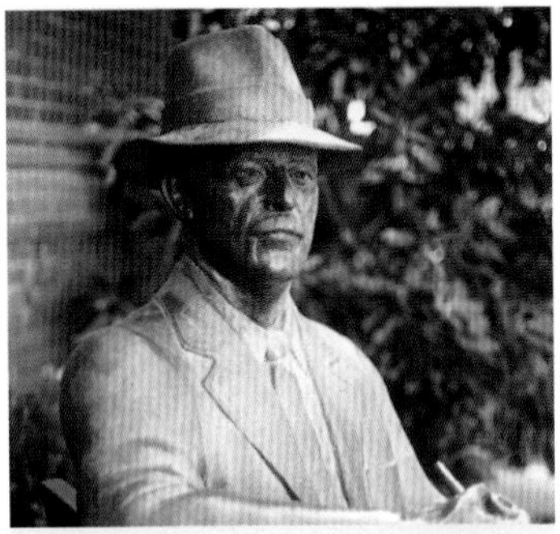

L & M's Kitchen and Salumeria

TUSCAN CAULIFLOWER

- ¼ cup extra virgin olive oil
- ½ cup diced red onion
- 2 cloves garlic, thinly sliced
- 1 head cauliflower, cut into medium-sized florets
- Kosher salt or sea salt and crushed black pepper to taste
- ⅛ teaspoon crushed red pepper
- ¼ cup finely chopped parsley
- ¼ cup breadcrumbs

In a large sauté pan heat oil over medium-high heat. Add onion and cook until soft, 1-2 minutes. Add garlic and cook until softened, but not browned. Add cauliflower and season with salt, pepper, crushed red pepper and parsley. Toss cauliflower in pan to coat well with oil. Sauté until cauliflower is tender, about 3 minutes. Remove from pan to individual bowls or plates. Sprinkle with breadcrumbs.

4 servings

CREOLE BUTTER BEANS

- 1 tablespoon canola oil
- 1 cup chopped celery
- 1 large green bell pepper, chopped
- 1 medium onion, chopped
- Garlic powder to taste
- Salt and pepper to taste
- 1 28-ounce can crushed tomatoes
- 2 cups fresh speckled butter beans
- ¼ cup water
- Hot cooked rice

In a large skillet or Dutch oven over medium-high heat, heat oil and add celery, green pepper and onion. Season to taste with garlic powder, salt and pepper. Sauté 1 minute. Add tomatoes, butter beans and ¼ cup water. Reduce heat to medium and cook, covered, adding water as needed, until butter beans are tender. Serve over rice.

6-8 servings

HERBED GREEN BEANS

1	pound green beans, snapped, blanched and drained	¼	cup minced celery
4	tablespoons unsalted butter	½	cup minced parsley
½	cup minced onion	1	teaspoon chopped, fresh rosemary
1	clove garlic, minced	¼	teaspoon dried basil
		¾	teaspoon salt

In a large pot of boiling salted water, cook green beans just until tender. Drain. In a large skillet over medium-high heat, melt butter and sauté onion, garlic and celery 5 minutes, stirring often. Add parsley, rosemary, basil and salt. Cover and simmer 10 minutes. Toss cooked beans with herbed butter and heat just before serving.

6 servings

Photo on page 42

HEARTY EGGPLANT

3	large eggplants, approximately 3 pounds	1	teaspoon salt
½	pound bulk, hot pork sausage	1	teaspoon pepper
1	cup hot water	½	teaspoon cayenne pepper
2	tablespoons olive oil		Tabasco sauce, optional
1	large onion, finely chopped	1	egg
4	cloves fresh garlic, minced	1	cup shredded Cheddar cheese
½	cup breadcrumbs		

Slice eggplants in half lengthwise, and bake them face down on an oiled cookie sheet until skins can be easily pierced with a fork, about 30 minutes. When cool enough to handle, scoop out and mince the insides and set aside. Reserve shells if desired. In a heavy skillet over high heat, brown sausage and drain oil. Pour 1 cup hot water over sausage and drain again. Set aside. In a large saucepan over low heat, heat olive oil and sauté onions until golden brown, about 30 minutes. Add garlic and cook 5 minutes. Preheat oven to 350°. To saucepan, add minced eggplant, breadcrumbs, salt, pepper, cayenne and Tabasco. Cook on low heat 10 minutes and remove from heat. Beat egg lightly and add to eggplant mixture, stirring quickly. Place in a greased baking dish or in reserved eggplant shells, sprinkle with cheese, and bake until heated through and cheese has melted, about 20 minutes.

May substitute shrimp or ham for sausage.

6 servings

For the next three days, we secured room #5 at the Oliver-Britt House on Van Buren Avenue. We rang in 2003 in the back room at the Yocona River Inn, and later we toasted the New Year upstairs at City Grocery. It was that holiday journey that led us to develop the plans for L & M's right here in Oxford.

~Dan Latham
Chef/Owner,
L & M's Kitchen and
Salumeria

To get rid of eggplant's bitter taste, peel and salt it and let it rest about 20 minutes.

To prevent it from turning brown, cut it immediately before using, or dip pieces in a mixture of water and lemon juice.

GREEN BEANS VINAIGRETTE

1	pound green beans, trimmed		Salt and pepper to taste
1	small red onion, finely chopped	¼	cup olive oil
2	tablespoons balsamic vinegar	2	tablespoons chopped, fresh cilantro (or basil or parsley)

In a colander or steamer over boiling water, steam the green beans until just tender, 4-6 minutes. Transfer beans to a serving bowl and toss together with onion. In a small bowl whisk together the vinegar, salt and pepper. Add olive oil in a stream, whisking until emulsified. Drizzle over beans. Add the coriander or other herb. Toss to mix, and serve warm or at room temperatur

EGGPLANT CASSEROLE

The best Sunday lunch in Oxford is undoubtedly at the church potluck; and after going down that long serving line of congealed salads, deviled eggs and caramel cake, everybody asks for this recipe.

3½	cups peeled, chopped eggplant	1	clove garlic, minced
2	cups water	½	teaspoon salt
½	cup plus 2 tablespoons unsalted butter	½	teaspoon cayenne pepper
1½	cups chopped onions, divided use	¼	teaspoon pepper
1½	cups fresh corn	2½	cups grated Cheddar cheese, divided use
2	eggs		
½	cup finely chopped green bell pepper	1¼	cups cracker crumbs

Preheat oven to 350°. In a saucepan over high heat, bring eggplant and water to a boil. Reduce heat, cover and simmer until eggplant is tender, about 30 minutes. Drain well, reserving 1 cup of the liquid. In a large skillet over medium-high heat, melt butter and sauté 1 cup of the onions until browned. Transfer onions to a large bowl. To same skillet add corn and cook over medium-high heat, stirring until lightly browned. To the large bowl add the sautéed corn, remaining ½ cup onions, drained eggplant, 1 cup of reserved eggplant stock, eggs, bell peppers, garlic, salt, cayenne, pepper, 1½ cups Cheddar and 1 cup cracker crumbs. Pour into a casserole, top with remaining 1 cup Cheddar and ¼ cup cracker crumbs. Bake until heated through and cheese is melted, about 40 minutes.

10 servings

ZUCCHINI CASSEROLE

2	pounds zucchini (about 3 medium), sliced
1	tablespoon unsalted butter
¼	cup sour cream
1	tablespoon grated Cheddar cheese
½	teaspoon salt
⅛	teaspoon paprika
1	tablespoon chopped chives
½	cup cracker crumbs
2	tablespoons unsalted butter, melted

Preheat oven to 350°. Boil zucchini in salted water until crisp-tender, about 5 minutes. Drain and place in greased casserole. In a saucepan over medium heat, melt butter. Stir in sour cream, cheese, salt and paprika. Cook over low heat, stirring constantly until cheese is melted. Remove from heat. Stir in chives and add to zucchini. In a small bowl toss cracker crumbs with melted butter and spread over zucchini. Bake uncovered 20 minutes.

6 servings

BUTTERNUT SQUASH CASSEROLE

SQUASH MIXTURE

2	cups baked, mashed butternut squash	⅓	cup milk
3	eggs, lightly beaten	1	teaspoon ground ginger
¾	cup sugar	½	teaspoon coconut flavoring
⅓	cup unsalted butter, room temperature	½	teaspoon salt

CRUNCHY TOPPING

1½	cups corn flake cereal	½	cup chopped pecans
¾	cup firmly packed brown sugar	¼	cup unsalted butter, melted

Preheat oven to 350°. In a large mixing bowl, combine squash, eggs, sugar, butter, milk, ginger, coconut flavoring and salt. Pour into a greased 8-inch square baking dish and bake, uncovered, 35 minutes.

For topping, in a small bowl combine all topping ingredients. Sprinkle topping over squash and bake an additional 10 minutes.

6-8 servings

Oxford's First Early Merchant

In 1853, Thomas Dudley Isom, age 16, was sent by his uncle, John J. Craig, to Lafayette County with a supply of goods to open a trading post. He opened for business in the Isom house on Jefferson and North 11th Street, becoming the first permanent settler to trade with the Indians.

~Will Lewis, Jr.

SPAGHETTI SQUASH PARMESAN

1	large spaghetti squash		Salt and pepper to taste
4	tablespoons unsalted butter	¼	cup finely chopped fresh parsley
2	tablespoons olive oil	½	cup grated Parmesan cheese
1	large onion, finely chopped	½	teaspoon thyme, optional
5	cloves garlic, chopped	1	cup seasoned breadcrumbs
1	red bell pepper, finely chopped	4	tablespoons unsalted butter, melted

Preheat oven to 325°. Spray cookie sheet with cooking spray. Cut squash in half and place on baking sheet, cut side down. Bake 1 hour. Scoop out seeds and discard. Scoop out flesh with a fork, reserving the shells. Place flesh in a mixing bowl and set aside. In a skillet over medium heat, melt butter and add olive oil. Sauté the onion, garlic, peppers, salt and pepper until onion is tender. Add to mixing bowl along with parsley, Parmesan cheese and thyme. Stir until combined. Spoon mixture into squash shells. In a small bowl toss together breadcrumbs and melted butter. Sprinkle over squash. Place stuffed squash on a greased cookie sheet and bake 30 minutes.

4-6 servings

COMPANY SQUASH

A wonderful summer dish, when yellow squash and tomatoes are at their best

8	medium yellow squash	1	tomato, sliced
½	cup chopped onion	1	cup breadcrumbs
1	cup sour cream	1	cup grated white Cheddar cheese
¾	teaspoon salt	½	cup unsalted butter, melted
¼	teaspoon pepper	4	slices bacon, cooked and crumbled
1	teaspoon chopped, fresh basil (or ½ teaspoon dried)		

Preheat oven to 300°. In a saucepan over high heat, cook squash and onions in salted water to cover. Drain well and mash. Transfer to a large bowl and add sour cream, salt, pepper and basil. Pour into a buttered 2-quart casserole and layer tomato slices on top. Combine breadcrumbs, cheese and butter. Sprinkle over tomatoes. Top with bacon and bake, uncovered, 30 minutes.

6-8 servings

Then in the lane, in the green middledusk of summer while the fireflies winked and drifted and the whippoorwills choired back and forth and the frogs thumped and grunted along the creek, he looked at his house for the first time, at the thin plume of supper smoke windless above the chimney....

~William Faulkner

Go Down, Moses

SPINACH AND WILD RICE

1 10.5-ounce can beef broth

1 cup water

4 tablespoons unsalted butter, divided use

1 6-ounce box seasoned long-grain and wild rice mix

2 10-ounce packages frozen, chopped spinach, cooked and drained

8 ounces cream cheese, room temperature

1 pound mushrooms, thinly sliced

Preheat oven to 350°. In a saucepan bring beef broth and water to a boil. Add 1 tablespoon butter and cook rice as directed on package. In a mixing bowl combine spinach and cream cheese. In a medium skillet over medium heat, sauté mushrooms in 3 tablespoons butter until golden. In a greased, 2-quart dish, layer half the rice, half the spinach and half the mushrooms. Repeat the layers and bake, covered, 40 minutes.

6 servings

ROASTED SWEET POTATOES

3 large sweet potatoes, peeled and cut into bite-sized chunks

¼ cup olive oil

1 clove garlic, minced

Kosher salt and freshly ground black pepper to taste

2 tablespoons chopped, fresh parsley or cilantro

2 tablespoons lime juice

Preheat oven to 400°. Toss cut sweet potatoes with olive oil and minced garlic. Season with salt and pepper. Place sweet potatoes in a 9 x 13-inch pan and roast 30-35 minutes, stirring once or twice. Remove from oven and cool 5 minutes. Sprinkle with parsley or cilantro and lime juice, turning to coat the potatoes completely.

4 servings

Photo on page 140

McCaslin watched him, still speaking, the voice, the words as quiet as the twilight itself was: "Courage and honor and pride, and pity and love of justice and of liberty. They all touch the heart, and what the heart holds to becomes truth, as far as we know truth."

~William Faulkner

Go Down, Moses

MARMALADE SWEET POTATOES

With a citrus tang, these sweet potatoes are a flavor treat,
a wonderful alternative to the traditional Southern sweet potato casserole.

When short on time, substitute one 16-ounce can sweet potatoes for 3 medium sweet potatoes.

6	medium sweet potatoes	2	tablespoons orange juice
2	tablespoons unsalted butter	1	tablespoon lemon juice
2	cups orange marmalade	⅛	teaspoon salt

Scrub potatoes and boil until tender, 25-30 minutes. Drain and cool. Peel potatoes and cut lengthwise into ½-inch slices and set aside. In a large skillet over high heat, melt butter and stir in marmalade, orange juice, lemon juice and salt. Bring to a boil. Reduce heat to medium. Add potatoes and cook, uncovered, 15 minutes, turning occasionally.

6-8 servings

SWEET POTATO CASSEROLE

SWEET POTATOES

4	pounds fresh sweet potatoes, boiled, peeled and sliced	1	teaspoon nutmeg
		5-6	tablespoons milk
2	teaspoons grated fresh orange zest	3	tablespoons orange juice
½	cup sugar	2	tablespoons sifted flour
½	cup packed brown sugar		Salt to taste
1	cup unsalted butter	1	egg, beaten
1	teaspoon cinnamon		

TOPPING

4	tablespoons unsalted butter	1	cup packed brown sugar
½	cup flour	1	cup chopped pecans

Preheat oven to 350°. In a large mixing bowl mash and stir sweet potatoes. Add orange zest, sugars, butter, cinnamon, nutmeg, milk, orange juice, flour and salt. Beat with a mixer until fluffy. Beat in egg just until blended. Pour into a buttered casserole.

For topping, in a small saucepan over medium heat, melt butter and stir in flour, brown sugar and pecans, cooking until well blended. Sprinkle over sweet potatoes. Bake until heated through, about 30 minutes.

10-12 servings

POTATOES SAUSALITO

2½ pounds russet potatoes
6 tablespoons unsalted butter, divided use
2 tablespoons chopped, fresh parsley

1 teaspoon salt
⅛ teaspoon freshly ground pepper
1 cup grated Swiss cheese
1¼ cups boiling beef broth

Preheat oven to 425°. Peel potatoes and thinly slice. Keep covered in cold water until ready to use. Butter a 2-quart baking dish with 2 tablespoons butter. Drain potatoes and dry thoroughly between paper towels. Overlap half of potatoes in baking dish. Dot with 2 tablespoons butter and sprinkle with half the parsley, salt, pepper and cheese. Add a second layer of potatoes, again overlapping them. Sprinkle with remaining parsley, salt, pepper and cheese. Dot with remaining 2 tablespoons butter. Pour boiling broth over potatoes. Bake, uncovered, until the potatoes are fork-tender, the top is well browned, and the broth has been absorbed, about 1 hour.

6-8 servings

ROOT VEGETABLE GRATIN

1 pound carrots
1 pound russet potatoes
1 large turnip
1 large sweet potato
3 beets
4 ounces grated Parmesan cheese

8 ounces grated Gruyère cheese
1½ cups heavy cream
¾ teaspoon fresh oregano
¾ teaspoon fresh thyme
1 teaspoon salt
¾ teaspoon black pepper

Wash and peel carrots, potatoes, turnip, sweet potato and beets. Slice all vegetables ⅛-inch thick and set aside. In a greased, 3-quart casserole, place a layer of vegetables followed by cheeses, cream, herbs, salt and pepper. Repeat layers. Cover and bake at 350° until tender, 60-70 minutes.

10 servings

Early Traffic Problems

In the late 19th century, two carriage routes from town to campus ran on Van Buren Avenue to South Fifth Street or on Fillmore Avenue to Eighth Street and then on to University Avenue. A swampy pond on University, in front of the current Oxford-University Methodist Church, was impassable except by foot on a wooden boardwalk. The Carolyn and Gary Carter house on Fillmore served as a stage stop and post office.

~Will Lewis, Jr.

Baked Green Peas

1 8-ounce jar sweet pickled onions, drained

1 pound frozen baby green peas, cooked and drained

½ cup unsalted butter

1 cup chopped pecans

¼ teaspoon dried rosemary

Preheat oven to 350°.
In a 9 x 12-inch baking dish toss together the drained onions and peas. In a saucepan over medium-high heat, melt butter and add pecans and rosemary. Sauté 2 minutes. Pour butter mixture over onions and peas. Bake covered 20 minutes.

8 servings

POTATO PURÉE SWIRL

1	pound red potatoes	1	teaspoon salt
1	pound sweet potatoes	½	teaspoon pepper
2	green onions, chopped		Nutmeg to taste
¼	cup unsalted butter	¼	cup fresh breadcrumbs
½	cup sour cream	2	tablespoons unsalted butter, melted
½	cup heavy cream	2	tablespoons minced, fresh parsley

Preheat oven to 350°. Boil, drain, and peel potatoes separately. Place red potatoes in 1 mixing bowl and sweet potatoes in another. In a skillet over medium heat, lightly sauté green onions in ¼ cup butter. In a small bowl mix sour cream, cream, salt, pepper, nutmeg and cooked green onions with butter from skillet. Stir to combine. Add half of sour cream mixture to each bowl of potatoes. Beat each potato mixture with an electric mixer until mixture is well combined and potatoes are mostly smooth. Transfer both potatoes to a greased casserole and swirl together gently. In a small bowl combine the breadcrumbs, 2 tablespoons melted butter and parsley. Spread over potatoes. Bake 30-35 minutes.

8-10 servings

The Flaky Baker

ITALIAN TOMATO TART

1	unbaked pastry shell	½	teaspoon salt
8	ounces mozzarella cheese, grated	¼	teaspoon pepper
¼	cup minced onion	¼	cup olive oil
2	tablespoons chopped, fresh basil	¼-½	cup grated Parmesan cheese
2-3	tomatoes, cut into ½-inch slices		

Preheat oven to 400°. Layer all ingredients in pastry shell in order listed. Sprinkle Parmesan cheese on top. Bake 30-40 minutes. Remove from oven and let stand 5 minutes before serving.

6 servings

TOMATO PIE

1	unbaked pastry shell	1	teaspoon Dijon mustard
2	large, ripe tomatoes, peeled and sliced	¼	cup chopped green onions
1	cup shredded Cheddar cheese	2	slices bacon, cooked and crumbled
¾	cup mayonnaise		

Preheat oven to 350°. Bake pie shell 10 minutes. Remove pie shell from oven and arrange tomatoes on bottom of crust. In a small bowl mix cheese, mayonnaise and mustard. Top tomatoes with cheese mixture. Sprinkle with green onions and bacon. Bake until cheese is golden brown, 20-30 minutes.

6 servings

One of the earliest accounts of the okra plant is from a Spanish Moor who traveled to Egypt in 1216. Today, Southerners use okra in stews and gumbos; its gluey sap thickens the broth.

STEWED TOMATOES AND OKRA

3	tablespoons bacon drippings	3	cups chopped okra
1	yellow bell pepper, chopped	½	cup water
1	green or red bell pepper, chopped	4	tomatoes, peeled and chopped
1	onion, chopped	½-1	teaspoon Creole seasoning
1	jalapeño pepper, seeded and minced	½-1	teaspoon salt

In a Dutch oven over medium-low heat, heat bacon drippings and sauté bell peppers, onions and jalapeño pepper until the onions are clear, about 30 minutes. Add okra, increase heat to medium, and cook, stirring, 5 minutes. Add water and cover. Reduce heat to maintain a simmer and cook about 1 hour, stirring often. Add tomatoes, seasoning and salt. Continue to simmer at least 1 hour, or as long as 3 hours.

8-10 servings

Roasted Vegetables

Cut a variety of vegetables into large chunks. Choose zucchini, yellow squash, tomatoes, onions, carrots, bell peppers or whatever your farmers' market offers. Pieces should be cut to approximately the same size. Toss with enough extra virgin olive oil to coat. Then toss with about 1 tablespoon sugar, kosher salt, pepper, minced garlic, fresh chopped herbs (such as marjoram or rosemary) and about ⅓ cup balsamic vinegar. Let rest about 30 minutes to soak up flavors. Drain vegetables and arrange in a single layer on a parchment-lined jelly-roll pan. Bake on the bottom rack of a preheated 425° oven until vegetables are caramelized and tender, about 15 minutes. For a crunchy texture, finish by broiling. Serve hot or at room temperature.

ROASTED TOMATOES

This savory side dish is made simple with the use of canned tomatoes to get all the flavor in half the time. While they make a flavorful side dish alone, these tomatoes add a wonderful taste to salads or pizza.

2	28-ounce cans whole tomatoes, drained, halved, and seeded	2	branches fresh rosemary leaves
⅓-½	cup olive oil	5	large cloves garlic, coarsely chopped
14	large fresh basil leaves, torn		Kosher salt and pepper to taste

Preheat oven to 300°. Spread tomatoes in large, shallow baking dish. Sprinkle with remaining ingredients and turn to coat. Bake about 2½ hours, basting and turning tomatoes several times. Tomatoes are done when they are a dark, scarlet red. Take care not to let tomatoes or garlic brown. Once done, transfer to glass or china bowl and allow the flavors to ripen at room temperature for up to 6 hours.

8-12 servings

GREEN TOMATO CASSEROLE

2-3	firm, green tomatoes, thinly sliced	1	cup shredded mozzarella cheese
	Salt and pepper to taste	½	cup bread or cracker crumbs
1	large onion, thinly sliced	½	cup grated Parmesan cheese
1	cup shredded Cheddar cheese		

Preheat oven to 350°. Grease a 2-quart covered casserole. Sprinkle tomatoes with salt and pepper. Arrange half of tomatoes on bottom of dish. Cover with half of onion slices and half of Cheddar and mozzarella cheeses. Repeat layers. Top with breadcrumbs and Parmesan cheese. Cover and bake 20-25 minutes. Remove cover and continue baking until liquid is fairly well absorbed and top is slightly browned, about 20 minutes. Remove from oven, cover, and let stand 5 minutes before serving.

4-6 servings

SWEET ONION PIE

6-8 large sweet onions	⅓ cup half-and-half
¼ cup unsalted butter	½ teaspoon nutmeg, or to taste
1 cup water, salted	1 teaspoon salt, or to taste
½ cup uncooked rice	½ teaspoon pepper, or to taste
1½ cups grated Cheddar cheese	Breadcrumbs

Preheat oven to 350°. Chop onions. (To chop in food processor, first cut each onion into 6 pieces. Process 2 onions at a time, pulsing briefly and being careful not to pulverize.) In a large skillet or Dutch oven over medium-high heat, sauté onions in butter until translucent. In a saucepan bring 1 cup salted water to boil. Stir in rice, reduce heat to low, and cook 5 minutes. (Rice will not be fully cooked.) In a mixing bowl combine onions, rice with any remaining water, cheese and half-and-half. Stir until combined. Season with nutmeg, salt and pepper. Put into greased 3-quart shallow casserole and sprinkle with breadcrumbs. Bake 1 hour.

8 servings

Artist Gay Graeber Artwork, page 157

Gay began her career in art at age four by painting her father's hunting dog a bright shade of yellow. She studied art in high school and received a BFA from Ole Miss. She is the curator of her family's 18th century Neopolitan crêche collection. She enjoys all media and is presently doing Styrofoam sculpture and oil portraits of animals.

CAJUN WHITE BEANS

2 pounds navy beans, soaked overnight in cold water to cover	¼ cup flour
1 cup chopped onion	1 teaspoon cayenne pepper, or to taste
2 cloves garlic, chopped	2 teaspoons salt
1 large ham bone with meat	2 cups chopped green onion tops
½ cup vegetable oil	5-6 cups cooked hot rice

Drain soaked beans in a colander. In an 8-10 quart stockpot, combine beans, onion, garlic and ham bone, adding enough water to cover. Bring to a boil over high heat. Reduce heat to low, cover, and simmer until beans are tender and a thick gravy has formed, 2-2½ hours. Add hot water as needed during the cooking process. Stir occasionally to prevent scorching. When stirring, use cooking spoon to mash tender beans against side of pot to create the gravy. Remove ham bone. In a heavy skillet over medium-high heat, heat oil and add flour. Stir constantly to make a light-brown roux, 3-5 minutes. Add roux to the beans along with cayenne and salt. Continue to cook beans slowly on low heat 15-20 minutes. Remove pot from heat, add green onion tops, cover, and let stand 5 minutes. Adjust seasonings. Serve over rice.

8-10 servings

VEGGIE AND BEAN BURRITOS WITH TOMATO MANGO SALSA

**Author Ace Atkins
Essay, page 158**

Alabama native, novelist, and former reporter for *Newsweek* magazine, the *Tampa Tribune*, and the *St. Petersburg Times*, Ace Atkins moved to Oxford in 2001 to teach journalism at the University of Mississippi. He was nominated for a Pulitzer Prize in 2000. Atkins is the author of four crime novels: *Crossroad Blues, Leavin' Trunk Blues, Dark End of the Street*, and *Dirty South*.

BURRITOS

1 tablespoon olive oil
1 medium onion, thinly sliced
1 jalapeño pepper, seeded and minced
1 tablespoon chili powder
2 cloves garlic, minced
2 teaspoons fresh oregano
1 teaspoon ground cumin
1 tablespoon water
1 large sweet potato, baked and diced (or 16 ounces canned yams, rinsed)

1 16-ounce can black beans, rinsed and drained
1 cup corn
1 green bell pepper, chopped
2 tablespoons lime juice
Whole wheat flour tortillas
Shredded Monterey Jack and/or Cheddar cheese
Sour cream

SALSA

1 small mango, peeled, seeded and chopped (about 1½ cups)
1 large tomato, peeled, seeded and chopped
⅓ cup chopped red onion

¼ cup minced fresh cilantro
1 small jalapeño pepper, seeded and chopped
2 tablespoons lime juice

Preheat oven to 350°. In a large skillet over medium-high heat, heat olive oil and sauté onion until golden brown. Add jalapeño, chili powder, garlic, oregano and cumin. Stir about 1 minute. Add 1 tablespoon water and stir. Remove from heat and transfer to a large mixing bowl. Add sweet potatoes, black beans, corn, green pepper and lime juice. Stir until combined. Spoon about 2 tablespoons filling onto the center of a tortilla. Sprinkle with cheese. Fold tortilla sides under to make a rectangle. Place seam sides down on a jelly-roll pan. Cover with foil and bake until heated through, 20-30 minutes. Serve with sour cream and salsa.

For salsa, in a small bowl combine all ingredients and refrigerate at least 2 hours.

12 burritos and 2 cups salsa

Farmers' Market by Gay Graeber ▸

TALES of a FOURTH GRADE FARMER

Ace Atkins

Before I moved to rural Mississippi, the last time I'd had any experience farming was in a fourth grade experimental school project for suburban kids in Detroit, Michigan. Unlike a lot of my classmates, I was completely familiar with goats and pigs and chickens. (My Alabama cousins used to pay me two dollars if I could catch a mean, quick-footed rooster at their farm. I still remember that angry-clawed bastard.)

The year after our school project, I talked my dad — who'd grown up the son of a sharecropper in Millport, Alabama — into tilling up our well-manicured lawn to let me plant a crop. My dad, who was at that time a defensive backfield coach for the Detroit Lions, thought this was a pretty odd request for our Bloomfield Hills neighborhood.

But he indulged me, and I continued a curiosity I had with farming. Maybe because my Alabama parents always tried to culture a Southern perspective for me in the cities I grew up in — Detroit, Buffalo, and San Francisco, among others — by helping with projects like this or in naming two of my dogs Rebel, complete with a dog house draped in the Stars and Bars.

That season we had carrots and lettuce (I'm not sure why I picked lettuce). We also had a big blackberry bush, the berries of which my mom picked to make pies now and then. I never thought about all this being a Southern thing until my Yankee neighborhood buddy, Bob Hastings, made fun of my mom baking pies from a bush in the yard and the way she pronounced things.

I had to whip his ass, which I guess was a Southern thing, too, but had little to do with farming.

I guess in those lean years between fourth grade and 32 years old, I thought about farming, or just growing things, a lot. We moved back South when I was about 12, but only to another well-tended suburb in Atlanta, a soulless place that had any real Southern feeling sucked out of it years ago.

But moving to Lafayette County and buying a farm made me think a lot about that experimental education project in Detroit. This may be a ridiculous notion, but I really believe I was so into raising my class's crops and caring for the farm animals because I was Southern.

If not bred, perhaps I learned from stories about my dad as a child in the Depression and his family having to grow their own crops to eat. His family even kept him out of school one year because they needed him to work the farm. (Not having a McDonald's or Burger King nearby was a completely foreign notion to me.)

In 2002, my fiancée and I bought a run-down little place in south Lafayette County. It was a farm house built by a man named T.W. Patton in 1895 and had fallen on hard times ever since the old man died about the time World War II had ended. The barns were falling apart; old rusted pieces of farming equipment lay scattered around the place.

That first spring, my fiancée's father — a lumbering, quiet man from North Carolina named Jack Moore — helped us pick out a good, solid section of land and corralled it with six-foot fencing to keep out the numerous deer who live in this little valley and like to eat.

We tilled.

We planted.

We had a terrible crop. Tiny tomatoes. Rotten watermelons. Weeds everywhere.

I felt perhaps this was *Green Acres* and here I was a writer trying to turn myself into a farmer. Maybe my memories of that garden in fourth grade and my powers as a Southern farmer (with God-given abilities through my Alabama lineage) had been exaggerated over time.

But the next year I tried again — this time seeking the advice and help from Mrs. Sybil King, my next door (well, yellin' distance, anyway) neighbor. Mrs. King has lived in the same house in this same valley and worked the same land here for 50 years.

I figured she was a pretty good bet.

The house she's shared with her husband of more than a half century, Joe Abb, would put any *Southern Living* garden to shame. In spring and early summer the lantana grow almost as tall as her house, which is also high with elephant ears, bright, huge zinnias, impatiens flowers, and day lilies.

The garden they work every year grows the juiciest tomatoes I've ever tasted and the hottest peppers. The sweet corn reaches to the sky.

To simply describe the kind of woman Sybil King is, the only thing you have to know is that a few days after we moved in, she brought us hot homemade sausage biscuits. A fine neighbor.

And that summer she provided us with those tomatoes, peppers, corn, and peas while our garden was suffering. She also made us homemade pear preserves from fruit she collected from our old Moonglow pear tree early that fall.

So the next year I took her advice and loaded in a good bit of production from my other neighbors — the cows of Jo Abb's brother, Gaylon. I also switched to other varieties of plants, thanks to the good folks down at O'Tuck's in Water Valley (it seems I was growing the wrong type tomatoes).

Last year was my best crop since fourth grade. My pride restored.

I don't need to explain how farm food is better than produce from Kroger or Wal-Mart. Some things just don't need to be explained — like those tasteless, pale, mealy, hard tomatoes you can buy at the local mega-store.

I also don't need to explain how growing your own food makes it taste better, too. Or maybe feel better.

But to be in the South and not take advantage of the kind of crops we can produce on our own is a real waste of time, space, and culture.

I could grow carrots and lettuce in Detroit.

But a plate of field peas, tomatoes, and sweet corn just tastes better here.

And if anyone says different, I'll have to whip their ass.

Cranberry Scones
Sweet Potato Biscuits
Cheese and Sour Cream Cornbread
Pumpkin Bread
Challah

BREAKFAST & BREADS

SPICY BRUNCH BACON

3	eggs	2	tablespoons tarragon vinegar
2	tablespoons dry mustard	1½	cups crushed buttery crackers
1	teaspoon cayenne pepper	1½-2	pounds bacon, ⅛-inch thick

Preheat oven to 350°. In a large bowl beat eggs and add dry mustard, cayenne and vinegar. In a large flat bowl, place cracker crumbs. One at a time dip bacon strips in egg mixture, then dredge both sides in cracker crumbs. Place bacon strips onto ungreased cookie sheets and bake 30-40 minutes. Bacon will remain flat when cooked.

8 servings

Photo on page 174

BACON TOMATO CUPS

1	10-ounce can diced tomatoes and green chilies, drained	8	slices cooked bacon, crumbled
½	cup mayonnaise	½	small onion, chopped
1	cup grated Swiss cheese	1	10-ounce can refrigerated flaky, layered biscuits
1	teaspoon dried basil		

Preheat oven to 375°. In a mixing bowl stir together the tomatoes, mayonnaise, cheese, basil, bacon and onion. Separate each biscuit into 3 layers. Press each layer into a lightly greased miniature muffin tin and fill with tomato mixture. Bake 10-12 minutes.

24 servings

Photo on page 25

The campus is only a few blocks down University Avenue. Here the town and Ole Miss seem to merge, little enclaves and outpockets and cul-de-sacs of youth and age. There is a loveliness to [the campus], an unhurried grace, with its gently curving drives, its shady bowers, its loops and groves and open spaces crowned with magnolias, oaks, and cedars and lush now with forsythia and dogwood and Japanese magnolias and the pear trees in early spring....

~Willie Morris

"The Ghosts of Ole Miss"

161

HEIRLOOM TOMATO, LEEK AND CHEESE TART

He goes to the
kitchen and builds a
fire in the stove, slowly,
clumsily; as clumsily
after twentyfive years as
on the first day he had
ever attempted it, and
puts coffee on…then
he finds that he is
preparing his usual
hearty breakfast….

~ William Faulkner

Light in August

PASTRY

2½ tablespoons unsalted butter, chilled

1 cup flour

Pinch salt

5 tablespoons ice water

FILLING

2 tablespoons unsalted butter

3 leeks, white part only, diced

¼ cup water

½ teaspoon salt

Flour for sprinkling

Fresh basil leaves, torn

1 cup grated sharp, white Cheddar cheese

2 large ripe heirloom tomatoes, cored and sliced into ⅛-inch rounds

Salt and freshly ground pepper to taste

Cut the butter into ¼-inch cubes. In a mixing bowl stir together cubed butter, flour and salt. Mix with fingertips until butter is coated with flour. Add ½ of the water. Using a pastry blender, cut butter into flour and water. Add remaining water, pouring it over the dry portions of the dough, continuing to mix until all flour is damp. Gather dough into a rough ball and dust with flour. Wrap with plastic wrap and refrigerate at least 1½ hours. Roll chilled dough on a well-floured board into a 12-inch circle. Place on a baking sheet and refrigerate about 30 minutes.

For filling, in a sauté pan over medium-high heat, melt butter. Add leeks and water and bring to a boil. Reduce heat, cover, and simmer until leeks are tender and water has completely evaporated, about 10 minutes. Add salt and let cool to room temperature.

To assemble, preheat oven to 400°. Dust surface of chilled pastry with flour. Sprinkle leeks over pastry, leaving a 1½-inch border around the edge. Scatter ½ of basil over leeks. Cover with cheese and remaining basil. Arrange tomatoes on top in a concentric circular pattern. Lightly season with salt and pepper. Fold the perimeter of the pastry over the edges of the tomatoes. Bake until pastry is golden brown, 40-50 minutes.

8 servings

Photo on page 175

SUNDAY BAKED EGGS

8	eggs		Kosher salt
8	teaspoons unsalted butter		Freshly ground black pepper
	Tabasco sauce	8	ounces Parmesan cheese

Preheat oven to 350°. Generously spray 8 individual muffin cups with cooking spray. Break one egg into each cup. Top each with 1 teaspoon butter and Tabasco, salt and pepper to taste. Sprinkle with 1 ounce of cheese. Bake until the egg yolk is slightly set, about 10 minutes. Remove from oven and run a knife along muffin cup edges to remove eggs.

8 servings

A frittata is an Italian omelet that looks like a crustless quiche. Usually the frittata is cooked on the stove like an omelet and then baked in the oven to finish.

ZUCCHINI AND TOMATO FRITTATA

2	tablespoons extra virgin olive oil	8	eggs
2	medium zucchini, cut into ⅛-inch-thick pieces	¼	cup freshly grated Parmesan cheese
1	small Vidalia onion, coarsely chopped	2	tablespoons minced chives
1	clove garlic, minced	½	teaspoon salt
2	Roma or plum tomatoes, seeded and chopped into 1-inch cubes	¼	teaspoon freshly ground pepper
			Grated Parmesan

Preheat oven to 350°. In a 10-inch nonstick, ovenproof skillet over medium-high heat, heat olive oil. Add zucchini and cook until softened, about 4 minutes. Add onion and garlic and cook until the onion softens, about 2 minutes. Stir in tomatoes and heat through, about 2 minutes. In a large bowl, whisk the eggs, Parmesan cheese, chives, salt and pepper. Pour over the vegetables. Reduce heat to medium-low. Cook uncovered until the bottom of the eggs are set, about 3 minutes. Transfer skillet to the oven. Bake until frittata feels set when pressed in the center, 12-15 minutes. Invert onto a serving plate. Serve hot, cool, or at room temperature. Serve with fresh, grated Parmesan.

8 servings

Ten O'Clock Coffee Club

This group of men or their predecessors meets Monday through Saturday mornings from 9:30 to 10:30. The number of members present on different days varies from about nine to 20. We first began meeting at Grundy's, next at Smitty's, and now at the Beacon. All these restaurants have been very hospitable, putting the group on the honor system, relying on the one who pays the bill each day to tell the cashier what is owed. We play a number game at 10:00, and no one wants to miss it. The loser of the game pays the bill and is then entitled to run the next day's game.

There are no requirements or qualifications for membership. Most of us are retired business people on

FRENCH TOAST SOUFFLÉ

10 cups cubed dense white bread (about 16 1-ounce slices)
8 ounces cream cheese, room temperature
8 eggs
1½ cups milk
⅔ cup half-and-half
1¼ cups maple syrup, divided use
½ teaspoon vanilla
2 tablespoons confectioners' sugar
Strawberries or other fresh fruit

Coat a 13 x 9-inch baking dish with butter and place bread cubes in dish. In the bowl of an electric mixer, beat cream cheese at medium speed until smooth. Add eggs one at a time, mixing well after each addition. Add milk, half-and-half, ½ cup maple syrup and vanilla. Mix until well combined. Pour cream cheese mixture over bread, cover, and refrigerate overnight. Preheat oven to 375°. Remove dish from refrigerator and let stand on counter 30 minutes. Bake until set, about 50 minutes. Sprinkle soufflé with confectioners' sugar and serve with remaining maple syrup and sliced fresh strawberries or other fruit.

12 servings

BROWN SUGAR STRATA

1 cup packed, dark brown sugar
½ cup unsalted butter
2 tablespoons light corn syrup
12 slices white bread, crust trimmed
1½ cups whole milk
6 large eggs
1 teaspoon vanilla
½ teaspoon salt
Assorted fresh fruit (strawberries, pineapple, kiwi)

Place sugar, butter and syrup in a small sauce pan. Stir over medium-low heat until butter melts and sugar dissolves. Bring to a boil. Pour into 9 x 13-inch baking dish. Coat bottom evenly. Cool. Place 6 bread slices in a single layer on top of caramel. Cover with remaining 6 bread slices. Whisk milk, eggs, vanilla and salt in bowl to blend. Pour over bread. Cover and chill overnight. Preheat oven to 350°. Bake strata uncovered until bread is puffed and light golden brown, approximately 40 minutes. Let stand a few minutes before serving. Loosen edges with a rubber spatula and invert onto a serving plate. Garnish with assorted fresh fruit.

6 servings

Photo on page 175

SUMMER FRUIT BOWLS

1½ cups cantaloupe balls

1½ cups honeydew melon balls

1½ cups fresh pineapple chunks

1   11-ounce can Mandarin oranges, drained

1   cup fresh strawberries

6   ounces frozen lemonade concentrate

¼   cup orange marmalade

2   tablespoons orange-flavored liqueur
     Mint leaves for garnish

In a large bowl combine fruit. In a small bowl combine lemonade, marmalade and liqueur. Pour over fruit and toss gently. Cover and chill 2 hours before serving. Spoon into stemmed dishes and garnish with mint leaves.

7 cups

SUGAR BAKED FRUIT

2   large bananas, sliced ⅜-inch thick

1   tablespoon lemon juice

1   cup strawberries, hulled and halved

2   oranges, peeled, seeded, and cut into bite-sized pieces

6   tablespoons butter, melted

1   cup firmly packed brown sugar

¾   cup slivered almonds

Preheat oven broiler. Toss bananas in lemon juice. Arrange in the bottom of a buttered 11 x 17-inch baking dish. Cover with strawberries and top with oranges. In a small bowl, stir together the butter, sugar and almonds. Sprinkle over fruit. Broil 6 inches from broiler until sugar melts and almonds are toasted.

6 servings

Photo on page 175

or near the Square: lawyers, judges, teachers, physicians, dentists, and engineers. Our ages vary from 50 to 90. Photos of deceased members adorn the walls of the meeting location, and members are just trying to stay "off the wall."

Conversation consists of jokes, gossip, information, and politics. Very little time is spent on international and other matters of substance. A lot of kidding goes on, and many coffee cups and glasses of water, tea, and Coke are turned over, which causes those nearby to scramble or get wet. Occasionally a member is half-jokingly told by the waitress that if he turns over anything else, he might not be allowed to come back.

~Tommy Ethridge

Adjust the proportions of the granola ingredients to suit your taste or add other ingredients as desired. Increased amounts will require longer cooking times. If you include more granola on the roasting pan, you can decrease the frequency of stirring. The concept is to dry out the ingredients without burning them.

GRANOLA

Not just for breakfast. This granola makes a good snack or hostess gift.
Top with chopped dried fruit, such as cranberries, cherries, golden raisins or apricots.

4	cups old-fashioned oats (not quick cooking), uncooked	1	cup raw sunflower seeds
2	cups sweetened, shredded coconut	½	cup ground flax seed, optional
¾	cup pecans, chopped	¾	cup canola or light olive oil
¾	cup almonds, chopped	¼	cup honey
¾	cup walnuts, chopped		Dried fruit

Preheat oven to 325°. In a large bowl combine oats, coconut, nuts and seeds. In a small bowl, whisk oil and honey together. Coat dry mixture with oil. Spread onto two 13 x 8-inch jelly-roll pans. Bake 25 minutes, stirring every 5 minutes, until the coconut is a golden brown. Watch carefully, as mixture will burn if not stirred frequently. Cool and store in an airtight container. Top with a mixture of dried chopped fruits.

about 10 cups

BAKED ORANGE CUPS

6	medium oranges	1	cup sugar
6	medium cooking apples, peeled and chopped	½	cup chopped pecans
1	8-ounce can crushed pineapple in its own juice	3	tablespoons unsalted butter, cubed

Preheat oven to 250°. Cut oranges in half, making a zigzag pattern in the tops. Cut out centers, leaving a thin layer of orange pulp inside. Remove orange seeds and reserve pulp and juice. In a large saucepan place orange pulp and juice, apples, pineapple and sugar. Cook over medium heat until very thick, about 10 minutes. Fill orange cups with mixture. Top with butter and pecans. Pour water about 1-inch up sides of a shallow pan and place orange cups in pan. Bake 30 minutes.

12 servings

TOMATO BREAD PUDDING

1½ loaves (12 ounces) French or Italian bread, sliced in ½-inch slices

1½ cups milk

1¼ cups half-and-half

1 cup heavy cream

3 eggs, lightly beaten

2 tablespoons chopped, fresh parsley

1 teaspoon chopped, fresh thyme

2 cups shredded Monterey Jack cheese, divided use

1 cup grated Parmesan cheese, divided use

3 cups fresh tomatoes (about 1½ pounds), seeded and sliced

Preheat oven to 350°. Butter a 9 x 13-inch baking dish and set aside. Arrange bread slices on a cookie sheet in a single layer and bake until lightly toasted, 5-8 minutes. In a large bowl, combine milk, half-and-half, cream and eggs. In a small bowl, combine parsley and thyme; set aside. Place toasted bread slices in a single layer on the bottom of the buttered dish. Top bread with 1 cup Monterey Jack cheese, ½ cup Parmesan cheese and ½ of the herb mixture. Pour ½ of milk mixture over the cheese. Layer ½ of the tomatoes on top and then repeat the layers with remaining bread, cheese, herbs, milk and tomatoes. With a spatula, press bread down to ensure it is completely covered by the milk mixture. Let stand for 5 minutes. Place pan on top of a cookie sheet and bake uncovered until a knife inserted in the center comes out clean, 30-40 minutes.

8-10 servings

WHOLE WHEAT ROLLS

1 tablespoon dry yeast

½ cup warm water

1¼ cups boiling water

⅔ cup shortening

¾ cup sugar or malt syrup (preferred)

3 cups bread flour, sifted

2 eggs

2 cups whole wheat flour

2 teaspoons salt

Dissolve yeast in ½ cup warm water. Set aside. In a large mixing bowl, pour boiling water over shortening. Add sugar or malt syrup. Stir to dissolve. Beat in 2 cups bread flour. Add eggs and beat again. While mixture is warm add the yeast mixture and mix well. Add whole wheat flour and salt. Add enough remaining bread flour while kneading to form a semi-stiff dough. Let the dough rise in a covered, well-greased bowl until doubled in size. Punch down. Divide dough and shape into 24 balls. Place on a well-greased cookie sheet and cover with a light cloth. Let the rolls rise until doubled in size. Preheat oven to 350° and bake rolls until golden brown, 12-15 minutes.

24 rolls

Active dry yeast is the most commonly used form of baker's yeast. It is sold in ¼-ounce envelopes and can be stored in the refrigerator or freezer. Before using, it should be brought to room temperature, then mixed with lukewarm (100-110°) water to activate it. To determine if yeast is still active, sprinkle it and a bit of sugar in lukewarm water and let it rest about 5 minutes. It should foam. Rapid-rise yeast makes dough rise in about half the time but may sacrifice flavor since bread develops flavor during the rising period. Salt stops the growth of yeast, so add it after the yeast has been proofed and a little flour has been added.

At Smitty's where I go
for breakfast, the talk
during the interminable
coffee breaks, among the
merchants of the Square,
and the legions of
lawyers (why do small
Southern towns have so
many lawyers?), and the
farmers from the farthest
reaches of Lafayette
County is about
Afghanistan, the crazed
Khomeini, the hostages,
the Russkies — one
morning coffee toasts
were exchanged to the
American ice hockey
boys — and the next
Ole Miss game....

~Willie Morris

"The Ghosts of Ole Miss"

ICE BOX ROLLS

2	ounces yeast	2	teaspoons salt
1	cup warm water	2	eggs
1	cup boiling water	6	cups flour
¾	cup sugar		

Dissolve yeast in 1 cup warm water and set aside. In the bowl of an electric mixer, pour 1 cup boiling water over sugar and salt. Mix until combined. Beat in eggs, one at a time, blending after each addition. When the mixture is lukewarm, stir in yeast mixture. Beat in flour, one cup at a time, blending well after each addition. Cover and refrigerate at least 1 day, up to 1 week. Using a floured cloth and roller cover, put about ⅓ of dough on cloth. Roll out to about ¼-inch thickness. Cut with round drinking glass and fold dough circles in half. Place rolls on greased or parchment-lined cookie sheet. Repeat with remaining ⅔ of dough. Cover rolls with a light cloth and allow to rise for several hours. If they don't seem to rise, put them in a cold oven with a pan of hot water under them. Preheat oven and bake at 425° until lightly browned, 10-15 minutes.

70 rolls

Photo on page 42

BUNDT BREAD

2	ounces yeast	¼	cup unsalted butter, melted and cooled
½	cup warm water	1	egg
¾	cup milk	3½	cups flour
¼	cup sugar		Sesame seeds
1	teaspoon salt		

Dissolve yeast in ½ cup warm water and set aside. In a saucepan over medium-high heat, pour milk and cook until bubbles form at the edges. Remove from heat and add sugar. Add salt and butter. Add dissolved yeast and egg and stir to blend. Add 2 cups flour and mix. Add remaining flour and mix. The dough will be soft and sticky. Cover and let rise until doubled in size, about 30 minutes. Punch down. Spoon into a well-greased Bundt pan. Let rise until doubled in bulk. Sprinkle with sesame seeds. Preheat oven and bake at 325° for 30 minutes.

1 loaf

ENGLISH MUFFINS

1	¼-ounce package rapid-rise yeast	4-4½	cups flour, sifted
¼	cup lukewarm water	½	cup self-rising cornmeal
1⅔	cups milk		Cornmeal for sprinkling
¼	cup solid vegetable shortening		Vegetable oil
3	tablespoons sugar		Melted butter
2	teaspoons salt		

Dissolve yeast in lukewarm water. In a large saucepan, combine milk, shortening, sugar and salt. Heat until shortening is melted and tiny bubbles form at the edges. Cool to lukewarm. Beat in 2 cups flour, cornmeal and yeast mixture. Stir in enough additional flour to make a soft dough. Turn out on lightly floured board and knead until smooth and satiny, about 10 minutes. Roll dough into a ball and place in greased bowl. Cover and let rise in warm place until doubled in size, about 1 hour. Punch dough down. Roll out to ¼-inch thickness on board heavily sprinkled with cornmeal. Cut with lightly floured 3-inch round cutter. Sprinkle waxed paper with remaining cornmeal. Invert dough circle onto waxed paper. Cover and let rise until nearly doubled in size, 35-60 minutes, depending on the temperature in the room. In a large skillet over medium heat pour just enough oil to cover the surface. Brown muffins in skillet on both sides. Drain on paper towels. Split horizontally, toast, and brush with melted butter. Muffins may be frozen in a zip-top bag after split and cooled.

12-15 muffins

■ *Downtown Grill* ■

CORNBREAD MUFFINS

1¾	cups self-rising cornmeal	3	eggs
¾	cup flour	2	cups buttermilk
1	teaspoon baking powder	2	tablespoons butter, melted
¼	teaspoon baking soda	1	tablespoon bacon grease plus additional for pan, melted
1	teaspoon salt		

Preheat oven to 400°. In a large bowl, stir together cornmeal, flour, baking powder, baking soda and salt. In a mixing bowl whisk together eggs and buttermilk. Stir in flour mixture, melted butter and 1 tablespoon bacon grease. Grease muffin tins with additional bacon grease. Place prepared pan in oven until very hot, about 5 minutes. Fill tins ⅔ full and bake until lightly browned, about 20 minutes.

12 muffins

He took the mule out and watered and fed it and only then went to the fence-corner and there it was — the pan of still-warm biscuit, the lard pail half full of milk, the tin worn and polished with scouring and long use until it had a patina like old silver — just as it had used to be.

~William Faulkner

Go Down, Moses

BUTTERMILK BISCUITS

1¾ cups White Lily self-rising flour
½ cup vegetable shortening, chilled
¾ cup buttermilk

Flour for dusting
¼ cup butter, melted

Preheat oven to 400°. In a mixing bowl combine the flour and shortening using a pastry blender until mixture is uniformly crumbly. Add buttermilk and blend with a fork until dough holds together. Turn onto a lightly floured board. Flour top of dough lightly and knead gently. Pat into a 1-inch-thick circle. With a biscuit cutter, cut biscuits any size. Arrange on a greased or parchment-lined cookie sheet and brush tops with melted butter. Bake until lightly browned, about 15 minutes.

12 biscuits

Photo on page 129

A substitute for 1 cup buttermilk is ⅔ cup yogurt mixed with ⅓ cup milk. Or, mix 1 tablespoon of lemon juice or vinegar with 1 cup milk and let it rest until it curdles, 5 to 10 minutes.

SWEET POTATO BISCUITS

2½ cups flour
½ cup brown sugar, firmly packed
1 tablespoon baking powder
½ teaspoon ground cinnamon
½ teaspoon ground ginger
½ teaspoon ground allspice

½ teaspoon salt
½ cup chilled lard, cut into pieces
1 cup cooked, mashed sweet potatoes
½ cup heavy cream
¼ cup coarsely chopped pecans

Preheat oven to 350°. In a large mixing bowl, whisk together the flour, brown sugar, baking powder, spices and salt. Add the lard and cut in with a pastry blender until mixture is uniformly crumbly. Add the sweet potato and stir until well blended. Add the cream and pecans and stir until dough is just moist. Transfer to a lightly floured work surface, roll dough to a 1½-inch-thick circle, and cut out rounds with a 2-inch biscuit cutter. Arrange biscuits on a greased or parchment-lined cookie sheet about 1 inch apart and bake on center oven rack until golden brown, 25-30 minutes. Serve warm.

12 biscuits

Photo on page 160

CHEESE BISCUITS

These are wonderful split, buttered and filled with thinly sliced ham.

3   cups White Lily self-rising flour

6   tablespoons unsalted butter, chilled
    and cut into pieces

6   tablespoons solid vegetable shortening,
    chilled and cut into pieces

¼   cup poppy seeds

2   cups grated Cheddar cheese

1   cup buttermilk

Preheat oven to 425°. In a large mixing bowl combine the flour, butter and shortening using a pastry blender, until mixture is uniformly crumbly. Stir in poppy seeds and cheese. Add just enough buttermilk to make a stiff dough. Turn out onto a floured board, and with minimal kneading, shape dough into a 1-inch-thick circle. Cut with a biscuit cutter. Bake on a lightly greased or parchment-lined cookie sheet until lightly browned, about 15 minutes.

12 biscuits

LEMON GLAZED TEA BREAD

BREAD

⅓   cup unsalted butter, melted

1   cup sugar

3   tablespoons lemon extract

2   eggs

1½ cups flour

1   teaspoon baking powder

1   teaspoon salt

½   cup milk

1½ tablespoons grated lemon zest

½   cup chopped pecans

LEMON GLAZE

¼   cup lemon juice

½   cup sugar

For the bread, preheat oven to 350°. Grease and flour a 9 x 5-inch loaf pan and set aside. In the bowl of an electric mixer, cream butter, sugar and lemon extract until fluffy. Add eggs, beating until mixture is blended. In a medium bowl, sift flour, baking powder and salt. Add flour mixture and milk alternately to butter mixture, beating well after each addition. Fold in lemon zest and pecans. Pour batter into prepared pan. Bake until toothpick inserted in center comes out clean, about 1 hour.

For the glaze, in a small bowl mix lemon juice and sugar until well combined. Pour slowly over hot bread, waiting for glaze to be absorbed into bread. Let stand 15-20 minutes and invert onto a rack to cool.

A double portion of the recipe makes 5 small loaf pans, 5¾ x 3¼ inches each.

12 servings

Pass the Biscuits, Dorothy

Before World War II, there were not many restaurants in town. Students usually ate at boarding houses when not dining on campus. One of the most popular boarding houses was at 210 South Fifth Street, a few blocks from campus.

~Will Lewis, Jr.

Father said clocks
slay time. He said time
is dead as long as it is
being clicked off by little
wheels; only when the
clock stops does time
come to life.

~ William Faulkner

The Sound and the Fury

CHEESE AND SOUR CREAM CORNBREAD

1½	cups self-rising cornmeal	8	ounces sour cream
⅔	cup canola oil	10	ounces Cheddar cheese, grated
2	eggs	4	tablespoons finely chopped onions
1	14-ounce can cream-style corn		

Preheat oven to 400°. In a large bowl, mix all ingredients well. Pour into a heated, greased 9 x 13-inch pan or cornstick pan (filling each compartment ⅔ full), and bake until golden brown, about 35 minutes.

16 servings

Photo on page 160

HUSHPUPPIES

	Vegetable oil for frying	3	eggs
2	onions, diced	1	cup buttermilk
2	cups cornmeal		Salt, pepper and hot sauce to taste
½	cup flour		

In a large skillet or fryer, heat oil to about 375°, or until water pops when sprinkled in the pan. In a large bowl, mix all ingredients together. Drop by the spoonful into hot oil and fry until browned. Serve hot.

18-24 hushpuppies

Mistilis Restaurant, mid 1950s

Bottletree Bakery

WHOLE WHEAT MUFFINS WITH FRUIT

MUFFINS

3½ cups whole wheat flour

¾ cup sugar

1 teaspoon baking powder

¾ teaspoon baking soda

½ teaspoon salt

¾ cup vegetable oil

1½ cups buttermilk

1 teaspoon lemon juice

1 teaspoon lemon zest

2 cups diced fresh fruit or berries

STREUSEL TOPPING

1 cup sugar

1 cup flour

½ cup unsalted butter, melted

Preheat oven to 350°. In a mixing bowl, sift together flour, sugar, baking powder, baking soda and salt. Set aside. In a separate bowl combine oil, buttermilk, lemon juice and zest. Gently stir diced fruit or berries into flour mixture. Make a well in the center and pour in buttermilk mixture. Stir until barely blended. Spoon into greased muffin tins.

For topping, in a small bowl combine sugar, flour and butter. Sprinkle muffins with topping. Bake 20 minutes.

18 muffins

When I was a student in the late 1950s, when few students had cars, we used to walk through the Grove to go to church or to shop on the square, the only real shopping venue in Oxford. We also took this path when we had dates to attend the Lyric or Ritz Theatres or to have dinner at Mistilis Restaurant or at the Mansion Restaurant, where we would sometimes see William Faulkner in the booth next to ours.

~Julie Hart Walton

East entrance to the University, 1902

Path through the Grove, early 1900s

SOUR CREAM BLUEBERRY MUFFINS

MUFFINS

1	cup flour	1	egg, lightly beaten
⅔	cup sugar	¼	cup unsalted butter, melted
1	teaspoon baking powder	½	cup sour cream
1	teaspoon cinnamon	1	cup blueberries
¼	teaspoon salt		

GLAZE

½	cup confectioners' sugar	1	teaspoon lemon zest
1	tablespoon fresh lemon juice		

For the muffins, preheat oven to 375°. In a large mixing bowl, sift together the flour, sugar, baking powder, cinnamon and salt. Add egg, butter and sour cream. Stir until just combined. Fold in blueberries. Line muffin tins with paper liners and fill with batter. Bake until muffins spring back to the touch, 25-30 minutes. Let cool.

For glaze, in a small bowl whisk together confectioners' sugar, lemon juice and zest. Spread 1 teaspoon over each muffin. Let stand until glaze hardens.

12 muffins

MENU ▶

BRUNCH ON THE GROUNDS AT COLLEGE HILL PRESBYTERIAN CHURCH

Heirloom Tomato, Leek
and Cheese Tart
Spicy Brunch Bacon
Brown Sugar Strata
Sugar Baked Fruit
Brown Sugar Pound Cake
Yoknapatawpha Tea

BREAD STICKS

Butter on Biscuits

In my parents' home we grew up around the chopping block, and the busier our hands were with whisks and spoons, the looser our tongues became. We learned responsibility by not letting sauces burn, confidence by flipping fried eggs. We swapped advice along with recipes, and without even knowing it, we learned to talk, to listen, and to put our moods into words.

Daddy and I discussed my fifth-grade troubles until the timer reminded us of a cake in the oven. Licking cookie dough off the beater, my sister and I exchanged countless secrets. And when we

COATING

2	tablespoons cumin seeds
¼	cup brown sugar
1	teaspoon cinnamon

½	teaspoon chipotle chili powder
⅛	teaspoon cayenne pepper

BREADSTICKS

1	ounce dry yeast
1	cup very warm water
3	cups flour
2	teaspoons salt

¼	cup plus 1 tablespoon extra virgin olive oil, divided use
	Cornmeal to coat pans
1	egg
1	teaspoon water

For coating, in a heavy small skillet, toast 2 tablespoons cumin seeds until they pop and give off aroma. Cool and grind to a fine powder in spice grinder. In a small bowl mix ground cumin seeds with brown sugar, cinnamon, chili powder and cayenne. Set coating aside.

For breadsticks, dissolve yeast in warm water and set aside. In a mixing bowl stir together flour and salt. Mix in ¼ cup olive oil. Stir in yeast mixture. Transfer dough to a floured work surface and knead to form a smooth ball. Coat the inside of a mixing bowl with remaining 1 tablespoon of olive oil. Transfer dough to bowl and turn to coat all dough surfaces with oil. Cover bowl with plastic wrap. Let dough rise at room temperature until doubled in size, about 1 hour. Transfer dough to floured surface and knead very lightly to form a ball; return to greased bowl. Cover with plastic wrap and let rise again in refrigerator 2 hours, or up to 24 hours. Preheat oven to 325°. Cover 3 cookie sheets with cornmeal. Transfer dough to floured work surface. Press into a 9-inch square and cut into 2 rectangles, 4½ x 9 inches each. Cut rectangles into ½ x 4½-inch strips, for a total of 36 strips. Cover strips with plastic wrap to prevent dough from drying out. One at a time, roll strips into narrow, 15-inch strips. Breadsticks can then be formed into straight, wavy or spiral shapes. Arrange them on prepared cookie sheets, ½ inch apart, and let them rest for 10 minutes. In a small bowl beat egg lightly with 1 teaspoon water. Brush bread sticks with egg wash and sprinkle coating on each stick. Bake until browned, 20-30 minutes. Cool and store in an airtight container.

36 breadsticks

Photo on page 38

CRANBERRY COFFEE CAKE

1 cup unsalted butter, room temperature	8 ounces sour cream
2 cups sugar	½ cup fresh cranberries, rinsed
2 eggs	½ cup chopped pecans
1 teaspoon vanilla	⅓ cup firmly packed light brown sugar
2 cups flour	1 teaspoon ground cloves
1 teaspoon baking powder	1 teaspoon cinnamon
½ teaspoon salt	

Preheat oven to 325°. In the bowl of an electric mixer, cream butter and sugar together until fluffy. Add eggs one at a time, blending after each addition. In a small bowl stir together flour, baking powder and salt. Add to butter mixture alternately with sour cream, mixing well until blended. Pour half of batter into a greased and floured 12-cup Bundt pan and spread evenly. Mix together cranberries, pecans, brown sugar, cloves and cinnamon; sprinkle over batter. Top with remaining batter. Bake until toothpick inserted in cake center comes out clean, about 50 minutes. Cool 10 minutes in the pan, run knife along pan edges, and invert onto cooling rack.

16 servings

STRAWBERRY BREAD

1½ cups vegetable oil	3 cups flour
4 eggs, beaten	1 teaspoon baking soda
2 cups sugar	3 teaspoons cinnamon
½ teaspoon red food coloring	2 pints fresh strawberries, chopped
1 teaspoon salt	¾ cup chopped pecans

Preheat oven to 350°. In the bowl of an electric mixer, cream together oil, eggs, sugar and food coloring. Mix in salt, flour, soda and cinnamon. Stir in strawberries and pecans. Pour into 2 greased and floured 9 x 5-inch loaf pans. Bake 1 hour and 10 minutes.

2 loaves

needed our parents, we looked in the kitchen first.

Upset, I'd pull up a stool and eat oranges while Mama started supper. She would hand me a knife and say, "Chop these bell peppers while you tell me about it." I'd talk until she started to butter the biscuits just out of the oven. Her pats of butter would melt into yellow puddles, sending up tiny puffs of Southern-fried incense. Then she'd send me to call the others for dinner, and I'd leave the kitchen skipping, my hands smelling of oranges and peppers.

~Susan Tyner

177

CHALLAH

Artist Marty Vinograd
Artwork, page 180

Marty Reed Vinograd's collages are known nationally. Primarily a portraitist, Vinograd uses dresses, fur, fabric, flax, leather, beads, wood, shower caps, and other objects with paint, pastel, pen and ink, gold, silver, and copper leaf — all to suffuse added life and personality into her subjects. Her portraits and other work are in the University of Mississippi Museums, the USS Decatur, Washington, D.C.'s Decatur House, VMI Museums, and the Israeli Heritage International Bank. Her work has also been featured in solo exhibitions in France, Memphis, New Orleans, Oxford, Santa Monica, Ohio, and Washington, D.C.

1½	cups milk	½	cup very warm water
¼	cup sugar	2	ounces yeast
3	teaspoons salt	6-7	cups sifted flour
⅓	cup unsalted butter	1	tablespoon water
3	eggs	2	teaspoons poppy seeds

In a small heavy saucepan over low heat, combine milk, sugar, salt and butter. Cook until butter melts. Cool to lukewarm. Beat eggs in a small bowl. Reserve 2 tablespoons for glazing the bread. In the bowl of an electric mixer, pour very warm water and sprinkle with yeast. Stir until yeast dissolves. Stir in milk mixture and eggs. Beat in 3 cups flour until smooth. Beat in enough remaining flour to make a soft dough. Turn dough out onto a lightly floured surface and knead until smooth and elastic, about 5 minutes, using only as much flour as needed to keep dough from sticking. The sticky-soft dough will absorb flour as it is kneaded and will become a velvety-soft dough. Place in a large greased bowl and turn to coat all over. Cover with a clean towel. Let rise in a warm place, away from draft, until doubled in bulk, about 1½ hours. Punch dough down and let rise again, until almost doubled, about 30 minutes. Punch dough down again, turn out onto lightly floured surface and knead a few times. Divide dough into 6 even pieces. Roll each piece into a rope about 15 inches long. Place 3 ropes on a greased cookie sheet and plait into a braid; pinch and tuck ends under to fasten securely. Repeat with remaining 3 ropes of dough. Let rise again in a warm place, away from draft, until double in bulk, about 1 hour. Preheat oven to 350°. Combine reserved 2 tablespoons egg and 1 tablespoon water. Brush egg wash over braid and sprinkle with poppy seeds. Bake until braids are golden and give a hollow sound when tapped, 25-30 minutes. Transfer to wire racks and cool completely.

2 large loaves

Photo on page 160

Off the Square, 1920s

CRANBERRY SCONES

1½ cups fresh cranberries, rinsed and picked over	½ cup unsalted butter, chilled and cut in pieces
3 cups White Lily self-rising flour	⅔ cup buttermilk
½ cup sugar	2 tablespoons cream, optional
½ cup solid vegetable shortening, chilled and cut in pieces	2 tablespoons coarse sugar, optional

Preheat oven to 425°. In a food processor chop cranberries coarsely and set aside. In large mixing bowl, stir flour and sugar together. Using pastry blender, cut in shortening and butter until mixture is uniformly crumbly. Stir in chopped cranberries. Mix in enough buttermilk to make a slightly sticky dough that holds together. Turn out dough onto a heavily floured surface and pat to a 1-inch thickness. Cut into rounds with a biscuit cutter, or into triangles with a sharp knife and arrange on a parchment-lined cookie sheet. Brush tops with cream and sprinkle with coarse sugar, if desired. Bake until tops are browned, about 15 minutes.

Dried cherries, currants or cranberries may be substituted for fresh cranberries. Reduce sugar to ⅓ cup. For cinnamon scones, add 3 teaspoons cinnamon to flour and reduce the sugar to ⅓ cup.

12 scones

Photo on page 160

PUMPKIN BREAD

2¾ cups flour	1 teaspoon nutmeg
2 cups sugar	½ teaspoon ground cloves
1 teaspoon baking powder	1 cup canned pumpkin
2 teaspoons baking soda	3 large eggs
1½ teaspoons salt	1 cup canola oil
1½ teaspoons cinnamon	⅔ cup water
1 teaspoon allspice	

Preheat oven to 350°. In a large mixing bowl stir together the flour, sugar, baking powder, soda, salt and spices. Add pumpkin, eggs, oil and water and mix well. Spray three 1-pound coffee cans with nonstick cooking spray and divide batter evenly among each can. Bake until toothpick inserted in center comes out clean, 50-60 minutes.

3 loaves

Photo on page 160

Author Robert Khayat
Essay, page 181

Robert is the 15th Chancellor of the University of Mississippi. He earned B.A. and J.D. degrees from Ole Miss and his L.L.M. from Yale University. He joined the law faculty of the University of Mississippi in 1969, was named Vice Chancellor for University Affairs in 1984, and became Chancellor in July 1995. Since then, the University has experienced a renaissance. Enrollment has increased, private support has soared, and a chapter of Phi Beta Kappa was chartered.

179

THE GROVE at OLE MISS

Robert Khayat

"*Where the trees reach high their branches, To the whispering southern breeze.*" This verse from the Ole Miss Alma Mater rings familiar to all who visit The Grove at Ole Miss: fourteen acres of gently rolling green space resting in the shade of oak, maple, dogwood, and sycamore of varying ages. For 157 years students, faculty, staff, alumni, and visitors have experienced the loving embrace of this hallowed ground. Best known to most as America's premier game-day picnic site, The Grove is a versatile sanctuary that accommodates young lovers, annually welcomes thousands of parents, relatives, and friends for commencement, provides an amphitheater for concerts, and a playground for weekend frisbee, football, and softball. Young parents strolling children, weddings and receptions, summer dance and cheerleader camps affirm the utility of the generous, beautiful space. It has been said that Ole Miss is "mood and spirit," and to a great extent The Grove inspired those words.

For the academic community, the tone of the campus is set by The Grove. Faculty and students recognize and draw from the serenity and beauty of the landscape which washes away the tensions of the outer world.

For commencement audiences, The Grove extends its arms and embraces celebrants by providing a stage worthy of the milestone in the lives of the graduates and their families. As the pre-processional music floats across the land and through the trees, the joy of the occasion suggests a victory song. The spectacle of 1,500 participants converging on the scene, clad in academic regalia, excites the audience of 8,000 family members, friends, and observers. A sense of communal achievement shines through the symbolism and formality of the program … an unexpressed but deeply felt awareness of the family journey begun at home, through kindergarten and twelve grades of structured education. Truly a moment to remember.

These graduates and thousands of others will participate time after time, year after year in pre-game picnics on beautiful autumn Saturdays. Friendships are renewed and the finest southern cuisine consumed to the melodies of the Pride of the South Ole Miss marching band, as thousands gather in colorful tents resting comfortably in the safety and sanctity of The Grove. The revelers begin to arrive before daylight to claim a small area for their tents, tables and chairs, and to spread the picnic fare. Regardless of the time the game is to begin, the party is underway early and lasts late into the evening.

Ostensibly, all have come to witness a football game. In reality, the picnic in The Grove is as much a part of the game as the blocking, tackling, running, passing, and kicking. Our old friend we call The Grove is the magnet that brings friends together across the nation to enjoy a day being fed by the unique relationships between the people and the land. Regardless of one's interest in football or one's school affiliation, life at Ole Miss is incomplete until you enjoy game day in The Grove.

Following a visit to the Grand Canyon, Mr. William Alexander Percy wrote:

"I almost died at the sight of it. It is God's most personal creation; you feel He has just walked off and is expected back any moment." I suspect the gentleman would have had a similar experience had he witnessed a sunrise across The Grove at Ole Miss.

VFV by Marty Vinograd

Bourbon Chocolate Cake
Coconut Cupcakes
Strawberries Cardinal
Fabulous Lemon Meringue Pie

DESSERTS

BOURBON CHOCOLATE CAKE

CAKE

2 cups flour

1 teaspoon baking soda

½ teaspoon salt

1¾ cups strong, hot coffee

¼ cup bourbon

5 ounces unsweetened chocolate, chopped

1 cup unsalted butter, room temperature, cut into small pieces

2 cups sugar

2 eggs, room temperature

1 teaspoon vanilla

½ teaspoon almond extract

GANACHE

8 ounces heavy cream

12 ounces semisweet chocolate chips or chopped bittersweet chocolate

2 teaspoons bourbon

Chocolate will keep up to one year in the pantry if wrapped well and kept dry. It can be frozen or refrigerated, but may form a "bloom," or white film. The bloom is caused by moisture and does not alter the taste.

Preheat oven to 275°. Grease and flour two 8-inch round pans with 2-inch-high sides. In a bowl, sift together flour, soda and salt. Set aside. In a large covered bowl, put hot coffee, bourbon, chocolate and butter. Let rest until the chocolate is melted. Whisk to blend, then whisk in sugar. In a small bowl, beat eggs lightly and blend in extracts. Whisk flour mixture into chocolate mixture alternately with eggs and extracts, beginning and ending with flour mixture. Pour batter into prepared pans and bake on center oven rack until a toothpick inserted in center of cakes comes out clean, about 45 minutes. Cool cakes 15 minutes in the pans, run a knife around the edges, and invert onto cooling racks to cool completely.

For ganache, in heavy medium saucepan, bring cream to a simmer. Put chocolate in a large metal bowl and pour hot cream over. Let rest for 5 minutes, then whisk to blend and stir in bourbon. Let cool to room temperature. Whip with electric hand mixer until of frosting consistency. Fill and frost cake layers.

12-16 servings

Photo on page 182

WHITE CHOCOLATE CAKE
WITH STRAWBERRY BUTTERCREAM

Buttercream can be made one week ahead and stored in the refrigerator or one month ahead and stored in the freezer. Cover well or place in an airtight storage bag or container. When ready to use, allow time for it to come to room temperature, then beat it with an electric mixer until it returns to its smooth consistency.

CAKE

1½	cups cake flour	¾	cup sugar
1	teaspoon baking powder	2	eggs
¼	teaspoon salt	1	teaspoon vanilla
3	ounces white chocolate, chopped	¼	teaspoon almond extract
½	cup unsalted butter, room temperature	½	cup milk

BUTTERCREAM

1	pint strawberries	¼	teaspoon cream of tartar
6	ounces white chocolate, chopped	¾	cup unsalted butter, room temperature
½	cup sugar	1	teaspoon vanilla
3	tablespoons water	4	ounces white chocolate, shaved or curled, for garnish
1	tablespoon light corn syrup		Whole strawberries for garnish
3	egg whites, room temperature		

For cake, preheat oven to 350°. Grease and flour a 9-inch round cake pan with 2-inch-high sides and line with waxed paper. Sift flour, baking powder and salt into a bowl and set aside. Melt white chocolate in top of double boiler over medium heat, or in heatproof bowl in microwave on low power, stirring until chocolate is smooth. Set aside. In the bowl of an electric mixer, cream butter and sugar until fluffy. Add eggs one at a time, beating well after each addition. Mix in white chocolate mixture and extracts. Add flour mixture alternately with milk, beginning and ending with flour mixture. Pour batter into prepared pan. Bake on center rack of oven until toothpick inserted in the cake center comes out clean, about 30 minutes. Cool cake in the pan 10 minutes, run a knife along edges of pan and invert cake onto a cooling rack. Peel off paper and cool completely.

For buttercream, purée strawberries in a food processor and strain through a sieve to remove seeds; set aside. Melt white chocolate in the top of a double boiler set over medium heat, or in heatproof bowl in microwave on low power, stirring frequently. Cool chocolate and set aside. In a heavy small saucepan over medium heat, stir sugar, water and corn syrup until sugar dissolves. Increase heat and boil until candy thermometer submerged in syrup mixture registers 238°, about 5 minutes. In the bowl of an electric mixer, beat egg whites and cream of tartar until soft peaks form. Gradually add boiling sugar syrup and continue beating until meringue is stiff and cooled to barely lukewarm, about 5 minutes. Add butter 1 tablespoon at a time, beating well after each addition. Gradually add melted white chocolate and vanilla and continue beating until thick and smooth.

WHITE CHOCOLATE CAKE WITH STRAWBERRY BUTTERCREAM *continued*

To assemble, mix 1½ cups buttercream with ½ cup seedless strawberry purée. Slice cake layer in half horizontally with long serrated knife. Spread bottom layer with strawberry buttercream. Top with second cake layer. Frost with remaining plain buttercream. Garnish with chocolate curls and whole strawberries. Chill.

12 servings

This unusual Brown Sugar Pound Cake won an award at the Yoknapatawpha Arts Council annual picnic in 2004.

BROWN SUGAR POUND CAKE

CAKE

3	cups flour	1	pound light brown sugar
½	teaspoon baking powder	1	cup sugar
¼	teaspoon salt	5	eggs
¾	cup unsalted butter, room temperature	1	cup milk
¾	cup vegetable shortening, room temperature	1½	teaspoons vanilla
		1	cup pecans, chopped

ICING

⅓	cup unsalted butter, room temperature	3	tablespoons milk
⅔	cup packed brown sugar	1-1½	cups sifted confectioners' sugar

Preheat oven to 325°. Grease and flour a 10-inch tube pan. In a large bowl, sift together flour, baking powder and salt and set aside. In the bowl of an electric mixer, cream butter and shortening until light and fluffy. Gradually add brown sugar and then sugar, mixing until light and creamy. Add eggs one at a time, beating well after each addition. Add the flour mixture alternately with the milk, beginning and ending with flour mixture and beating each addition just until blended. Stir in vanilla and nuts. Spoon into prepared pan and bake on the center rack of oven until toothpick inserted in cake center comes out clean, about 1 hour, 10 minutes. Cool cake in the pan 10 minutes, run knife along pan edges, invert onto cooling rack, and cool completely.

For icing, melt butter in a heavy medium saucepan over medium heat. Stir in brown sugar. Boil 2 minutes. Add milk and confectioners' sugar and return to a boil, stirring constantly. Cool to lukewarm. Drizzle over cake.

14-16 servings

Photo on page 175

LE GÂTEAU AU CHOCOLAT

A dense, not-too-sweet chocolate cake with a bit of rum flavor

When shaving or curling chocolate, use a large block of smooth chocolate and a very sharp knife or vegetable peeler. Using extreme caution, hold the chocolate with one hand, and with the other hand, hold the knife or peeler at a 45° angle while pushing *away* from your body and across the top of the chocolate. A knife makes larger shavings, and a peeler smaller ones.

CAKE

6	1-ounce squares semisweet chocolate	1½	teaspoons baking soda
2	egg yolks, beaten	½	cup unsalted butter, room temperature
1	cup buttermilk	1⅓	cups packed brown sugar
3	cups flour	1	cup strong coffee
1	teaspoon salt	2	teaspoons vanilla

GLAZE

¼	cup unsalted butter, room temperature	½	cup rum
⅔	cup sugar		

FILLING

6	ounces semisweet chocolate chips	1	egg, beaten
½	cup evaporated milk		

FROSTING

2	cups heavy cream	Chocolate curls and shavings, for garnish
4	tablespoons sifted confectioners' sugar	
1	teaspoon vanilla	

For cake, preheat oven to 325°. Grease, flour, and line with waxed paper two 9-inch cake pans with 2-inch-high sides. In the top of a double boiler set over medium heat, melt chocolate squares and stir until smooth. Add egg yolks and stir to combine. Gradually stir in buttermilk and cook until mixture is the consistency of pudding, about 7 minutes. Cool. In a large bowl, sift together the flour, salt and soda and set aside. In the bowl of an electric mixer, cream the butter and sugar until light and fluffy. Mix in the flour mixture alternately with the coffee, beginning and ending with flour mixture. Mix in chocolate mixture and vanilla. Batter will be thick. Spoon batter into prepared pans and bake on the center oven rack until toothpick inserted in center of cakes comes out clean, about 30 minutes. Cool cakes in the pans 10 minutes. Run a knife along pan edges and invert cakes onto cooling racks.

For glaze, in a medium heavy saucepan over medium heat, cook butter, sugar and rum until sugar is dissolved.

For filling, in a medium heavy saucepan over medium heat, stir chocolate chips and evaporated milk together until chocolate is melted and smooth. Add egg, mix well, and chill until thick enough to spread.

LE GÂTEAU AU CHOCOLAT *continued*

- For frosting, in the chilled bowl of an electric mixer, whip cold cream until stiff peaks form. Whip in sugar and vanilla.

- To assemble, poke holes in cake layers with a toothpick and slowly pour half the glaze over each layer, waiting for glaze to be absorbed into the cake. Place one cake layer on serving plate and spread half of filling over the top. Top with second cake layer and the rest of the filling. Frost entire cake with frosting and garnish with chocolate curls and shavings. Refrigerate.

12-16 servings

Make sure that your dessert is healthy as your entrée. Carrots not only have benefits to eyesight, but also can lower cholesterol and prevent heart attacks and cancer.

CARROT CAKE

CAKE

2½ cups flour	1 8-ounce can crushed pineapple
1 teaspoon baking soda	3 eggs, lightly beaten
1 teaspoon cinnamon	2 teaspoons vanilla
1 teaspoon salt	2 cups grated carrots
2 cups sugar	1 cup chopped walnuts
1½ cups vegetable oil	

FROSTING

½ cup unsalted butter, room temperature	4 cups confectioners' sugar
16 ounces cream cheese, room temperature	4 teaspoons vanilla
	Chopped walnuts, optional

- Preheat oven to 350°. Grease, flour, and line with waxed paper two 9-inch round cake pans with 2-inch-high sides. In a large bowl, combine flour, baking soda, cinnamon, salt and sugar. Add oil, pineapple, eggs and vanilla and stir to combine. Add carrots and walnuts and stir to combine. Pour into prepared pans and bake on center oven rack about 35 minutes, or until toothpick inserted in cake center comes out clean. Cool in pans 10 minutes, run knife along pan edges, and invert cakes onto cooling racks to cool completely.

- For frosting, in the bowl of an electric mixer, cream butter and cream cheese. Mix in confectioners' sugar and vanilla and beat until of spreading consistency. If necessary, thicken with more confectioners' sugar or thin with milk or cream. Fill and frost cake and garnish with walnuts, if desired.

12-16 servings

RATTLING RUM CAKE

A trip to town on Saturday was a big event. The Square in Oxford has changed some, true, but by and large it still retains the image I have of it from thirty years ago. It is still lined with stores and parked cars, and the big oaks still stand on the courthouse lawn, and the Confederate soldier is still standing there high above everything so that you can see him first when you come up the long drive of South Lamar. What has changed is the nature of the town. A long time ago you could find people selling vegetables from the backs of their trucks, and you could go in Winter's Café and get a hamburger and a short-bottled Coke for sixty-five cents. You can't even buy an Egg McMuffin on University Avenue for that.

~Larry Brown

Billy Ray's Farm

SPONGE CAKE

6	eggs, lightly beaten	1	cup flour
1	cup sugar	¼	cup unsalted butter, melted and cooled

SYRUP

6	tablespoons light rum	6	tablespoons liqueur of choice (such as Grand Marnier, Amaretto or Frangelico)

FROSTING

3	cups heavy cream	½	cup sugar

FILLING

⅔	cup toasted, chopped almonds	8	ounces bittersweet chocolate, finely chopped

OPTIONAL GARNISH

Chopped nuts

Chocolate curls

Toasted coconut

For cake, preheat oven to 350°. Grease, flour, and line with waxed paper three 8-inch round cake pans with 2-inch-high sides. In a large mixing bowl, combine eggs and sugar. Place bowl over a large pan of simmering water, being careful not to let the bowl touch the water. Slowly heat the egg mixture until it is just warm, stirring frequently. Remove from heat and beat mixture with electric mixer on high speed until thick and more than doubled in volume. Sprinkle flour about ⅓ cup at a time over egg mixture and gently fold until well combined. Fold in butter. Pour batter into prepared pans and bake on the center rack of oven until cake is just light brown around the edges, 20-25 minutes. Cool cakes in pans 10 minutes, run knife around pan edges, and invert onto cooling racks. Cool completely.

For syrup, in a small bowl combine rum and liqueur.

For frosting, in the chilled bowl of an electric mixer, whip cream, gradually adding sugar until stiff peaks form.

To assemble, place one cake layer on serving plate. Brush with ⅓ of syrup, spread liberally with sweetened whipped cream, and top with ½ of the nuts and ½ of the chopped chocolate. Repeat with the second layer. Top with third cake layer and frost cake with remaining sweetened whipped cream. If desired, garnish cake by pressing chopped nuts, chocolate curls and toasted coconut into the sides and top of cake.

12-16 servings

HAROLD'S COCONUT CAKE

CAKE

2⅔ cups cake flour

4 teaspoons baking powder

¼ teaspoon salt

1 cup unsalted butter, room temperature

2 cups sugar

4 eggs, separated

1 cup milk

1 teaspoon vanilla

FROSTING

1 egg yolk

1 cup milk

1 cup sugar

1 tablespoon cornstarch

1 teaspoon vanilla

1 coconut, grated or one 7-ounce bag frozen coconut

The Ole Miss Drive Inn was one of very few restaurants in Oxford in the 1950s. It was on West Jackson Avenue, which at the time seemed way out of town.

Preheat oven to 375°. Grease, flour and line with waxed paper three 8-inch round cake pans with 2-inch-high sides. In a large bowl, combine flour, baking powder and salt. Set aside. In the bowl of an electric mixer, cream butter and sugar. Add egg yolks one at a time, blending well after each addition. Blend in the flour mixture alternately with milk, beginning and ending with flour mixture. Blend in vanilla. In another bowl, beat egg whites with an electric mixer until stiff peaks form. Fold egg whites into batter and pour batter into prepared pans. Bake on the center oven rack until a toothpick inserted into cake center comes out clean, 20-25 minutes. Cool cakes in pans 10 minutes, run a knife along pan edges, and invert cakes onto cooling racks to cool completely.

For frosting, in a heavy medium saucepan over medium heat, combine egg yolk, milk, sugar and cornstarch. Cook, stirring constantly, until mixture thickens to pudding consistency, about 7 minutes. Remove from heat and add vanilla and coconut. Cool. Spread frosting between and on top of layers, but not on sides.

12-16 servings

Ole Miss Drive Inn, 1950s

RED VELVET CAKE

CAKE

2¼	cups flour		2	eggs
½	teaspoon salt		1	teaspoon vanilla
2	ounces liquid red food coloring		1	cup buttermilk
2	tablespoons cocoa powder		1	teaspoon baking soda
½	cup unsalted butter, room temperature		1	tablespoon white vinegar
1½	cups sugar			

FROSTING

½	cup unsalted butter, room temperature		1	teaspoon milk
8	ounces cream cheese, room temperature		1	tablespoon vanilla
1	pound confectioners' sugar, sifted		1	cup chopped pecans, optional

For cake, preheat oven to 325°. Grease and flour two 9-inch round cake pans with 2-inch-high sides. In a small bowl, sift flour and salt together and set aside. In another bowl, combine red food coloring and cocoa powder and set aside. In the bowl of an electric mixer, cream butter and sugar. Blend in eggs one at a time. Stir in cocoa mixture and vanilla. Mix in flour mixture alternately with the buttermilk, beginning and ending with flour mixture. Fold in baking soda and vinegar. Pour batter into prepared pans and bake on center oven rack until a toothpick inserted in cake center comes out clean, 20-30 minutes. Cool in the pans 10 minutes, run a knife along pan edges, invert cakes onto cooling racks, and cool completely.

For frosting, in the bowl of an electric mixer, cream butter and cream cheese. Gradually add confectioners' sugar, milk and vanilla, beating until of spreading consistency. Stir in pecans, if desired. Fill and frost cake layers.

12-16 servings

Neilson's Department Store, about 1940

MERINGUE CAKE WITH RASPBERRY SAUCE

This recipe originated in Baltimore and has traveled to Virginia, Ohio, West Virginia, and now Mississippi. It makes a terrific no-flour cake for Passover.

CAKE

Soft butter and sugar for coating pan
12 egg whites, room temperature
⅛ teaspoon cream of tartar

2¼ cups sugar
2 teaspoons vanilla
1 teaspoon almond extract

FROSTING

1 cup heavy cream
3 tablespoons confectioners' sugar

1 teaspoon vanilla

SAUCE

2 cups frozen raspberries, thawed
¾ cup sifted confectioners' sugar

¼ cup orange-flavored liqueur
1 tablespoon frozen orange juice concentrate

Raspberries don't have to be fresh to be nutritious. According to health experts, frozen raspberries may retain nutrients better than fresh ones that have been shipped or kept in cold storage.

For cake, preheat oven to 450°. Butter a 10-inch tube pan and dust with sugar. In the bowl of an electric mixer, beat egg whites and cream of tartar until frothy. Gradually add sugar, beating until stiff peaks form. Fold in extracts. Gently spoon batter into prepared pan and place in center of hot oven for 1 minute. Turn oven off and leave the door closed for 6-8 hours. Remove cake from oven and run knife along edges of pan. Invert cake onto serving plate.

For frosting, in the chilled bowl of an electric mixer, whip cream, gradually adding confectioners' sugar and vanilla, beating until stiff peaks form.

For sauce, place all ingredients in a food processor or blender and process until smooth. Using the back of a spoon, push the mixture through a sieve to remove seeds. Chill.

For assembly, frost the cake with frosting and serve raspberry sauce alongside.

10-12 servings

St. Peter's Episcopal Church, about 1900

THE BEST POUND CAKE

The Best Pound Cake was an award winner at the 2004 Yoknapatawpha Arts Council picnic. Serve with Raspberry Sauce (page 191) and sweetened whipped cream for an outstanding dessert.

1 cup unsalted butter, room temperature	3 cups flour, sifted
16 ounces cream cheese, room temperature	¼ teaspoon baking soda
3 cups sugar	1 tablespoon vanilla
6 eggs	1 teaspoon almond extract or 2 teaspoons lemon extract

Preheat oven to 325°. Grease and flour a 10-inch tube pan. In the bowl of an electric mixer, cream butter and cream cheese. Gradually add sugar and cream until light and fluffy. Mix in eggs, one at a time, blending after each addition. Mix in flour, baking soda and extracts. Spoon into prepared pan and bake on the center rack of oven until toothpick inserted in cake center comes out clean, about 1 hour. Cool in the pan 15 minutes, run knife along pan edges, and invert onto cooling rack.

14-16 servings

KILLER CUPCAKES

CUPCAKES

4 ounces semisweet chocolate	1 teaspoon vanilla
1 cup unsalted butter	1 cup flour
4 eggs	¼ teaspoon salt
1½ cups sugar	

FILLING

8 ounces cream cheese, room temperature	1 egg, lightly beaten
¼ cup sugar	1 dash salt
	1 cup semisweet chocolate chips

For cupcakes, preheat oven to 350°. Line muffin tins with paper liners. In a heatproof bowl, melt chocolate and butter together in the microwave on low power or in a heavy saucepan on the stove over lowest heat, stirring frequently. Set aside to cool. In the bowl of an electric mixer, beat the eggs until thick and lemon-colored. Beat in the sugar, vanilla, flour and salt. Beat in cooled chocolate mixture. Spoon into prepared muffin tins, filling ⅔ full.

For filling, mix cream cheese, sugar, egg and salt until just blended. Stir in chocolate chips. Drop a rounded teaspoonful of filling onto the top of each cupcake. Bake 30 minutes.

20-22 cupcakes

COCONUT CUPCAKES

CUPCAKES

1½	cups flour	3	eggs
½	teaspoon baking powder	¾	teaspoon vanilla
¼	teaspoon baking soda	¾	teaspoon almond extract
¼	teaspoon salt	½	cup buttermilk
¾	cup unsalted butter, room temperature	3½	ounces sweetened, shredded coconut
1	cup sugar		

FROSTING

¾	cup unsalted butter, room temperature	½	teaspoon vanilla
8	ounces cream cheese, room temperature	¼	teaspoon almond extract
2½	cups confectioners' sugar, sifted	3½	ounces sweetened, shredded coconut

For cupcakes, preheat oven to 325°. In a small bowl, combine flour, baking powder, soda and salt and set aside. In the bowl of an electric mixer, cream butter and sugar until light and fluffy. Add eggs one at a time, blending after each. Blend in extracts. Blend in flour mixture alternately with the buttermilk, beginning and ending with flour mixture. Fold in coconut. Line muffin tins with papers and spoon batter almost to the top of each cup. Bake until tops are golden brown and a toothpick inserted into center of cupcakes comes out clean, 20-25 minutes for oversized cupcakes, or 15-20 minutes for standard ones. Cool in the pan 15 minutes, then remove onto cooling racks to cool completely.

For frosting, in the bowl of an electric mixer, cream butter and cream cheese and blend in confectioners' sugar and extracts until of spreading consistency. Frost cupcakes and sprinkle with coconut.

9 oversized cupcakes or 18 standard cupcakes

Photo on page 182

Thompson House, about 1900

Inell's Chocolate Icing

Inell Carter has cooked for my family for 35 years. She puts this icing on devil's food cake. It has been our family birthday cake for as long as I can remember.

~Ginny Self Terry

1 (5.33-ounce) can evaporated milk

4 ounces semisweet chocolate

½ cup unsalted butter

1 teaspoon vanilla

In the top of a double boiler, put milk, chocolate and butter. Simmer until mixture melts and thickens, stirring often. Remove from heat and stir in vanilla. Spread on cooled cakes.

1½ cups

DINNER PARTY APPLE PIE

This pie smells great while cooking, and is simple and delectable. Serve it with vanilla or butter pecan ice cream.

3	tart apples, peeled, cored and sliced	1	teaspoon cinnamon
	Juice of 1 lemon	¾	cup unsalted butter, melted
2	teaspoons bourbon	1	cup sifted flour
¾	cup plus 2 tablespoons sugar, divided use	¼	teaspoon salt
		1	egg, lightly beaten

Preheat oven to 350°. Sprinkle apple slices with lemon juice and arrange them in a 9-inch buttered pie pan. Sprinkle with bourbon, 1 tablespoon sugar and cinnamon. In a small bowl, mix melted butter with ¾ cup sugar, flour, salt and egg. Stir until smooth. Spread batter over apples and sprinkle with 1 tablespoon sugar. Bake until crusty and pale gold, about 40 minutes.

6-8 servings

Three excellent varieties of tart apples for cooking are Granny Smith, Cortland and York.

BLACKBERRY COBBLER

This delicious comfort dessert is easy to prepare and gets rave reviews. Serve warm with vanilla ice cream.

3	cups fresh or frozen blackberries, thawed	2	teaspoons baking powder
1½	cups sugar, divided use	¼	teaspoon salt
½	cup unsalted butter	½	teaspoon cinnamon
¾	cup flour	¾	cup milk
		2	tablespoons fresh lemon juice

In a large glass or plastic bowl, put berries and sprinkle with ½ cup sugar. Let rest to extract juice from berries. Preheat oven to 350°. Put butter in a 9 x 12-inch baking dish and place in the oven just until butter is melted. In a mixing bowl, whisk together remaining sugar, flour, baking powder, salt and cinnamon. Whisk in milk and lemon juice. Pour batter evenly over melted butter. Do not stir. Spoon fruit evenly over batter. Do not stir. Bake in upper ⅓ of oven until golden brown, about 45 minutes.

8 servings

FABULOUS LEMON MERINGUE PIE

CRUST

1½ cups graham cracker crumbs

7 tablespoons unsalted butter, melted

FILLING

1 15-ounce can sweetened condensed milk

½ cup fresh lemon juice

1 teaspoon grated lemon zest

2 egg yolks

MERINGUE

5 egg whites, room temperature

¼ teaspoon cream of tartar

10 tablespoons sugar

For crust, preheat oven to 350°. Mix graham cracker crumbs with melted butter and press onto bottom and sides of 9-inch pie pan. Bake until crust is lightly browned on the edges, 10-15 minutes. Cool crust.

For filling, blend all ingredients and pour into prepared crust. Set aside.

For meringue, in the bowl of an electric mixer, beat egg whites until frothy. Add cream of tartar and beat until soft peaks form. Gradually add sugar, beating until stiff peaks form. Spoon meringue onto pie filling. Bake until tips of meringue are lightly browned, 10-15 minutes. Cool to room temperature.

7-8 servings

Photo on page 182

To make a fabulous lime pie, substitute lime juice and lime zest for the lemon juice and zest. Pour filling into prepared crust and bake 10 minutes. Cool pie to room temperature, then refrigerate. Top with sweetened whipped cream instead of meringue.

CRANBERRY TART

1½ cups fresh cranberries, rinsed and picked over

1¾ cups sugar, divided use

1½ cups flour

½ teaspoon salt

2 eggs, lightly beaten

½ cup unsalted butter, melted

Walnut halves, optional

Sweetened whipped cream

Preheat oven to 325°. Grease a 9-inch pie plate. Pour cranberries into pie plate and sprinkle with ¼ cup sugar. In a small bowl, stir together flour, remaining 1½ cups sugar, salt, eggs and butter. Press dough evenly over cranberries. Decorate top with walnut halves and bake on center oven rack 1 hour. Cool until warm and serve with sweetened whipped cream.

8 servings

People often confuse tarts and tortes. A tart is similar to a pie and has a shallow pastry crust with a filling. A torte is a layer cake made with breadcrumbs, cake crumbs, or ground nuts, and can be filled with whipped cream, jam, or buttercream.

PEACH CRISP

To peel fresh, ripe peaches, submerge them in boiling water for 1-2 minutes, then immediately place them in an ice bath. The skin will rub off easily.

4   cups peeled and sliced fresh peaches
¾   cup sugar, divided use
½   teaspoon cinnamon
1   cup flour

¼   teaspoon salt
½   cup cold unsalted butter, cut into small pieces
    Vanilla, cinnamon or rum ice cream

Preheat oven to 375°. Grease a 9-inch square baking dish. Sprinkle peaches with about half the sugar and ½ teaspoon cinnamon and spoon them into prepared baking dish. In a medium bowl, stir together the flour, salt and remaining sugar. Cut the butter into the flour mixture with a pastry blender or two forks until mixture resembles oats. Sprinkle over the peaches and bake 30 minutes or until golden brown. Serve warm with ice cream.

6 servings

UPSIDE-DOWN APPLE PECAN PIE

This clever presentation of the classic apple pie is best served warm with vanilla ice cream.

4   tablespoons unsalted butter, room temperature
1   cup packed brown sugar, divided
⅔   cup pecan halves
2   prepared pie crusts
6   cups peeled, sliced apples

    Juice of 1 lemon
1   tablespoon flour
½   teaspoon cinnamon
½   teaspoon nutmeg
¼   teaspoon salt

Preheat oven to 450°. In a small bowl, combine butter and ⅔ cup brown sugar and spread evenly in the bottom of a 10-inch pie pan. Arrange pecan halves in a design on the pie pan bottom, pressing into the sugar mixture. Roll out each pie crust to about a 10-inch diameter. Cover pecans with 1 pie crust leaving ½-inch of pastry hanging over the sides. In a mixing bowl, sprinkle the apples with lemon juice and set aside. In another bowl, combine remaining ⅓ cup brown sugar, flour, cinnamon, nutmeg and salt. Add the apples and stir well. Pile apples on the pie crust, making as level a surface as possible. Cover with the second pie crust. Fold top crust over bottom crust, wetting the edges to seal as you go. Flute edges and prick top crust with a fork. Bake 10 minutes, then reduce oven temperature to 350° and bake 45 minutes longer, covering the top with foil if necessary to prevent excess browning. Remove from oven. When syrup in the pan stops bubbling, place serving plate over pie and invert. Remove pie pan.

7-8 servings

CARAMEL COBBLER

½ cup unsalted butter

1½ cups self-rising flour

1½ cups sugar

¾ cup milk

1 teaspoon vanilla

1½ cups packed light brown sugar

1½ cups hot water

Ice cream or sweetened whipped cream

Preheat oven to 350°. In a 9 x 13-inch pan, place butter and put in the oven just until butter melts. In a mixing bowl, combine flour, sugar, milk and vanilla. Stir to combine. Pour over melted butter and do not stir. Sprinkle brown sugar over batter. Add water slowly and do not stir. Bake until golden brown, about 35 minutes. Serve warm with ice cream or sweetened whipped cream.

12-15 servings

FRENCH SILK CHOCOLATE PIE

CRUST

4 tablespoons unsalted butter

½ cup finely chopped pecans

1 cup shredded coconut

FILLING

½ cup unsalted butter, room temperature

¾ cup sugar

2 ounces unsweetened chocolate, melted and cooled

1 teaspoon vanilla

2 eggs

Sweetened whipped cream

For crust, in a heavy skillet over medium-high heat, melt butter. Add pecans and coconut. Cook, stirring frequently, until golden brown. Press into a 9-inch pie pan and cool.

For filling, in the bowl of an electric mixer, cream butter and sugar until light and fluffy. Blend in chocolate and vanilla. Add eggs one at a time, beating 5 minutes after each addition. If mixture appears grainy after beating in the second egg, continue to beat until smooth. Spoon into pie shell and chill. Serve with sweetened whipped cream.

7-8 servings

It is the proximity of Oxford and the Ole Miss campus, each populated with about 10,000 souls, which has given my homecoming its poignance, for both have tender resonances of an older past. Youth and age are in healthy proportion, and the loyalty of the town to the university is both exuberant and touching.

~Willie Morris

"Coming on Back"

Miss Daisye Wade Hampton is a four star general in a predominately female Southern army that wages war against fathers, grandfathers, husbands, sons, and even against its own kind in defense of its cause: the absolute abstaining of everybody from alcohol.

The Miss Daisyes of this world are clean livers who have never sipped an alcoholic beverage and do not intend to. Yet something strange happens in kitchens all over the South as the holiday season approaches. These devout supporters of the Women's Christian Temperance Union haul out the Bacardi, the Jack Daniels, the George Dickel called for in their recipes, and pour them with as heavy a hand as a

Bottletree Bakery

GERLACH PUMPKIN PIE

1	15-ounce can pumpkin	¼	teaspoon ginger
1	15-ounce can sweetened condensed milk	¼	teaspoon nutmeg
1	egg	½	cup California sherry
½	teaspoon salt	½	cup hot water
½	teaspoon cinnamon	1	9-inch unbaked pastry shell

Preheat oven to 375°. In a large bowl, combine all ingredients and beat vigorously until well blended. Pour into unbaked pastry shell and bake on center oven rack 50 minutes, or until golden brown.

7-8 servings

BUTTERMILK CHESS PIE

First-place winner at "Pie Bake à la Oxford," at the Mid-Town Farmers' Market

2	cups sugar	½	cup butter, melted
2	tablespoons flour	1	teaspoon vanilla
5	eggs, lightly beaten	1	unbaked 9-inch pastry shell
⅔	cup buttermilk		

Preheat oven to 350°. In a large bowl, combine sugar and flour. Add eggs and buttermilk, stirring until blended. Stir in butter and vanilla and pour mixture into pastry shell. Bake until set, about 45 minutes. Cool.

7-8 servings

Ladies at the Depot, 1920s

POTS DE CRÈME

6	ounces semisweet chocolate chips	1	tablespoon rum, Kahlúa or vanilla
¾	cup milk	1	teaspoon instant coffee granules
1	egg		Pinch salt
2	tablespoons sugar		

In a blender, put chocolate chips. In a heavy, small saucepan, bring milk to a simmer and pour over chocolate chips. Add egg, sugar, flavoring, coffee granules and salt. Blend on high for 1 minute. Pour mixture into sherbet glasses and chill until cold, about 4 hours.

6-8 servings

WHITE CHOCOLATE MOUSSE WITH STRAWBERRIES

CRUST

2	cups vanilla wafers	¼	cup unsalted butter, room temperature
⅓	cup sugar	1	cup toasted almonds

MOUSSE

6	ounces white chocolate, melted and cooled	¾	cup chilled heavy cream
2	tablespoons Cointreau	1	pint strawberries, washed, hulled and sliced

For crust, preheat oven to 350°. In food processor put vanilla wafers, sugar, butter and almonds. Pulse until combined. Divide crumb mixture among 6 heatproof bowls (we use McCarty pottery cups), pressing crumbs to cover the bottom and up the sides about an inch. Bake 8 minutes.

For mousse, in a small bowl combine melted chocolate and Cointreau and set aside. In the bowl of an electric mixer, whip cream until stiff peaks form. Fold cream into chocolate mixture. Divide mousse among prepared dishes. Refrigerate at least 4 hours. Arrange strawberries on top of mousse just before serving.

4-6 servings

country club bartender on New Year's Eve.

Perhaps it is the uninhibiting, festive air of the season that so affects them. But there is also a refusal on their part to recognize, much less admit, that the same demon that lurked in Big Dad's rum bottle could possibly be released on a bright sunny morning in *their* kitchens. Nothing could be wrong with a liquid that looks and smells that good, not if it's thoroughly beaten into a batter of flour, sugar, eggs, vanilla, and cream. Served their way, 90 proof Jack Daniels becomes little more than a kissing cousin to vanilla extract.

~Dean Faulkner Wells

"Letter from South Lamar"

199

CHOCOLATE PÂTÉ

18 ounces semisweet chocolate, chopped
½ cup unsalted butter
5 eggs, separated
½ teaspoon cream of tartar

2 cups heavy cream, chilled
3 ounces rum, Kahlúa, or your favorite liqueur
Berries
Sweetened whipped cream

Line a 5 x 9-inch loaf pan with parchment paper and spray with nonstick cooking spray. Chill pan in freezer. Melt chocolate and butter slowly in top of double boiler and set aside. In the bowl of an electric mixer, whip egg whites with cream of tartar until stiff peaks form. Set aside. In a chilled bowl, whip the cream until stiff peaks form. In a large bowl, mix egg yolks with liqueur, then stir in melted chocolate. Fold egg whites into chocolate mixture until mostly blended, then fold in cream and mix just until blended. Spoon into prepared loaf pan, freeze until firm, unmold, and slice onto dessert plates. Top with berries and sweetened whipped cream.

For a smoother cooking experience, see tips at left.

12 servings

■ Make sure to dry the pan thoroughly before melting the chocolate, and don't melt the chocolate all the way over heat. Melt it only two-thirds of the way, then remove from heat to finish.

■ There should be no fat in the bowl used for beating egg whites, or they will not stiffen well.

■ Make sure the cream is very cold. Put the bowl, beaters and cream in the freezer for ten minutes before beating.

■ *Main Street Grill, Water Valley* ■

COSMOPOLITAN BREAD PUDDING

10 eggs
1 quart half-and-half
2 cups sugar
Grated zest of 1 lime

1½ cups dried cranberries
2 quarts cubed stale white bread with no seeds

Preheat oven to 350°. Grease a 9 x 13-inch glass baking dish. In a large mixing bowl, add eggs and beat lightly. Add half-and-half, sugar, lime zest and cranberries and stir to combine. Add bread and mix well. Pour into prepared pan and cover with foil. In a larger baking pan, pour hot water until pan is filled about 1 inch up the sides. Put pudding in water bath and bake 45 minutes. Remove foil and bake until lightly browned on top, 5-7 minutes. Serve with Duke's Boiled Custard, page 201.

12 servings

MOCHA VELVET TORTE

A rich, smooth, intense chocolate dessert

GANACHE

1   cup heavy cream

8   ounces bittersweet chocolate, finely chopped

TORTE

½   cup coffee

½   cup Kahlúa

1½ cups sugar

2½ cups semisweet chocolate chips

1½ cups unsalted butter, melted

6   eggs

1   teaspoon vanilla

For ganache, in a heavy medium saucepan over high heat, bring cream just to a simmer. Turn off heat and add chopped chocolate. When chocolate has melted, whisk to blend. Set aside to cool and thicken slightly.

For torte, preheat oven to 225°. Grease bottom and sides of a 9-inch springform pan and line bottom with greased waxed paper. In a heavy medium saucepan over medium heat, bring coffee and Kahlúa to a simmer. Add sugar and cook, stirring, until sugar dissolves. Set aside. Position metal blade in food processor bowl and add chocolate chips. Process until chocolate is finely chopped. Pour hot coffee mixture through food chute with processor running. Pour melted butter through food chute with processor running. Add eggs through food chute one at a time, pulsing after each until blended. Add vanilla and pulse to blend. Open food processor, scrape down sides and stir mixture. Pour into prepared pan and bake until slightly firm, about 2½ hours. Cool completely on a wire rack. Run a knife along pan edges, release springform pan sides, and invert onto an 8-inch cardboard circle.

On a rack over a shallow pan, pour ganache over torte, covering top and sides. Chill 8 hours before serving.

16 servings

Photo on page 42

Duke's Boiled Custard

9 egg yolks

3 cups sugar

4 cups half-and-half

4 cups whole milk

2-3 tablespoons vanilla

In the bowl of an electric mixer, beat egg yolks and sugar until lemon yellow. Set aside. In a large saucepan over medium low heat, pour half-and-half and milk. Stir constantly with a whisk until milk mixture forms tiny bubbles at the edges. Pour 2 cups of hot milk mixture into the egg mixture and stir. Pour egg mixture back into the saucepan and cook, stirring with a whisk, until custard is thick enough to coat the back of a spoon. Remove from heat and add vanilla to taste. Chill.

about 3 quarts

Yocona River Inn

CRÈME BRÛLÉE

Do not be intimidated by the length of this recipe.
It is actually very simple to prepare this classic baked custard.

4	cups heavy cream	½	cup vanilla sugar (see note)
	Grated zest of 1 lemon or orange		Sugar for sprinkling
7	egg yolks		

Prepared custard may be refrigerated before baking for up to one week. Pour it in the smallest possible container and put plastic wrap directly on the surface of custard. Before baking, remove custard from refrigerator, leave plastic wrap on, and allow it to come to room temperature. Remove plastic wrap and put custard dish(es) in a cold oven, then turn oven to 300° and expect 10 minutes more baking time.

Preheat oven to 300°. In a heavy large saucepan over lowest heat, put cream and zest. Heat slowly until tiny bubbles form at the edges. Remove from heat. In a large mixing bowl, whisk together egg yolks and sugar until evenly distributed. Slowly drizzle in warm cream mixture while stirring with the whisk. Continue drizzling until outside of bowl is hot to the touch, then pour in remainder of cream mixture all at once and stir until well blended. Pour custard through a fine sieve to remove any lumps. Pour strained custard into individual baking dishes or one large baking dish, making sure that custard is not more than 1-inch deep. Place dish(es) in a large pan deep enough to hold water halfway up sides of custard dish(es). Pull out top oven rack a few inches, place large baking pan filled with custard dish(es) on the rack, and fill pan with boiling water to about half the depth of custard dish(es). Carefully slide oven rack into the oven, making sure that no water spills into custard. Bake custard until it jiggles uniformly when shaken, like gelatin cubes. Cooking time will vary depending on dish size. Check after 30 minutes, then again every 15 minutes. Watch custard to see that it does not brown too much, covering with foil if necessary. When custard has reached the gelatinous stage, remove baking pan from oven, dry outside of custard dish(es), cover with plastic wrap and refrigerate at least 2 hours.

Up to an hour before serving, sprinkle surface of custard lightly with sugar. Using a handheld torch, carefully caramelize the sugar, moving flame constantly to dissolve sugar without burning. Serve immediately or refrigerate up to 1 hour. (It is possible to caramelize the sugar using the oven's broil setting instead of a torch. Be sure to turn the custard frequently under the broiler and watch carefully. If using the oven, refrigerate custard after broiling since the oven tends to warm the custard more than does a torch.)

Vanilla sugar is granulated sugar that has been stored with a vanilla bean in it, allowing the sugar to soak up the flavor of the vanilla. To substitute granulated sugar for vanilla sugar, scrape the seeds from half a vanilla bean into the cream and omit zest from the recipe.

10-12 servings

MANDY'S KEY LIME CHEESECAKE

A friend saw this cheesecake at a restaurant and asked me to recreate it. It's now one of my most requested items!

CRUST

½ cup shredded coconut

1¾ cups graham cracker crumbs

¼ teaspoon salt

1 tablespoon sugar

½ cup unsalted butter, melted

FILLING

24 ounces cream cheese, room temperature

1 cup packed brown sugar

3 eggs

1 cup sour cream

½ cup Key lime juice

■ For crust, preheat oven to 350°. In food processor put coconut and pulse a few times to chop. In a small bowl combine coconut, graham cracker crumbs, salt, sugar and butter. Stir until combined. Press on the bottom and 2 inches up the sides of a 9-inch springform pan. Bake 10 minutes. Cool on a wire rack.

■ For filling, in the bowl of an electric mixer, place cream cheese and beat until smooth with the paddle attachment. Scrape down the sides and add brown sugar. Beat 1 minute more. Add eggs one at a time, beating until combined. Beat in sour cream and lime juice. Pour filling into crust. Bake on center oven rack in a water bath 1 hour or until set. Center of cheesecake will still jiggle and top will not be brown. Once set, turn oven off and let cheesecake sit 30 minutes in oven. Cool on a wire rack. Refrigerate 12 hours or overnight. When ready to serve, transfer cheesecake to serving platter and remove springform sleeve.

12 servings

To ensure a creamy texture throughout a cheesecake, bake it in a water bath. Cover the bottom and sides of the springform pan with a large sheet of heavy duty aluminum foil to prevent leaking and a soggy crust. Place springform pan in a baking dish that is at least 4 inches wider and no deeper than the springform pan. Pour boiling water into the baking dish until about half full. Carefully place in the oven so that no water spills into the cheesecake.

WWI Soldiers in Formation on the Square, 1917

HOKA CHEESECAKE

The Hoka of the Mississippi Oxford, named after the tenacious Chickasaw princess, is situated across an alleyway from a bar reconverted from an old cotton gin. One is witness in this boondocks avant-garde coffeehouse to the true variety of Ole Miss and Oxford life, as opposed to the enclaves of Sorority and Fraternity Rows. It is presided over by Ron Shapiro, a much beloved St. Louis transplant, a kind of white Jewish Rastaman, and one Jim Dees, a Deltan who writes essays under the nom-de-plume "Dr. Bubba." The auditorium in back will have the classic European and American movies. Up front B. B. King will be on the stereo, or the Grateful Dead, or Hank Williams, or Elvis....Two or three of the village dogs will wander in

CRUST

1 cup graham cracker crumbs	1 cup sugar
½ cup unsalted butter, melted	¼ teaspoon cinnamon

FILLING

24 ounces cream cheese, room temperature	½ cup plus 1 tablespoon unsalted butter, melted and cooled
1 cup sugar	3 eggs
	3 tablespoons vanilla

TOPPING

½ cup sour cream	2 tablespoons sugar
1 tablespoon vanilla	

■ For crust, preheat oven to 375°. Mix graham cracker crumbs, butter, sugar and cinnamon until combined. Reserve ¼ cup for topping. Press remainder onto the bottom and halfway up the sides of a 9-inch springform pan.

■ For filling, in the bowl of an electric mixer, beat cream cheese and sugar until creamy. Beat in butter, eggs and vanilla. Pour onto crust and bake 60 minutes or until firm. Cool 10 minutes on a wire rack.

■ For topping, in a small bowl combine sour cream, vanilla and sugar. Spread over cheesecake and bake an additional 5 minutes. Sprinkle reserved crumbs on top. Refrigerate 12 hours. When ready to serve, remove springform sleeve and transfer cheesecake to serving platter.

12 servings

Photo by Hamp Overton

The Hoka, 1987

■ *Old Venice Pizza Kitchen* ■

TIRAMISU

Tiramisu, which means "pick me up" in Italian, uses
espresso to help moisten and flavor the crisp ladyfinger cookie layers.

1 cup plus 1 tablespoon sugar, divided use	¼ cup Kahlúa
⅔ cup sweet Marsala wine	3 cups warm espresso
8 egg yolks	Ladyfingers
24 ounces mascarpone cheese	1½ tablespoons cocoa powder

In a medium metal bowl whisk 1 cup sugar, wine and egg yolks. Set bowl over a pan of gently boiling water, being careful not to let the bottom of the bowl touch the water. Whisk mixture constantly until a candy thermometer reaches 165° and mixture thickens, about 4 minutes. Remove bowl from heat. Gradually add mascarpone, whisking until well blended. Set aside. In a medium bowl combine 1 tablespoon sugar, Kahlúa and espresso. Stir until sugar is dissolved. Dip each ladyfinger in espresso mixture for 1 second, shake off excess liquid and place in a 9 x 13-inch dish, repeating until the bottom of the dish is covered with one layer of ladyfingers. Spoon half the mascarpone mixture over the ladyfingers, spreading to cover. Repeat a layer of ladyfingers in the same fashion and cover with remaining mascarpone mixture. Sift cocoa powder evenly over the top. Refrigerate 8 hours.

12 servings

SEBELLE'S LEMON DESSERT

1 cup sugar	Grated zest of 1 lemon
3 tablespoons flour	Juice of 1 lemon
1 cup milk	¼ teaspoon salt
2 eggs, separated	Sweetened whipped cream

Preheat oven to 350°. Grease a soufflé dish or 4 individual baking dishes. In a large mixing bowl combine sugar and flour. Stir in milk. Beat egg yolks well and add to sugar mixture. Stir in lemon zest and juice and salt. In a separate mixing bowl, beat egg whites until stiff peaks form. Carefully fold egg whites into sugar mixture. Pour into prepared dish(es) and set dish(es) in a larger pan of warm water. Bake until a knife comes out clean, about 35 minutes. Serve warm and top with whipped cream, if desired.

4 servings

expecting a sampling of the cheese nachos or a nibble from the most popular sandwich of the place, called mysteriously "The Love at First Bite." … there are cinnamon coffee, bagels, and New Orleans-style beignets. The mood is mischievous but well-behaved, and some of the soliloquies are lyrical. On the walls are posters and circulars announcing rock concerts in the Delta, or blues festivals in the darkest canebrakes, indigenous sculptures, and photographs of Mississippi's writers.

~Willie Morris

"My Two Oxfords"

Store strawberries and blueberries in the refrigerator without washing them. Moisture serves to accelerate the development of mold.

STRAWBERRIES CARDINAL

Make this dessert only when strawberries are at their best.

1½ quarts fresh strawberries

¼ cup plus 2 tablespoons sugar, divided use

1 10-ounce package frozen raspberries, thawed

1 tablespoon orange liqueur

1 teaspoon fresh lemon juice

Fresh mint sprigs, for garnish

Wash, hull, and dry strawberries. If they are small, leave them whole; if large, slice in half. Place berries in a large glass or plastic bowl and sprinkle ¼ cup sugar over. Stir gently. Cover with plastic wrap and refrigerate several hours. In a blender place raspberries with their juice and remaining 2 tablespoons sugar and blend at high speed until thoroughly puréed and slightly frothy. Strain through a sieve to remove seeds. Stir liqueur and lemon juice into strained raspberries. Cover and chill. To serve, spoon strawberries into individual serving dishes and cover with just enough raspberry sauce to coat lightly. Garnish with mint sprigs.

6 servings

Photo on page 182

■ *Downtown Grill* ■

KAHLÚA MOCHA PARFAIT PIE

CRUST

2 cups flaked coconut

2 tablespoons flour

½ cup chopped pecans

½ cup unsalted butter, melted

FILLING

½ gallon Angel Food Coffee Chip ice cream, soft

Chocolate syrup

Kahlúa

For crust, preheat oven to 325°. In a mixing bowl combine coconut, flour and pecans. Add butter and mix well. Put crust mixture into a 10-inch metal pie pan, pressing with the back of a spoon to pack firmly and cover entire pan surface evenly. Bake until golden brown, 20-25 minutes. Cool completely.

For filling, pack cooled crust with ice cream and freeze. Drizzle with chocolate syrup and serve with Kahlúa in cordial glass on the side.

8 servings

TORTONI SQUARES

½	cup almonds, toasted and chopped	1	teaspoon almond extract
3	tablespoons unsalted butter, melted	3	pints vanilla ice cream, soft
1	cup graham cracker crumbs	1	12-ounce jar apricot preserves

In a medium bowl combine almonds, butter, graham cracker crumbs and almond extract. Set aside ¼ of mixture for topping. Line an 8-inch square pan with foil. Spread half of the remaining crumb mixture on the foil. Spread half the ice cream over crumbs. Drizzle half the preserves over ice cream. Repeat with remaining crumbs, ice cream and preserves and top with reserved crumb mixture. Freeze until firm.

8 servings

JUSTINE'S PINEAPPLE MINT ICE CREAM

This recipe is from the old Justine's in Memphis. Many in north Mississippi
and the Delta for whom Memphis was the Big City will remember enjoying it as children.

1½	cups sugar	1½	cups pineapple juice
1½	cups water	2	cups milk
2	cups fresh mint leaves	½	cup white crème de menthe
½	cup light corn syrup	¼	cup fresh lemon juice
2	cups canned crushed pineapple in its own juice	2	cups heavy cream

In a heavy medium saucepan over medium high heat, combine sugar and water. Boil until syrup reaches the soft ball stage, about 5 minutes. Add mint leaves and corn syrup and simmer 10 minutes. Remove from heat and cool. Pour syrup into a blender and purée. Strain through a sieve into a large mixing bowl. Purée pineapple in blender and add it to the syrup. Stir in pineapple juice, milk, crème de menthe, lemon juice and cream. Refrigerate until cold and freeze in ice cream freezer according to manufacturer's instructions.

10-12 servings

It would be no question of choosing, having to choose between the champagne or whiskey and the sherbet, but all of a sudden (it would be spring then, in that country where he had never spent a spring before and you said North Mississippi is a little harder country than Louisiana, with dogwood and violets and the early scentless flowers but the earth and the nights still a little cold...) you find that you don't want anything but that sherbet and that you haven't been wanting anything else but that....

~William Faulkner

Absalom, Absalom!

Solid chocolate can be purchased in the following forms. Unsweetened chocolate has up to 70% or more chocolate liquor. Semisweet or bittersweet has 35% chocolate liquor. Milk chocolate contains 10% chocolate liquor. White chocolate has no chocolate liquor but is made of cocoa butter and milk solids.

CHOCOLATE TOFFEE COOKIES
Wonderfully rich and chewy

½	cup flour	1¾	cups packed brown sugar
1	teaspoon baking powder	4	eggs
¼	teaspoon salt	1	tablespoon vanilla
1	pound bittersweet or semisweet chocolate	8	ounces milk chocolate toffee bits
¼	cup unsalted butter	1	cup walnuts, toasted and coarsely chopped

In a small bowl combine flour, baking powder and salt. Set aside. In the top of a double boiler, or in a heatproof bowl in the microwave, slowly melt chocolate and butter together and set aside to cool. In the bowl of an electric mixer, beat sugar and eggs until thick, about 5 minutes. Beat in chocolate mixture, vanilla, flour mixture, toffee bits and walnuts. Chill batter until firm, about 45 minutes. Preheat oven to 350° and line 3 cookie sheets with parchment paper. Scoop batter with an ice cream scoop (2 tablespoons) onto cookie sheets, spacing cookies at least 2½ inches apart. Bake until tops are dry and cracked but still soft to touch, about 15 minutes. Cool on cookie sheets.

24 cookies

ORANGE CHOCOLATE CHIP COOKIES

1	cup unsalted butter, room temperature	1¾	cups flour
⅔	cup brown sugar	¼	teaspoon salt
2	eggs	½	teaspoon baking soda
2	teaspoons vanilla	2	cups semisweet chocolate chips
1	teaspoon orange extract	1	cup walnuts, finely chopped, optional
3	tablespoons grated orange zest		

Preheat oven to 350°. In the bowl of an electric mixer, cream butter and sugar at high speed for about 2 minutes. Add eggs one at a time, blending well after each addition. Beat in extracts and orange zest. In a small bowl sift together flour, salt and soda. Add flour mixture to the butter mixture, blending well. Mix in chocolate chips and optional walnuts. Drop by rounded teaspoons onto lightly greased or parchment-covered cookie sheets. Bake until lightly browned, about 12 minutes.

40 cookies

SNICKERS SURPRISE

3½ cups flour
1 teaspoon baking soda
½ teaspoon salt
1 cup unsalted butter, room temperature
1 cup creamy peanut butter
1 cup light brown sugar
1 cup sugar

2 eggs
1 teaspoon vanilla
1 13-ounce package Snickers miniature candy bars, unwrapped
Powdered sugar
6 ounces milk chocolate chips, melted

In a mixing bowl stir together flour, soda and salt. Set aside. In the bowl of an electric mixer, cream the butter, peanut butter and sugars until light and fluffy. Add eggs one at a time, beating well after each addition. Beat in vanilla and mix until combined. Add flour mixture and beat until combined. Wrap dough in plastic wrap and chill 2-3 hours. Preheat oven to 300°. Divide dough into 1-tablespoon sized pieces. Flatten each dough piece and wrap 1 piece around each miniature Snickers. Bake on greased or parchment-lined cookie sheets 10-12 minutes. Cool completely. Sprinkle with powdered sugar. Drizzle with melted chocolate.

40 cookies

SOUR CREAM COOKIES

1 cup unsalted butter, room temperature
2 cups sugar
2 eggs
5 cups flour
1 teaspoon salt

1 teaspoon baking soda
1 teaspoon lemon extract
1 teaspoon vanilla
1 cup sour cream

In the bowl of an electric mixer, cream butter and sugar until light and fluffy. Add eggs one at a time, beating well after each addition. Mix in extracts. Sift together flour, salt and soda. Add flour mixture to butter mixture alternately with sour cream. Divide dough into 3 equal sections and roll each into a 2-inch diameter log. Wrap with plastic wrap and chill at least 30 minutes. Preheat oven to 375°. Slice dough rolls into ¼-inch circles and place on parchment-lined or greased cookie sheets. Bake until lightly browned on the bottom but not yet brown on top, about 8 minutes.

45 cookies

Oxford, Mississippi, belongs to William Faulkner, and one hot July week in Oxford I was moved to spend an afternoon walking…. I like the way they sell chicken and pit-barbecue and fried catfish in the little stores next to the service stations…. I like the way strangers on the Square or the Levy's Jitney Jungle finish your sentences for you.

~Willie Morris

"The Ghosts of Ole Miss"

Vanilla Frosting

3 cups sifted
confectioners' sugar

¼ teaspoon salt

5 tablespoons half-and-half

2 tablespoons
unsalted butter, melted

1 teaspoon vanilla

In the bowl of an
electric mixer, combine
all ingredients. Blend
until of spreading
consistency.

MO'S SUGAR COOKIES

1	cup unsalted butter, room temperature	1	teaspoon almond extract
2	cups sugar	4	cups flour
3	eggs	2	teaspoons baking powder
1	teaspoon vanilla	½	teaspoon salt

In the bowl of an electric mixer, cream butter and sugar until light and fluffy. Add eggs one at a time, beating well after each addition. Mix in extracts. In a mixing bowl combine flour, baking powder and salt. Blend flour mixture into butter mixture until well combined. Wrap in plastic wrap and refrigerate until firm, about 45 minutes. Preheat oven to 350°. Working with about ⅓ of dough at a time, roll with a rolling pin to about ⅛-inch thickness. Cut with cookie cutters and bake on greased or parchment-lined cookie sheets until lightly brown at the edges, 8-10 minutes. Sprinkle with colored sugar while still hot, or cool and ice.

24 large or 48 small cookies

Photo on page 25

TEA CAKES

1	cup solid vegetable shortening	2¾	cups flour
1½	cups sugar	1	teaspoon baking soda
2	eggs	½	teaspoon salt
1	teaspoon vanilla	2	teaspoons cream of tartar

Preheat oven to 350°. In the bowl of an electric mixer, cream shortening and sugar. Add eggs and vanilla and beat well. In a medium bowl, combine flour, baking soda, salt and cream of tartar. Beat flour mixture into shortening mixture until well combined. Roll dough into walnut-sized balls and place 2 inches apart on ungreased cookie sheets. Bake until lightly browned, about 12 minutes. Cool on paper towels.

60 cookies

ROSEMARY ORANGE SHORTBREAD

1	cup unsalted butter, chilled	½	teaspoon salt
1	tablespoon finely chopped fresh rosemary	2½-3 cups flour	
2	teaspoons finely grated orange zest	1	egg white
½	cup sugar		Sugar for sprinkling

In the bowl of an electric mixer, combine butter, rosemary, orange zest and sugar. Beat with the paddle attachment on medium speed until ingredients are combined and butter is very smooth. Mix in salt and enough flour to make a cohesive dough. Do not over mix. Turn dough out onto a floured work surface and roll it into a ½-inch thick rectangle. Cut into 2 x 2-inch bars and arrange them on parchment-lined cookie sheets. Refrigerate at least 30 minutes. Preheat oven to 350°. Brush cookies with egg white and sprinkle with sugar. Bake until cookies are a very light tan, about 25 minutes.

30 cookies

Shortbread recipes date back to the 16th century. During festive occasions, special flavorings like citrus peels or sugared nuts were added to the dough. The earlier recipes contained finely ground oats, and the shortbread was often round and cut from the center to form triangles, symbolizing the sun and its rays, a leftover practice from the early days of sun-worshipping.

ROSEMARY PEPPER SUGAR COOKIES

1	cup unsalted butter, room temperature	2-3 teaspoons finely minced, fresh rosemary	
¾	cup sugar	½	teaspoon salt
1	egg, room temperature	½	teaspoon freshly ground black pepper
1	teaspoon vanilla		Coarse sugar
2½	cups sifted flour		

In the bowl of an electric mixer fitted with the paddle attachment, cream butter and sugar on medium speed until light and fluffy. Scrape down sides and mix in egg and vanilla, beating until well combined. Add flour, rosemary, salt and pepper. Mix on low speed until just incorporated. Stir dough by hand, then turn out onto floured work surface. Divide dough into 2 equal sections, then roll each section into a 1½-inch-diameter log. Wrap logs in waxed paper or plastic wrap and refrigerate or freeze until firm, about 1 hour. Preheat oven to 375°. Roll each log in coarse sugar to coat completely. Slice logs into ¼-inch-thick circles and bake on parchment-lined cookie sheets until edges are golden, 15-20 minutes.

60 cookies

SUNFLOWER SEED COOKIES

Sunflower seeds are high in protein, low in carbohydrates, and good source of Vitamin E. They made an excellent heart-healthy snack.

2	cups sugar	1	teaspoon baking powder
1	cup unsalted butter, room temperature	2¾	cups flour
1	teaspoon baking soda	1	cup sunflower seeds

Preheat oven to 350°. Mix together all ingredients in order given. Mixture will be crumbly. Roll into 1-inch balls and arrange on ungreased cookie sheets. Press balls flat with a fork. Bake until straw-colored, 12-15 minutes.

70 cookies

KAHLÚA BROWNIES

BROWNIES

1	19.8-ounce package fudge brownie mix (for a 9 x 13-inch pan)	3	eggs
		⅓	cup vegetable oil

ICING

½	cup plus 6 tablespoons unsalted butter, divided use	2	tablespoons Kahlúa liqueur
2	cups confectioners' sugar	1	cup semisweet chocolate chips

Preheat oven to 350°. In a large mixing bowl, mix brownie mix, eggs and oil until well combined. Bake in a greased 9 x 13-inch pan until set, about 25 minutes.

Cool brownies completely. In a glass bowl melt ½ cup butter in the microwave. Stir in confectioners' sugar and Kahlúa. Stir until smooth and spread evenly over brownies. Chill 1 hour. In a small heatproof bowl melt 6 tablespoons butter and chocolate chips in the microwave on low power. Stir until smooth and spread over frosted brownies. Chill at least 1 hour before cutting.

24 brownies

RASPBERRY BROWNIES

1	cup unsalted butter	1¼	cups flour
5	ounces unsweetened chocolate, chopped	1	teaspoon baking powder
2	cups sugar	½	teaspoon salt
4	eggs	1	cup chopped walnuts, toasted
2	teaspoons vanilla	½	cup raspberry preserves

In a heavy large saucepan over low heat, melt butter and chocolate, stirring constantly until smooth. Remove from heat. Whisk in sugar, eggs and vanilla. In a small bowl mix flour, baking powder and salt. Add to chocolate mixture, whisking to blend. Stir in nuts. Pour 2 cups of batter into a greased 9 x 13-inch pan, reserving remainder of batter. Freeze until firm, about 10 minutes. Preheat oven to 350°. Spread preserves over chilled batter in pan. Spoon remaining batter over preserves. Let stand 20 minutes at room temperature to thaw bottom layer. Bake until a toothpick inserted in center comes out clean, about 35 minutes. Cool completely and cut into squares.

24 brownies

Square Table has included three award-winning brownie recipes from the 2004 Yoknapatawpha Arts Council picnic.

THE ULTIMATE GANACHE BROWNIE

4	ounces unsweetened chocolate	½	cup flour
½	cup unsalted butter	¼	teaspoon salt
2	eggs	1	cup chopped walnuts or pecans
1½	cups sugar	7	ounces semisweet chocolate, chopped
1	teaspoon vanilla	½	cup heavy cream

Preheat oven to 350°. In a heatproof bowl melt chocolate and butter on low power in the microwave. Stir until blended and cool slightly. In the bowl of an electric mixer, beat eggs and sugar until well combined. Beat in chocolate mixture and vanilla. Mix in flour and salt, just until blended. Stir in nuts. Spread batter in a greased and floured 8 x 8-inch pan. Bake until set, 20-25 minutes. Cool completely in the pan. Place semisweet chocolate in a small heatproof bowl. In a small heavy sauce pan over high heat, bring the cream to a boil and pour over chocolate. Whisk until chocolate is melted and mixture is smooth. Chill 15 minutes. Spread evenly over brownies and chill at least 1 hour before cutting into squares.

16 brownies

Brittle was perhaps one of the first candies of the ancient Middle Easterners. The original brittle contained honey and sesame seeds, which were readily available. The basic concept was easily adapted to regional preferences and the availability of ingredients. Brittle recipes have evolved to include sugar, molasses, almonds, peanuts, and pecans. Although Almond Cookie Brittle is not a true brittle, it is a perfect example of how recipes evolve.

ALMOND COOKIE BRITTLE

1	cup unsalted butter, room temperature	1½	teaspoons almond extract
1	cup sugar	2	cups flour
1	teaspoon salt	1	cup sliced almonds

Preheat oven to 350°. In the bowl of an electric mixer, cream butter, sugar, salt and almond extract until creamy. On low speed beat in flour gradually, mixing just until combined. Stir in nuts. Press dough ⅜-inch thick onto the bottom of a 10 x 15-inch jelly-roll pan. (Dough will fill only ¾ of pan surface, but will not spread during baking.) Bake 15-20 minutes. (A longer baking time makes a crispier texture.) Cool in the pan. Break into pieces as you would peanut brittle.

20-25 pieces

CRANBERRY DATE BARS

Perfect for the holidays, this recipe comes from the kitchen of dear friend Susan Burkett.

BARS

12	ounces fresh cranberries, rinsed and picked over	2	cups rolled oats
8	ounces chopped dates	1½	cups packed brown sugar
2	tablespoons water	½	teaspoon baking soda
1	teaspoon vanilla	½	teaspoon salt
2	cups flour	1	cup unsalted butter, melted
		½	cup chopped pecans or walnuts, optional

GLAZE

2	cups confectioners' sugar	½	teaspoon vanilla
2-3	tablespoons orange juice		

Preheat oven to 350°. In a covered heavy saucepan over low heat, simmer cranberries, dates and water for 15 minutes. Stir occasionally until cranberries pop. Remove from heat, stir in vanilla and set aside. In a large bowl combine flour, oats, brown sugar, baking soda and salt. Stir in butter until well blended. Press half of flour mixture onto bottom of an ungreased 9 x 13-inch pan. Bake 8 minutes. Spread cranberry mixture over crust. Stir chopped nuts into remaining flour mixture. Sprinkle over cranberries and pat down gently. Bake until lightly browned, 25-30 minutes. Cool completely and cut into bars.

For glaze, in a small bowl stir together confectioners' sugar, orange juice and vanilla. Drizzle over bars.

24 bars

PECAN SQUARES

CRUST

1 cup flour	½ cup unsalted butter, chilled
2 tablespoons confectioners' sugar	

FILLING

1¼ cups packed brown sugar	¾ cup chopped pecans
2 eggs	1 teaspoon vanilla
2 tablespoons flour	Confectioners' sugar for sprinkling
¾ cup sweetened flaked coconut	

Preheat oven to 400°. In a small bowl combine flour and confectioners' sugar. With two forks or a pastry blender, cut in butter until mixture resembles rolled oats. Press onto the bottom and ¼ inch up sides of a greased 8 x 11-inch pan. Bake 10 minutes.

For filling, in a large bowl stir together all filling ingredients except confectioners' sugar until well blended. Pour onto crust, reduce oven temperature to 350° and bake until a toothpick inserted in the center comes out almost clean, about 20 minutes. Cool, sprinkle with confectioners' sugar and cut into squares.

15 squares

Photo on page 129

CINNAMON TRIANGLES

Good with homemade ice cream

1 cup unsalted butter, room temperature	2 cups flour
½ cup firmly packed brown sugar	1 tablespoon cinnamon
½ cup sugar	½ teaspoon salt
1 egg, separated	1½ cups pecans, chopped

Preheat oven to 300°. In the bowl of an electric mixer, beat butter, sugars and egg yolk at medium speed until light and fluffy. In a mixing bowl combine flour, cinnamon and salt. Add flour mixture to butter mixture, beating until blended. Dough will be stiff. Spread evenly in a greased and floured 10 x 15-inch jelly-roll pan. Beat egg white with a fork until foamy. Spread evenly over dough. Sprinkle with nuts and press lightly. Bake 40-45 minutes. While still hot, cut into 3-inch squares and then cut diagonally across each square. Cool in the pan.

30 triangles

**Artist Darri Mansel
Artwork, page 217**

Darri Dubberly Mansel has a B.S. in Interior Design from the University of Alabama, and has been making art since childhood. Citing her primary influences as French and Russian Impressionism, her late friend Lynn Green Root, and her Southern roots, she works in oil, acrylic, collage, and mixed media. Mansel was born in Quitman, Georgia, and grew up in Greenville, Mississippi. She lives with her husband, Keith Mansel, with whom she has two daughters, Ferriday and Jane.

**Author Beth Ann Fennelly
Essay, page 218**

Beth Ann is the
author of two poetry
collections: *Open House,*
awarded the 2001
Kenyon Review
Prize in Poetry for
a First Book, and the
recently published *Tender
Hooks.* Her poems have
appeared in the Best
American Poetry Series
and other anthologies.
She received a 2003
Creative Writing
Fellowship in Poetry
from the National
Endowment for the Arts.
An assistant professor of
English at the University
of Mississippi, Fennelly
lives with her husband,
writer Tom Franklin, and
their two children
in Oxford.

TOFFEE

*You will have to work quickly to take advantage of
this speedy technique for making toffee. Have all ingredients at your fingertips.*

1	cup chopped almonds, toasted	¼	teaspoon salt
1	cup unsalted butter	12	ounces semisweet chocolate chips
1	cup sugar	1	cup ground pecans, toasted

Line a 9 x 12-inch baking sheet with nonstick aluminum foil. Spread almonds evenly over foil and set aside. In a heavy medium saucepan over medium high heat, combine butter, sugar and salt. Bring to a boil and cook until mixture turns light brown, about 7 minutes. Working quickly while the butter sauce is still very hot, pour it over the almonds and spread to the edge of the pan with a heatproof spatula. Quickly spread the chocolate chips over the hot butter sauce, using spatula to smooth chocolate until melted. Immediately top with ground pecans, pressing lightly to adhere. Refrigerate until thoroughly chilled, 6-8 hours. Break into pieces.

15 servings

AMARETTO BALLS

Pack these little gems in a decorative container for the perfect gift.

½	cup unsalted butter, room temperature	4	tablespoons amaretto liqueur (can substitute bourbon)
1	pound confectioners' sugar		
1	cup ground pecans	8	ounces semisweet chocolate
		1-3	tablespoons paraffin wax, melted

In the bowl of an electric mixer, cream butter and sugar. Blend in pecans and liqueur. Chill until firm, about 45 minutes. Cover a large baking sheet with waxed paper. Roll dough into ½-inch-diameter balls and arrange on baking sheet. Place a toothpick into center of each ball and transfer them to the freezer on the baking sheet. Freeze until firm, about 1 hour.

To cover with chocolate, in a heavy medium saucepan over low heat, slowly melt chocolate, stirring constantly. Add just enough melted paraffin wax to thin chocolate slightly. Keep the burner on lowest heat. Remove dough balls from freezer and, using the toothpick as a handle, dip ball into melted chocolate and return to baking sheet. If chocolate is too thick to coat ball, add more paraffin wax. Continue until all balls are coated. Remove toothpicks. Using a teaspoon, drop a small amount of melted chocolate on the holes left by the toothpicks. Return to freezer until firm. Store in a cool place.

60 balls
Cakewalk Around the Square by Darri Mansel ▶

THE GENIE in the BOTTLE of RED FOOD COLORING

Beth Ann Fennelly

The first time I came to the South I was twenty-four and heading to the University of Arkansas to get my MFA in poetry writing. My family in Chicago kept talking about my move to "the deep South" with wonder and trepidation — to them, yuppified Fayetteville was just down the river from Deliverance country.

At the same time I was making my trip South, my future husband, Tom Franklin, was leaving his home in Alabama to head to the same University on his first trip "way Up North," as his family called it, also with wonder and trepidation — for them, Fayetteville was just down the road from the gang warfare of St. Louis.

Here's the short version of what happened next: we met the first day of school, and we fell in love, and I never really went back North again.

Understanding my new home in the South meant, of course, coming to understand its foods. I easily adopted grits, fried okra, and yams. But these were rather superficial adoptions; mostly I ate and cooked what I always had eaten and cooked. That's not acculturation. Acculturation, as acculturated folks know, involves pain. My story of acculturation begins with an innocent offer: what type of cake would Tommy like for his birthday? Here I will brag that I make wonderful cakes, probably because I have a determined sweet tooth so I've grown cagey at gratifying it. Invite me to a dinner party, for example, and I'll not ask, "Can I bring something?" but "Can I bring dessert?" which prevents the postprandial surprise of the host passing sliced strawberries at the table. Friends — strawberries, unless dipped in white chocolate, are not a dessert, they're a *garnish*. Dessert means chocolate, preferably dark, what someone with a less distinguished palate might call "too rich." So would Tommy perhaps enjoy my chocolate almond ganache with crème anglaise? My bitter chocolate hazelnut torte? Dacquoise? Génoise? Anything that rhymes with "awe"?

"Um, how about red velvet?" he asked.

"Um, sure," I replied. But not only had I never heard of this concoction, I couldn't find it in either my batter-splatted *Elegant Desserts* or *The Cake Bible*. Finally I went to The Source: my future mother-in-law, who was only too happy to share the recipe. Now that I think of it, perhaps it was that phone call that began our deep friendship, because Betty saw that her son's Yankee girlfriend wanted to make him happy.

But there was a problem with the recipe. More than one, in fact. First, when I sprinkled the vinegar on top of the baking soda, it hissed at me. The cakes I baked did not require safety goggles. The cakes I baked did not talk back. I discovered the second, bigger problem when the batter was almost finished and I realized just how much red food coloring was in the four ounce bottle the recipe called for. Should I phone again and ask my potential mother-in-law to recheck her recipe? "The cake's supposed to be dark red," Tommy said.

"How red?" I asked.

"You know, like a dead armadillo on the roadside." And I'd been in the South exactly long enough to know how red that was.

All my sweet husband-to-be wanted for his birthday was a red velvet cake, but, I confess, he didn't get one. I tried — Lord knows I tried. But as the bottle of food coloring hovered over the batter, my hand just couldn't commit to tilting. What was in this stuff anyway? I brought the bottle close: propylene glycol, propylparaben, and FD&C Red #40. I let three fat drops fall into the batter, stirred it to a lovely cherry blossom pink, then shoved the pans in the oven.

And so July 7, 1995, the pink velvet cake was born. I have made it each July 7 since for Tommy's birthday. The last three years, I've also made it May 19, our daughter's birthday. Claire, unlike her Mama, has never known anything but Southern cuisine. Her first solid food was yams, and her favorite vegetable is "fried Oprah." Claire enjoyed her first dessert, like most babies, at her one-year birthday party. We held the celebration at the Grisham Visiting Writer house on Old Taylor Road, having moved to Oxford for my husband to serve as writer-in-residence at Ole Miss for the year. At that point, Claire's little rosebud palate was pure of processed sugars, not to mention FD&C Red #40. When the moment for her debauchery arrived, I held up the baby fork with a crumb of the cake on it. She stuck out a tentative tongue, touched the icing, then slipped her tongue back in her mouth. An expectant hush overtook the solemn party guests wearing conical hats. Then, as if the glorious gates of sugar-rush paradise trumpeted open before her, Claire leaned forward in her highchair and, with both hands, yanked the fork into her mouth. Next she was tearing into the cake with both fists, smearing cake up her nostrils and into her eyelashes. The following morning, as I got Claire ready for the day, I was reliving the memory of a party so successful that its clean up involved swabbing Q-tips in my daughter's ears. But as I began to change her diaper, I felt a panicked sickness at finding a bloody mess inside of it. I was heading for the car to take Claire to the doctor before I realized it was just the red food coloring.

Of course, all of this brings up a thorny question—by adapting Southern food and foodways for my New South family, am I merely diluting them, bleaching them, producing pale pink when crimson is called for? Perhaps. But I also know that healthy traditions can accept adaptations, in the same way that healthy animals and plants systems do, and in the same way language does, for we think of language as a closed system, but it is no fossil, it is an organic, seething marvel, continuously created and recreated, tumbling into the future with its bundle of blanks and redundancies. The only languages that are perfected are those that are dead. And if I've learned one thing living in the South, it's that Southern cuisine is anything but dead.

Back to my story now: Girl meets boy. Girl meets delicious Southern Boy, and they have themselves a delicious Southern Child, and each day is a Glad Day. Well, where does that leave the Girl? I know, as much as I'd like to call myself one, I'm not a Southerner. But I'm also no longer a Yankee, at least not the kind my husband was warned against. Oh, I don't claim to admire everything about the South, or understand it — I still think the term "Fry Daddy" sounds more like a rapper's handle than a kitchen appliance. And my thighs hope I keep it that way. But I'm learning where I fit in the South, and where the South fits in me. Learning what to adopt, and what to adapt.

And learning that, sometimes, one moves through the pain of acculturation to come out on the other side in a rainbow of pleasure. If you don't believe me, stop by my house May 19 or July 7 for what I guarantee is the best pink velvet cake you've ever had.

Mo's Sugar Cookies

VALENTINE'S DAY

I LOVE YOU FOND DOO

FUDGE DIPPING SAUCE

1 cup hot fudge sauce

2 tablespoons water

¼ cup chocolate-flavored syrup

CARAMEL CHOCOLATE DIP

8 ounces caramel candies

2 ounces semisweet chocolate, chopped

½ cup milk

DIPPERS

2 pints strawberries, washed and dried

4 ripe bananas, peeled and cut into chunks

1 10-ounce bag jumbo marshmallows

1 prepared angel food cake,
sliced and cut with a heart cookie cutter

For fudge sauce, in a small saucepan over medium-low heat, mix all ingredients and cook, stirring until well combined and smooth. Transfer to dipping bowl.

For caramel sauce, in a heavy saucepan over low heat, heat caramels, chocolate and milk, stirring until melted and smooth.

Place a dipping bowl filled with fudge or caramel chocolate dip in the center of a large platter. Surround the bowl with an arrangement of strawberries, bananas, marshmallows and cake.

Makes 8 servings.

MELT-YOUR-HEART PEANUT BUTTER MARSHMALLOW SANDWICHES

2 cups peanut butter	2 cups light corn syrup
1 7-ounce jar marshmallow crème	1 loaf sliced bread 1 heart-shaped cookie cutter

In a mixing bowl, combine peanut butter, marshmallow crème and corn syrup until well blended. Spread on bread slices and make sandwiches. Cut sandwiches into heart shapes. Makes 10 sandwiches.

CUPID'S KISS SANDWICH COOKIES

Little ones will love creating their own treats.

6 ounces white or chocolate candy coating	50-55 cream-filled, chocolate sandwich cookies Assorted candy hearts, sprinkles or decorations

In microwave-safe bowl or heavy saucepan, melt candy coating, stirring until smooth. Spread over cookie tops and decorate immediately. Place on waxed paper to harden. Makes 50-55 cookies.

HOMEMADE FINGER PAINT

Painting love notes is fun when it's hands-on!

3 tablespoons sugar	Liquid food coloring
½ cup cornstarch	Ivory Liquid dish soap
2 cups cold water	Small disposable cups

In saucepan over low heat, mix sugar and cornstarch. Add water and cook, stirring until thick. Remove from heat and spoon into cups. Add a drop or two of desired food coloring to each cup and a drop of dish soap to each portion. Stir and let cool. Makes 2½ cups.

EASTER BRUNCH

FRUIT AND CHEESE KABOBS

These colorful and healthy snacks are perfect for
Easter egg hunters to assemble and munch on before the big hunt.

KABOBS

1 8-ounce can pineapple chunks, drained

12 fresh strawberries, hulled

12 green seedless grapes

12 cubes mild Cheddar cheese

12 slices banana

12 6-inch thin plastic drinking straws

DIP

8 ounces sour cream

4 tablespoons packed light brown sugar

For kabobs, thread fruit and cheese onto straws. For dip, mix sour cream and sugar. Chill and serve with kabobs.

12 kabobs

EASTER BASKET EGG BUNDLES

1 tablespoon butter

12-18 bacon strips

6 eggs

Parsley, for garnish

Preheat oven to 325°. Lightly grease six oversize muffin cups with butter. In skillet, cook bacon over medium heat until cooked, but not crisp. Drain bacon on paper towels. Cut bacon strips in half widthwise. Line the bottom of each muffin cup with 2 pieces of bacon. Line the sides of each muffin cup with 1 or 2 bacon strips. Break an egg into each cup. Bake, uncovered until whites are completely set and yolks begin to thicken, but are not firm, 12-18 minutes. Run a knife along muffin cup edges to release egg bundles. Garnish with parsley.

6 servings

GRAN'MAMA'S CINNAMON ROLLS

1 10-ounce package refrigerated biscuits

1 cup cinnamon sugar

1 cup confectioners' sugar

1 tablespoon unsalted butter, melted

⅛ teaspoon salt

Water

Pat biscuits flat. Dip both sides in the cinnamon/sugar mixture. Stretch biscuit, roll around finger, and bring 1 end up through the circle to form a knot. Place in a greased, 8-inch pie pan. Bake according to directions. In a small bowl, mix confectioners' sugar, melted butter, salt and water until spreading consistency. Drizzle over warm rolls.

10 rolls

FOURTH OF JULY

TOSS ICE CREAM

A must for children of all ages! Include as many participants as you wish. Allow about 30 minutes for this activity—perfect for a hot, lazy afternoon, a birthday party or family reunion. Small children will need assistance.

1 quart zip-top bag	1 gallon zip-top bag
½ cup milk	2-3 cups crushed ice
1 tablespoon sugar	½ cup ice cream salt
¼ teaspoon vanilla	1 plastic spoon

Multiply the ingredients by the number of children being served. Place the ingredients in the above order along a picnic table. Give each child a quart zip-top bag. As each child moves down the table, help him add the milk, sugar and vanilla to his bag. Zip the quart bag closed. Add crushed ice and salt to the gallon bag. Place the filled quart bag inside the gallon bag. Shake and toss the bag for about 5 minutes. Test the ice cream consistency by squeezing the bag. When the ice cream is ready to eat, remove the quart bag from the large bag and hand out spoons. Makes 1 serving.

FIZZY FIREWORKS FRUIT DRINK

⅓ cup sweetened strawberry Kool-Aid powder	3 cups ginger ale
	Fresh strawberries and blueberries

Pour Kool-Aid powder into blender. Add ginger ale, cover and blend until smooth. Pour into clear tumblers filled with ice. Garnish with blueberries and strawberries. Makes 4 servings.

FIREWORKS AT SUNSET HOT DOGS

Celebrate the Fourth of July with this festive treatment of their favorite foods—hot dogs and macaroni and cheese.

8 hot dogs
8 servings macaroni and cheese

Starting about 1-inch from the top, slice hot dog in half length-wise. Then slice the 2 strips length-wise to make 4 strips. Cut each of those strips in half vertically to make a total of 8. Drop hot dogs into boiling water and cook until hot dog heats and strips fan apart to create a firework shape. Spoon a serving of macaroni and cheese into a bowl and top with a hot dog firework burst. Makes 8 servings.

SEASIDE VEGGIE DIP

2 cups sour cream	Celery, carrots and cucumber, cut into sticks
1 1-ounce package ranch salad dressing mix	
1 cup grated Cheddar cheese	1 beach pail
¼ cup bacon bits	8 bowl-shaped seashells, washed

In a mixing bowl, stir together sour cream, ranch dressing mix, cheese and bacon bits. Refrigerate at least 2 hours. Arrange vegetables in beach pail. Spoon dip into seashells. Makes 8 servings.

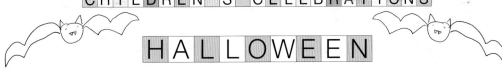

HALLOWEEN

CANDY CORN PIZZA

3 tablespoons chicken broth
3 tablespoons mascarpone cheese
Salt and pepper to taste

1 10-ounce package refrigerated pizza crust
2 cups shredded Cheddar cheese, divided

2 tablespoons paprika
½ cup shredded mozzarella cheese
⅓ cup tomato sauce

In a small saucepan over low heat, combine chicken broth and mascarpone cheese. Stir until cheese is melted. Season to taste with salt and pepper. Preheat oven to 400°. Spray a 13-inch pizza pan with cooking spray and spread dough on pan. In a small bowl toss 1 cup Cheddar cheese with paprika until cheese is evenly coated. Spread mascarpone mixture in center of pizza in a 4-inch circle. Put mozzarella cheese on top of mascarpone circle. Spread a 3-inch ring of tomato sauce around white center circle. Sprinkle paprika-colored cheese on top of tomato sauce. Use the remaining 1 cup Cheddar cheese to create a 1½-inch border around edge of pizza. Bake until cheese is melted, 12-15 minutes. Slice pizza into wedges that look like candy corn. Makes 1 pizza.

WITCH HAT CANDY CONES

1 16-ounce can milk chocolate frosting
12 sugar cones
12 fudge stripe cookies

3 12.5-ounce bags candy corn
1 16-ounce can vanilla frosting
Orange food coloring

In a heatproof bowl melt chocolate frosting in microwave until smooth, about 1 minute. Dip sugar cones and fudge cookies in melted frosting. Fill each cone with candy corn. Place a cookie on top of each cone. Invert onto waxed paper and allow to dry. In a small bowl stir vanilla frosting until of spreading consistency. Stir in orange food coloring. Fill a zip-top plastic bag about ⅓ full with orange frosting. Cut a tiny hole in 1 corner of the bag and pipe an orange frosting band at the base of the hat, where cone meets cookie, and a bow on the front of each hat. Makes 12 servings.

MONSTER MOUTH

4 green apples
1 cup peanut butter

Slivered almonds

Place apple, stem side up, on cutting board. Cut away 2 large slices from 2 sides of apple, leaving a 1-inch thick center with stem and core. Discard center slice. Cut each slice vertically into 4 wedges. Repeat with remaining apples. Spread 2 teaspoons peanut butter on each apple wedge. Top with another apple wedge, aligning edges to resemble jaws. Insert almonds to make fangs. For a realistic effect, use a crinkle cutter garnishing tool to create a toothy look. Makes 16 mouths.

WICKED WITCH CUPCAKES

These not-so-scary cupcakes are perfect for Halloween parties.

1 18.25-ounce box yellow cake mix
1 16-ounce can vanilla frosting, tinted green
1 16-ounce can chocolate frosting

1 1-pound bag M & M's
6 green spearmint candy slices, cut into fourths
1 thin red rope licorice
24 fudge-striped cookies
24 chocolate kisses

Prepare cake mix as directed on box, making 24 cupcakes. Allow to cool completely. Frost each cupcake with green frosting to make witch's face. Pipe chocolate frosting on top and 2 sides of witch face to resemble hair. Place M & M's for the witch's eyes, green candy for nose, and a piece of red licorice for lips. To make the witch's hat, adhere 1 kiss with chocolate frosting to the center of 1 fudge-striped cookie. Place hat over witch hair. Makes 24 cupcakes.

MEAN GREEN CHILLER

10 footed water goblets
¼ cup honey or corn syrup
12 drops red food coloring
4 cups chilled pineapple juice

1 6-ounce container frozen limeade concentrate
3 cups chilled ginger ale

In shallow pan, combine honey and food coloring. Mix until well blended. Dip rims of 10 goblets into mixture, one at a time, coating rim of each glass. Turn upright and allow mixture to drip down sides of glass. (Place paper towel around base of glass to catch drips.) To serve, combine pineapple juice and limeade in punch bowl. Stir until limeade dissolves. Stir in ginger ale. Fill each blood-dripped goblet with lime chiller. Makes 10 servings.

BOUNTIFUL CHOCOLATE CAKE

Children will love the marshmallow center in these rich, gooey bars.

CAKE

1 cup unsalted butter
⅓ cup cocoa
4 eggs
1½ cups sugar
1½ cups flour
¼ teaspoon salt
¼ teaspoon vanilla

1 cup chopped pecans
1 6-ounce package semisweet chocolate chips
1 10-ounce package mini marshmallows

ICING

¾ cup unsalted butter, room temperature
½ cup cocoa
¼ cup milk

2 teaspoons vanilla
⅛ teaspoon salt
1 pound confectioners' sugar

Preheat oven to 350°. In a small heatproof bowl, melt butter in the microwave. Stir in cocoa and set aside. In a mixing bowl combine eggs, sugar, flour, salt and vanilla. Add cocoa mixture and stir until combined. Pour into a well-greased 12 x 18-inch jelly-roll pan. Bake until middle is just beginning to set, 13-15 minutes. Remove from oven and sprinkle evenly with pecans, chocolate chips, and marshmallows. Return to oven for 5 minutes. Remove and cool completely.

For icing, in the bowl of an electric mixer, beat butter, cocoa, milk, vanilla and salt until smooth. Gradually beat in confectioners' sugar. Spread icing over cooled cake. Cut into 2-inch squares and serve. Makes 24 servings.

APPLE-GUMDROP TURKEYS

6 green apples
30 short wood skewers

90 medium gum drops of assorted colors
6 cherries with stems
Toothpicks

Place 5 skewers in 1 side of each apple in a fan shape to form tail. Put 3 gumdrops in assorted colors on each skewer. With a toothpick attach a cherry to resemble turkey's head with stem pointing down to resemble the wattle. Makes 6 servings.

EGG CUSTARD WITH A TWIST

4 hot dog buns
½ cup unsalted butter, melted
1 cup sugar

2 cups milk
4 eggs
1 teaspoon vanilla

Preheat oven to 350°. Open buns and lay them face down in a greased 13 x 9-inch baking pan. Pour melted butter slowly over buns and press down with the back of a spoon. In a mixing bowl, combine sugar, milk, eggs and vanilla. Mix well and pour over buns. Bake until set, about 20 minutes. Makes 6 servings.

PEANUT BUTTER PLAY DOUGH

What child doesn't like to sneak a lick while helping in the kitchen? This fun and tasty recipe is great for creating and also for eating.

1 cup nonfat dry milk powder

½ cup peanut butter
¼ cup honey

In a large bowl combine all ingredients and stir well. After playtime discard leftovers. Makes 1½ cups.

CHRISTMAS

HOLIDAY HOT CHOCOLATE MIX

A great gift for children to package and give to friends.

- 1 25.6-ounce package nonfat dry milk
- 1 15-ounce container hot cocoa mix
- 4 cups confectioners' sugar
- 1 6-ounce jar powdered nondairy creamer
- ½ cup cinnamon

In a large bowl combine all ingredients. Mix well and store in an airtight container. To prepare hot chocolate, place ¼ cup mix in a mug and stir in ¾ cup boiling water until blended. Makes 17 cups of mix.

BLIZZARD IN A BOWL TRAIL MIX

Trail mix they can use to create a winter wonderland

- 1 16-ounce bag large marshmallows
- 1 10.5-ounce bag small marshmallows
- 1 12.5-ounce bag candy corn
- 1 12-ounce bag semisweet chocolate chips
- 1 11-ounce bag pretzel sticks

In a large bowl toss together all ingredients. Put individual portions in snack-sized zip-top plastic bags. Children can make snowmen from the marshmallows with chocolate chips for eyes, pretzels for arms and candy corn for a nose. Makes 15 servings.

CHOCOLATE-COVERED CHRISTMAS SPOONS

- 1 6-ounce package semisweet chocolate chips
- 24 metal or plastic spoons
- Peppermint and/or chocolate mint candies, chopped

In a heatproof bowl slowly melt chocolate chips in the microwave. Stir until smooth. Dip spoons into chocolate. Tap the handle of spoon on edge of the bowl to remove excess chocolate. Place on waxed paper. Sprinkle with chopped candies and let stand until set. Makes 24 spoons.

WINTER FUN PLAY DOUGH

This inedible dough is soft and pliable. If stored in a zip-top plastic bag, it will keep for weeks without drying out.

- 1 cup flour
- ½ cup salt
- 2 teaspoons cream of tartar
- 1 teaspoon oil
- 1 cup water
- Food coloring

In a medium saucepan over medium heat, combine flour, salt, cream of tartar, oil and water. Cook, stirring constantly, until the mixture pulls away from the sides of the pan. Remove to countertop until cool enough to handle. Knead food coloring into the dough. Store in a zip-top plastic bag. Makes 2 cups.

City Hall and Sights by Reid Beasley Mallette,
second grader at Oxford Elementary School

IN THAT KITCHEN

Ann Fisher-Wirth

She fed so many children for so many years. *Can I pour you some milk? Would you like some peach pie? Tch, no one ate them and now the bananas have blackened.* Now it's come down to two sons, home for the moment. And the one, 19, sleeps all day and parties all night; he mostly just wants fast food, even when he's said what she could cook for him. And the other, 25, works construction, comes home covered with dust and sweat and sometimes too tired to eat, sits smoking on the porch for hours, staring off into the leaves, his Great Dane on the dog-smelling cushion beside him. The boys are healthy, yes, but they smoke too much and eat too little, their chests and ribs are bony. She's laying down food that doesn't get eaten, though her husband tries. Some nights it's so hot the thought of food sickens, and all they want is fritos or beer or those ice cream sandwiches from Kroger, mint ice cream between chocolate cookies.

So the ceiling fan churns slowly. The windows her older son painted, like bits of Aegean Sea set in ripply heartpine, are full of summer—redbud, willow oak, star-shaped leaves of the maple they planted five years ago, spreading leaves of the gingko they planted twelve years ago. The trees flash scarlet with the liquid calls of cardinals. It's August in that kitchen. Surrounded by silent men, her life is full of beauty and her life is full of love, yet she doesn't know where she's going.

Being the mother was a long rapture, a long abandonment. Abandonment of what? Of herself? Of silence? But how much love can flow through your hands, did flow through her hands, into the cakes, the pies, the sandwiches and stews. And thence into their bones, their bodies. It's quiet now. Her husband reads, her sons are heading out for the night. She's dying to ask her menfolk if they'd like some quesadillas.

A widely published author and environmental essayist and professor of English at the University of Mississippi, **Ann Fisher-Wirth**, moved to Oxford in 1988. Fisher-Wirth's first book of poems, *Blue Window*, appeared in 2003, and her chapbook of poems, *The Trinket Poems*, was runner-up in the 2003 Quentin R. Howard Poetry Chapbook Competition. Fisher-Wirth won the 2003 *Malahat Review* Long Poem Prize for the first section of *Carta Marina*. In July 2004, she won the 2004 Rita Dove Poetry Award from the Salem College Center for Women Writers for a prose poem from *Dream Cabinet*. Her book *William Carlos Williams and Autobiography: The Woods of His Own Nature* (1989) contains numerous essays on American literature and the environment. She has published more than 70 poems in journals, including *The Kenyon Review*, *The Georgia Review*, *The Malahat Review*, *Diner*, *The Connecticut Review*, *Flyway*, and *Natural Bridge*.

ACKNOWLEDGEMENTS

The *Square Table* committee gratefully acknowledges the generous assistance of the following businesses, organizations, and individuals.

Ann Abadie
Dale Abadie
Leslie Abadie
Palmer Adams
Jennifer Aronson
Shannon Brown
Martha Cofield
College Hill Presbyterian Church
Betty Cordell
Ann DeVoe
Linda Dupree
Patsy Farris
Elizabeth Fisher
Bill Griffith
Dino Grisanti
Ann Hawthorne
Blair Hobbs
Dorothy and Tom Howorth

Richard Howorth
Katherine Hudspeth
Lisa Ivy
Kelly Tidwell Kornegay
Nathan Latil
Tom Levidiotis
Will and Patty Lewis
Mayo Mallette PLLC
Missy Morrison
Bruce Newman
Ron Nurnberg
Joe Osgoode
Oxford Floral
Oxford Insurance
Tim and Kim Phillips
Shelby Powers
Suzie Rao
Susie Reagan

Red Eye Catering
Rebecca Reyenga
Margaret Seicshnaydre
Sir Speedy
Southside Gallery
Star Package
Jim Stephens
St. Peter's Episcopal Church
Dorothy Lee Tatum
Two Stick
University Florist
University Museums
The University of Mississippi
Gerald Walton
Dean Faulkner Wells
Curtis Wilkie
Will Wilkins
Nila Williams
Willie Price University Nursery School

106 South Lamar

Libbie Kakales Patterson

Libbie Patterson grew up in Oxford, where her parents owned Dino's Restaurant on the Square. She is an attorney who stays at home with her young boys.

COMMITTEE MEMBERS

CO-CHAIRS
Dorothy Walton Laurenzo
Caroline Hawthorne McIntosh

RECIPE SELECTION
Beth Doty
Lenore Hobbs
Sharon Hunt
Patty Tatum

TESTING CHAIR
Liza Dolby Mallette

RECIPE EDITORS
Ellen Meacham
Renée Moore
Ginny Terry
Julie Walton

LITERARY EDITORS
Mary Ann Percy
Linda Spargo
Jimmy Thomas
Lynn Wilkins

ART AND DESIGN
Vontese Farmer
Gay Graeber
Sloan Stribling Hunter
Cory Lewis
Darri Mansel
Molly Meisenheimer
Norma Parks

PUBLISHING CONSULTANT
Melanie Tatum Thompson

SECTION CHAIRS
Marie Barksdale: Appetizers & Beverages
Mona Mills: Soups
Mary Tucker Myres: Salads
Jennie Vieve Richardson: Pasta & Grains
Tracy Morgan: Poultry
Lynn Riley: Meat & Game
Beth Little: Fish & Seafood
Liza Frugé: Vegetables
Judy Whitehurst Riddell: Breakfast & Breads
Katrina Hourin: Desserts
Eleanor Davis and Angela Hinton:
    Children's Celebrations

MARKETING AND SALES CO-CHAIRS
Marty Swartzfager Dunbar
Mary Ann Frugé
Patty Tatum

MARKETING
Julie Chadwick
Robbye Chandler
Beth Doty
Margaret Fancher
Julie Field
Lea Ashley Fyfe
Caroline Grisanti
Lenore Hobbs
Sarah Hollis
Phyllis Johnson
Anne Ketchum
Dorothy Walton Laurenzo
Leighton McCool
Rosie Adams McDavid
Ellen Meacham
Lee Mitchell
Mary Tucker Myres
Renée O'Neill
Cindy Semmes
Robyn Tannehill
Ginny Terry
Susan Thomas
Melody Webb
Suzanne Wilkin
Lisa Williams
Sally Street Williams
Jade Yoder

SALES
Jessica Yoste Dennis
Paula Farese
Dotsy Fitts
Liza Frugé
Roane Rayner Grantham
Katrina Hourin
Phyllis Johnson
Meredith Latham
Caroline Hawthorne McIntosh
Cherri Mayo
Paige Rayburn
Amy Scruggs
Diane T. Scruggs
Lynn Wilkins

He rose to his feet.
"I gonter tell you something
to remember: anytime you wants to
git something done, from hoeing out
a crop to getting married, just get the
womenfolks to working at it. Then
all you needs to do is set down and
wait. You member that."

~William Faulkner
Go Down, Moses

Apologies to Jimmy Thomas

RECIPE TESTERS

Margie Abel
Priscilla Adams
Katie Anderson
Janice Antonow
Elise Atkins
Marian Barksdale
Camie Bianco
Ellen Bourdeaux
Emily Callicutt
Heather Card
Lisa Carwyle
Julie Chadwick
Buffy Choinski
Lisa Chow
Sally Clancy
Jean Crawford
Eleanor Davis
Nan Davis
Mike Dolby
Barbara Dollarhide
Beth Doty
Marty Dunbar
Cyd Dunlap
Carol Dunn
Carol Dye

Sonya Dye
Margaret Fancher
Molly Ferguson
Vicki Ferguson
Julie Field
Dorrie Fitzhugh
Katherine Flouhouse
Marnie Frost
Liza Fruge
Lea Fyfe
Kara Giles
June Goza
Gay Graeber
Sarah Frances Hardy
Betty Harrington
Sylvia Harvey
Robin Hendrickson
Dee Anna Hill
Angela Hinton
Mary Helen Hitt
Betty Hoar
Lenore Hobbs
Sarah Hollis
Katrina Hourin
Beckett Howorth, III

Mary Hartwell E. Howorth
Cris Hughes
Sharon Hunt
Lisa Ivy
Virginia Johnson
Maura Klingen
Alyce Krouse
Dorothy Laurenzo
Kathy Laurenzo
Erin Levidiotis
Liza Mallette
Reese Mallette
Darri Mansel
Jodie Marsalis
Caroline Mayo
Cherri Mayo
Leighton McCool
Rosie McDavid
Caroline McIntosh
Michele McNeely
Ellen Meacham
Molly Meisenheimer
Lydia Moak
Elizabeth Monteith
Renee Moore

Tracy Morgan
Shelly Mott
Mabel Murphree
Kendra Myers
Mary Tucker Myres
Vivian Neill
Brenda Norman
Mary Lou Owens
Norma Parks
Leita Patton
Ann Peeler
Mary Ann Percy
Roy Percy
Sandra Perkins
Helen Phillips
Wanda Reid
Julia Rholes
Jennie Vieve Richardson
Judy Riddell
Sarah Robinson
Michele Rogers
June Rosentreter
Caroline Rosser
Mardi Russell
Margaret Seicshnaydre

Ann Paige Shull
Denise Smith
Lu Ann Smith
Elizabeth Speed
Vicki Stevens
Robyn Tannehill
Linda Tatum
Patty Tatum
Leigh Ann Teague
Ginny Terry
Jimmy Thomas
Madeleine Walker
Julie Walton
Melody Webb
Suzanne Wilkin
Lynn Wilkins
Franklin Williams
Sally Williams
Suzy Wise
Ken Wooten
Cathy Yates
2003-04 2nd grade
    Friday Insights
    Class, Oxford
    Elementary School

BIBLIOGRAPHY

Brown, Larry. *Billy Ray's Farm.* Chapel Hill: Algonquin Books of Chapel Hill, 2001.

Faulkner, William. *Faulkner in the University: Class Conferences at the University.* Eds. F. L. Gwynn and J. L. Blottner. Charlottesville: University of Virginia Press, 1995. Reprinted with permission of the University of Virginia Press.

Faulkner, William. *Light in August.* Copyright 1932 and renewed 1960 by William Faulkner. Used by permission of Random House, Inc.

—. *Go Down, Moses.* Copyright 1940 by William Faulkner and renewed 1968 by Estelle Faulkner and Jill Faulkner Summers. Used by permission of Random House, Inc.

—. *Absalom, Absalom!* Copyright 1936 by William Faulkner and renewed 1964 by Estelle Faulkner and Jill Faulkner Summers. Used by permission of Random House, Inc.

—. *The Sound and the Fury.* Copyright 1929 and renewed 1957 by William Faulkner. Used by permission of Random House, Inc.

—. *Requiem for a Nun.* New York: Random House-Vintage, 1975.

Hannah, Barry. *High Lonesome.* New York: The Atlantic Monthly Press, 1996.

Morris, Willie. *Homecomings.* Jackson: University Press of Mississippi, 1989.

—. *Terrains of the Heart.* Oxford: Yoknapatawpha Press, 1981.

—. *My Two Oxfords.* Iowa: Yellow Barn Press, 1993.

Wells, Dean Faulkner. "Letter from South Lamar." *They Write Among Us.* Ed. Jim Dees. Oxford: Jeffereson Press, 2003.

Wilkie, Curtis. *Dixie.* New York: Scribner, 2001.

RECIPE CONTRIBUTORS

Ann Abadie
Leslie Abadie
Ann Abbott
Linda Adams
Aileen Ajootian
Susie Allen
Karen Anderson
Janice Antonow
Louisa Arico
Louise Avent, deceased
Vada Baird
Charlene Baker
Susan Burkett, deceased
Marie Barksdale
Marion Barksdale
Janet Barnes
JoAnn Bell
Antoinette Bethea
Vasser Bishop
Modine Bolen
Sally Booke
Laurel Boone
Charlene Bosarge
Cathy Brown
Julie Brown
Paula Tatum Brown
Susan L. Brown
Mollie Brewer
Kaye H. Bryant
Maralyn Howell Bullion
Harvey R. Bullis
Martha Burnett
Ann Burrow
Lil Carson
Sally Carson
Buffy Choinski
Lisa Chow
Ellen S. Clayton
Joan Cleary

Annabelle Brady Covington
Eleanor Davis
Nan Davis
Ann DeVoe
Beth Doty
Jane Dubberly
Heidi Hopkins Ducote
Marty Dunbar
Gerry Pankratz Duvall, deceased
Charlene E. Dye
Martha Elkins
Steve Elkins
Katherine Elliott
Doug Fancher
Margaret Fancher
Vontese Farmer
Mandy P. Ferrington
Julie Field
Ann Fisher-Wirth
Teresa Flautt
Katherine Flouhouse
Bill Forrester
Elizabeth Fortune
Geri Ellen Foster
Bertha Fountaine
Debi Freeman
Marnie Frost
Mary Ann Frugé
Liza Frugé
Lee Fyfe
Kara Giles
Ann Gill
Duke Goza
June Goza
Gay Graeber
Frances Graeber
Ann V. Greenlee
Bill Gurley
Carole Haney

Tim Hargrove, deceased
Betty Harrington
Ruby Hartman, deceased
Amos W. Harvey
Ann Hawthorne
Patti Herndon
Dewey Hickman
Susan Hill
Angela Hinton
Tricia Parker Hipp
Betty Hoar
Blair Hobbs
Lenore Hobbs
Lillian Hoffman
Mil Murray Hopkins
Margaret Hornsby
Katrina Hourin
Beckett Howorth
Dorothy Howorth
Lisa Howorth
Cris Hughes
Katherine Hudspeth
Sharon Hunt
Sheila Hunt
Lisa Ivy
Michael Jacobson
Virginia Johnson
Lou Jones
Dixie Jordan
Larry Kegley
Jimmy Kennedy
Maya Kennedy
Margaret Khayat
Mary King
Maura Klingen
Patricia Krueger
Frances W. Laird
Margaret Laney
Dorothy Laurenzo

Kathy Laurenzo
Kyle League
Rosebud Stone Leatherbury
Thomas S. Leatherbury
Jennie Lee
Madison Foster Lees
Erin Levidiotis
Cory Lewis
Mary Lexa
Beth Little
Joanne Logar
Sara Lovelace
Carol Lutken
Leighton McCool
Rosie McDavid
Jane McIlwain
Caroline McIntosh
Mary Howell McIntosh
Mozelle McIntosh
Michele McNeely
Linda MacCormack
Margaret MacPhearson
Liza Mallette
Diane Mangus
Jim Manning
Sudie Manning
Darri Mansel
Ann Mason
Kate Massey
Elizabeth Miesner
Joel Miller
Marion Miller
Jo Dale Mistilis
Maggy Mistilis
Martha Mitchell
Rob Mitchell
Lydia Moak
Elizabeth Monteith
Carroll C. Moore

233

Hal Moore
Melanie Moore
Nancy Moore
Shelly Mott
Kendra Myers
Karen Namorato
Beverly Neale
Vivian Neill
Walter Neill
Emily Newcomb
Jeanette Newell
Brenda Norman
Charles E. Noyes
Renée O'Neill
Amy Foster Overby
Mary Lou Owens
Linda Peterson
Ann Peeler
Farish Percy
Shirley H. Perry
Ann Phillippi
Helen Phillips
Bonnie Poole
Mary Poole
Lucy Evelyn Privett
Julia Reed
Jennie Vieve Richardson
Judy Riddell
Mike Riley
Sara Robinson
Michele Rogers
Nancy McLeod Rogers
June Rosentreter
Carolyn Jones Ross
Gusta Russell, deceased
Kay Schiller
Elaine Hoffman Scott
Rosemary Scott
Russell Scott
Amy R. Scruggs
Diane Scruggs
Leo Seicshnaydre
Jean M. Shaw

Ella Hughes Griffin Sides,
    deceased
Yvette Sirker
Denise Smith
Sue Sneed
Alexis Solomon
Darrell Solomon
Linda Spargo
Brenda Spencer
Lisa Spraggins
Betty Povall Staub
Jeanne Stennett
Madge Stubblefield
Jack Stubbs
Pat Williams Stubbs
Molissia Swaney
Sara Love Swaney
Pat Tate
Dorothy Lee Tatum
John Hederman Tatum
John Reagan Tatum
Pat Tatum
Patty Tatum
Marilyn Taylor
Ginny Terry
Mary Sue Tettleton
Jimmy Thomas
Melanie Tatum Thompson
Mardra Thompson
Perry A. Thompson, Jr.
Perry A. Thompson, Sr.
William A. Thompson
Mary Torbert
June Truly
Susan Tyner
Tor Valenza
Ron Vernon
JoAnn Walker
Julie Walton
Ruby Elizabeth Walton,
    deceased
Mel Warren
Ann Tipler Watson

Elizabeth Watson
Virginia Watson
Vivian Watson
Isabella Watt
Sandy Webb
Charmie L. Weeks
Martha Whitwell
Sylvia Wiez
Bobbye Wiley
Curtis Wilkie

Jane Pelegrin Wilkie
Suzanne Wilkin
Liz Williams
Nila Williams
Mary Jane Zander
First Presbyterian Church
    Cookbook
The Deli at Sav-Rex Drugs,
    Pascagoula, Mississippi
Lib Wight Quirk

Oxford Square, early 1960s

Photo by Martin J. Dain

234

INDEX

239

Southwest Corner

Janet Barnes

Janet Barnes is a registered nurse who has also studied painting and graphic design. She has lived in Oxford for 18 years.